THE YANKS FORGET TO

WWII

THE PEOPLE'S STORY

MENTION DROPPING FIRE BOMBS ON

TOKYO EARLY 1945.
THE YANKS DROPPED THEM

WWII

THE PEOPLE'S STORY

NIGEL FOUNTAIN

GENERAL EDITOR

Reader's
Digest

The Reader's Digest Association, Inc.
Pleasantville, New York/Montreal

WWII
THE PEOPLE'S STORY

A Reader's Digest Work

Interview text copyright © 2003 Imperial War Museum Sound Archive
Interview text copyright © 2003 State Historical Society of Wisconsin

The credits and acknowledgments on pages 318–320 are hereby made part of this copyright page.

READER'S DIGEST

U.S. PROJECT EDITOR: Robert Lockwood Mills
U.S. PROJECT DESIGNER: George McKeon
U.S. CREATIVE DIRECTOR: Michele Laseau
EXECUTIVE EDITOR, U.S. TRADE PUBLISHING: Dolores York
DIRECTOR, U.S. TRADE PUBLISHING: Christopher T. Reggio
VICE PRESIDENT & PUBLISHER, U.S. TRADE PUBLISHING: Harold Clarke

MICHAEL O'MARA BOOKS

PROJECT EDITOR: Rod Green
PROJECT DESIGNER: Ron Callow, Design 23
COPY EDITOR: Dominique Enright
INDEXER: Rhian McKay
PRODUCTION CONSULTANT: David Bann
PRODUCTION MANAGER: Joanne Rooke

CONTRIBUTORS

PICTURE RESEARCH: Jackum Brown, Mirco Decet, Rachel Irwin, Judy Palmer
IMAGE TREATMENT: Yves Lachance
SPECIAL FEATURES TEXT: Rod Green
COLOUR ORIGINATION: Matthew Axten

Address any comments about *WWII: The People's Story* to:
The Reader's Digest Association, Inc.
Adult Trade Publishing
Reader's Digest Road
Pleasantville, NY 10570-7000

For more Reader's Digest products and information,
visit our online store at

rd.com

Library of Congress Cataloging-in-Publication Data
WWII : the people's story / general editor, Nigel Fountain.p. cm.
Includes index.
ISBN 0-7621-0376-0
    1. World War, 1939-1945. I. Title: World War II, the people's story.
II. Title: World War Two, the people's story. III. Title: World War 2,
the people's story. IV. Fountain, Nigel.
    D743.W79 2003
    940.53--dc21
                                        2003043172

Printed in China by Toppan Printing Co.

3 5 7 9 10 8 6 4 2

CONTENTS

FEATURE PAGES

"The pages of *World War II: The People's Story* are filled with hundreds of these stories from ordinary people caught in extraordinary circumstances…These personal stories resonate with us today as we create our own stories in an increasingly troubled world."

FOREWORD

Everyone has a story. My decades of broadcast journalism experience have taught me many things, but this is one of the greatest lessons I have learned: that the stories come not just from politicians, movie stars, generals, and scam artists but from ordinary people living everyday lives. If you dig a little and ask the right questions, you can be rewarded with surprising stories from completely unexpected sources.

The pages of WORLD WAR II: THE PEOPLE'S STORY are filled with hundreds of tales from ordinary people caught in extraordinary circumstances: fighter pilots, soldiers at the front, resistance fighters, evacuees, nurses, POWs, and more. These first-hand accounts of battles won and lost, of children shipped from city to countryside, of strategic military successes and blunders, of Navajo code talkers, and of concentration camp survivors bring an immediacy to the conflict that is missing in traditional accounts of the Second World War. These personal stories resonate with us today as we create our own stories in an increasingly troubled world.

I encountered everyday heroes when I served in the U.S. Navy during World War II, and I wish I had met many of those who people these pages: the fighter pilot who continued attacking a battleship alone despite the intense attack from the Germans; the ten-year-old boy, sent from Wales to New York, who survived the frigid waters of the Atlantic when the ship transporting him across the ocean was torpedoed; the nurse preparing to attend to the wounded at Pearl Harbor; the British war artist who carried a wounded soldier to safety; the female Special Operations Executive who parachuted into France dressed in a black coat and skirt and silk blouse in order to evade detection; the sailor who found the Enigma Machine, complete with that day's German naval code setting. Their words not only tell us their engrossing stories but also add a touch of humanity in what were too often inhumane times.

Different readers will learn different lessons and take different inspiration from this book. I have used these words to form a more personal image of the war that shaped our world and to derive encouragement from the men, women, and children who found strength within themselves in the most uncertain circumstances. Whether you dip in and out of sections of this book or read it from cover to cover, I believe you may find your own inspiration in these pages.

Mike Wallace
Senior Correspondent, CBS News

INTRODUCTION

What follows, on paper and on disc, are voices from another world, a world separated from us not by space but by time. It is a different world because it was a place not troubled by war—as ours is today—but consumed by it. Every day for six years between September 1, 1939, when the Nazis invaded Poland, and September 2, 1945, when the Japanese surrendered onboard the United States battleship *Missouri* in Tokyo Bay, over 25,000 people died—were murdered—by war.

The voices in *World War II: The People's Story* hail from North America, Australia, Great Britain, Ireland, Austria, France, Italy, and Germany. But they could have come from anywhere and still told stories of the war, because no place on Earth escaped the conflict.

Each year, fewer people have direct memories of living in that world. Yet images left to us flicker on in our heads, perpetuated by a thousand movies, books, newsreels, and television documentaries, filtered through our background, nationality, and age. They fascinate us, they repel us, they bore or inspire us: Stuka dive-bombers over Poland; the dome of St. Paul's Cathedral unscathed amid the bombing of London; blazing warships at Pearl Harbor in the wake of the Japanese air attack; Canadians coming ashore at Dieppe; the beaches of Normandy; Australians in the jungle of New Guinea; the raising of the Stars and Stripes over Iwo Jima; the incomprehensible horror of the death camps; G.I.s and Red Army soldiers meeting on the Elbe; the terrible cloud of August 1945 rising above a stricken Japanese city. Single words still trigger memories: Rotterdam, Coventry, Bataan, Stalingrad, Warsaw, Dresden, Belsen, Auschwitz, Dachau, Hiroshima, Nagasaki. But isolated images and words can deceive. Only beyond them, obscured in the haze, can individuals remember their place in history. That is what *World War II: The People's Story* is about.

For the last couple of years I have been gathering interviews with women and men touched by the conflagrations of the last century. Listening to their voices, remembering moments when history turned, I had a startling, obvious, but still curious realization: People did not live and die in the heroic myths of Pearl Harbor, Bataan, Dieppe, or the Battle of the Bulge. Myth came later, even if, sometimes, only a day later. They endured not the myth but the reality of such places. They survived, painfully, in their present, getting by, making out, usually with no clear agenda, no guarantee that fate would put them on the winning side. . . .

When the ship carrying 18-year-old New Yorker James Goodson back to the United States was torpedoed in the Atlantic, on the day in 1939 that Great Britain declared war on Germany, history had not ruled that he would even make it back to dry land—let alone stand in the blazing ruins of Berlin under bombardment in 1945. When, in Newfoundland that same day, 15-year-old Patrick Lewis celebrated the outbreak of hostilities and enjoyed John Wayne dreams of heroism, it was not predestined that he would face death in France four years later. When 35-year-old journalist Stanley Baron stood, transfixed, amid the blazing, blitzed city of London on Christmas Day 1940, he was not to know that his trail of the bombing's perpetrators would lead, four years later, to a slave camp-cum-rocket factory under a German mountain.

The voices here provide cautionary tales—news of wars, battles, bereavements, joys, incidents that, five decades later, few remember—in places hardly anyone has heard of, because there was no reporter within 500 miles, no relevant newspaper within 2,000 miles, or because it just didn't seem much of a story then.

Other battles took place on the home front, in factories, on farms. For all these people the war was beyond the far horizon, and only those who came later could appreciate their heroism or understand their sacrifice in comfort. The 55 million warriors, civilians, and children who died had no happy ending, and left behind lifelong grief—and fleeting joyous memory—for relatives, lovers, husbands, and wives.

War, as the voices explain, brought a lot of other things. There was the boredom of sitting around, being seasick on built-in-a-week Liberty ships making their first Atlantic crossings, the grayness of rationing, lineups, pubs with no beer, and "sold out" signs. There were strange places that, before the war, Canadian farm boys, London nurses, New Zealand pilots, Alabama sharecroppers, and Wisconsin workers could never have dreamed—or feared—of seeing. There was also the excitement of new loves, new music, and jitterbugging. At home, people found liberation from dead-end jobs, African-Americans migrated to the industrial north and west of the United States, and women followed Rosie the Riveter into the workplace.

World War II: The People's Story is not a history of the war. But it does provide signals from that lost world, a world whose gravity still pulls on our present.

—NIGEL FOUNTAIN

My good friends, for the second time in history a British prime minister has returned from Germany bringing peace with honor. I believe it is peace for our time. . . .

BRITISH PRIME MINISTER NEVILLE CHAMBERLAIN
on his return from the Munich Conference
September 1938

ONE DAY IN SEPTEMBER

On September 3, 1939, 71-year-old Prime Minister Neville Chamberlain addressed the people of Great Britain on BBC Radio.

> I am speaking to you from the Cabinet Room at 10 Downing Street.
>
> This morning the British ambassador in Berlin handed the German government a final note stating that unless we heard from them by 11 o'clock that they were prepared at once to withdraw their troops from Poland, a state of war would exist between us. I have to tell you that no such undertaking has been received, and that consequently this country is at war with Germany.

Thus ended all hope that Chamberlain may have harbored for the "peace for our time" which he had announced on his return from the Munich Conference a year before.

The British people listened in thrall as their prime minister's broadcast continued:

You can imagine what a bitter blow it is to me that all my long struggle to win peace has failed. Yet I cannot believe that there is anything more or anything different that I could have done and that would have been more successful.

Up to the last it would have been quite possible to have arranged a peaceful settlement between Germany and Poland. But Hitler would not have it. He had evidently made up his mind to attack Poland whatever happened, and although he now says he put forward reasonable proposals which were rejected by the Poles, that is not a true statement.

The proposals were never shown to the Poles, nor to us, and, though they were announced in a German broadcast on Thursday night, Hitler did not wait to hear comments on them, but ordered his troops to

Neville Chamberlain, below, announces the declaration of war in his famous radio broadcast; Hitler's birthday parade, at right, in Berlin, 1936. On the previous pages: British Prime Minister Neville Chamberlain in Munich, 1938. In the background, a Nazi rally in Nuremberg, 1933

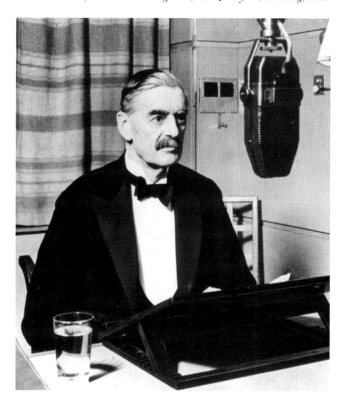

cross the Polish frontier. His action shows convincingly that there is no chance of expecting that this man will ever give up his practice of using force to gain his will. He can only be stopped by force.

We and France are today, in fulfillment of our obligation, going to the aid of Poland, who is so bravely resisting this wicked and unprovoked attack upon her people. We have a clear conscience. We have done all that any country could do to establish peace, but a situation in which no word given by Germany's ruler could be trusted and no people or country could feel themselves safe had become intolerable. And now that

1938

MARCH 12
Hitler occupies Austria and declares it a province of the Third Reich

APRIL 10
Socialist Édouard Daladier becomes prime minister of France

we have resolved to finish it, I know that you will all play your part with calmness and courage.

At such a moment as this, the assurances of support that we have received from the Empire are a source of profound encouragement to us.

Now may God bless you all and may he defend the right. For it is evil things that we shall be fighting against, brute force, bad faith, injustice, oppression and persecution. And against them I am certain that right will prevail.

The British government had hesitated sending its ultimatum to Adolf Hitler until the morning of September 2, 1939. The day before, the Nazis had invaded Poland and, pressed by the House of Commons, Chamberlain, his Foreign Secretary Lord Halifax, and his cabinet had stumbled uneasily into action.

Across the Atlantic in St. John's, Newfoundland, 15-year-old Patrick Lewis missed the broadcast and picked up the news on the street.

I was on my pedal bike going down a hill in St. John's and this woman came running out of her door screaming, "War has been declared! War has been declared!" I felt like John Wayne. I wanted to join up straight away and be a hero. And they told me to clear off and get back to school.

Hitler salutes as troops march past in Adolf Hitler Platz, Nuremberg, 1938

MAY 3

Hitler begins state visit to Rome

AUGUST 28

British Parliament passes Emergency Powers (Defence Act) leading to recruitment and mobilization of ARP (Air Raid Precautions) personnel as well as Territorial Army and RAF Volunteer Reserve

1938

A newspaper vendor at left spreads the word on September 3, 1939; special constables above restrain crowds cheering the declaration of war in Downing Street

Yvonne Cormeau was 29, recently married, with a small child and working in London.

> I can't say it was a surprise. We could see, with friends and relations living abroad, that things were building up, and being able to listen to certain speeches I could understand that something was going to happen indeed. It seemed to me the only way we could honorably stand up to our promises.

Josephine Pearce, a nurse, was organizing evacuees.

> I was standing on a rural bridge admiring the trout. And I heard somebody's wireless, through one of their cottage windows, when Chamberlain was announcing that war was declared, that we were now at war with Germany. And the whole bottom fell out of everyone's life. We really were at war. Something terrible was suddenly happening.

Hardly had the prime minister finished speaking, when the air-raid sirens went off. Ellen Harris was a young journalist, working at the House of Commons.

> The first day I remember very well indeed, the announcement, "This country is now at war," and my saying—I was living in north London—to my husband, "I shall have to get up to the office quickly, they'll be ringing but I'll get ready and go." He said, "Well, I'll come with you. I can't allow you to go up there alone."
>
> Well, we got a bus and we'd gone about two or

1938

SEPTEMBER 30

Prime ministers Chamberlain of Britain and Daladier of France meet with Hitler and Mussolini in Munich and agree to Germany annexing Sudetenland, a German-speaking area of Czechoslovakia

OCTOBER 1

First Lord of the Admiralty, Alfred Duff Cooper, resigns in protest against the Munich accord

three hundred yards, I suppose. And we got as far as Islington Green and the sirens went. And nobody knew—this was the first time ever. We'd had drill and training and what was impressed upon everybody was the gas mask. So now, here was the first warning, your mind immediately flew to the worst of everything. We were all turfed off the buses, people didn't know what to expect, you see, drivers, conductors, everybody, went down into a shelter. And this is where the driver stopped, right outside Islington Green shelter which went right under the Green.

And as we all went in, mothers carrying little babies, even little babies with their gas masks on—immediately put on, you see—and the wardens were calling out, "Mind the live wires!"—they hadn't finished the shelter. That to me was the first shock. I thought, What a terrible thing. I wonder if this has happened all over the country?

Well we were there for a time and then it turned out to be a false alarm. They'd seen something off

The colors are paraded at the Nazi Party rally in Nuremberg, 1938

OCTOBER 30

Orson Welles's realistic radio dramatization of H. G. Wells's "The War of the Worlds" causes widespread panic in the United States

NOVEMBER 9

Kristallnacht—Jewish shops, synagogues and other premises across Germany have their windows broken, are looted and set afire by mobs in a violent escalation of the persecution of Jews

1938

A German column above pauses for a rest break while advancing eastward

Jewish shopkeepers at right pick up the pieces in the wake of Kristallnacht, November 1938

DECEMBER 1

National Register for War Service is established in Britain

JANUARY 26

Spanish Civil War rages on as General Francisco Franco's Nationalists wrest Barcelona from the Republicans

AND NOW MAY GOD DEFEND THE RIGHT: See P. 11

THE FASTEST EVER
Sir Malcolm Campbell & Mr. John Cobb
both used
K·L·G
SPARKING PLUGS

DAILY SKETCH

LATEST WAR NEWS

No. 9,464   MONDAY, SEPTEMBER 4, 1939   ONE PENNY

The King's Message

"STAND calm, firm and united!" That was the keynote of the message broadcast by the King to the Empire last night.

"In this grave hour," said the King, "perhaps the most fateful in our history, I send to every household of my people, both at home and overseas, this message, spoken with the same depth of feeling for each one of you as if I were able to cross your threshold and speak to you myself.

"For the second time in the lives of most of us we are at war.

"Over and over again we have tried to find a peaceful way out of the differences between ourselves and those who are now our enemies.

"But it has been in vain. We have been forced into a conflict. For we are called, with our Allies, to meet the challenge of a principle which, if it were to prevail, would be fatal to any civilised order in the world.

"It is the principle which permits a state, in the selfish pursuit of power, to disregard its treaties and its solemn pledges; which sanctions the use of force, or threat of force...

Britain (since 11 a.m. yesterday) and France (since 5 p.m.) at war with Germany

Lord Gort leads British Expeditionary Force

Churchill in War Cabinet as First Lord

The day after the declaration of war, the Daily Sketch's *front page above included quotes from King George's radio broadcast to the Empire. Below, a somber President Franklin Delano Roosevelt*

the coast and this alarm was given, put the wind up everybody, but there was no raid. So that was my first introduction to wartime London.

In Washington, D.C., the president had been awakened in the middle of the night on September 1 to be told of the German invasion of Poland by the U.S. ambassador in France, William Bullitt. Two days later, in his radio "fireside chat," Franklin Delano Roosevelt addressed the American people.

When peace has been broken anywhere, the peace of all countries everywhere is in danger. It is easy for you and for me to shrug our shoulders and to say that conflicts taking place thousands of miles from continental United States, and, indeed, thousands of miles from the American hemisphere, do not seriously affect the Americas—and that all the United States has to do is to ignore them and go about our own business. Passionately though we may desire detachment, we are forced to realize that every word that comes through

MARCH 15
Hitler expands out of Sudetenland and occupies the rest of Czechoslovakia

MARCH 28
Civil war ends in Spain when Franco takes Madrid

1939

the air, every ship that sails the sea, every battle that is fought does affect the American future.

Let no man or woman thoughtlessly or falsely talk of America sending its armies to European fields. At this moment, there is being prepared a proclamation of American neutrality. This would have been done even if there had been no neutrality statute on the books, for this proclamation is in accordance with international law and in accordance with American policy. This will be

Such was the fear of a gas attack that masks were issued to British civilians, like the little girl below, a year before war broke out. The evacuation of children from major cities was a logistical nightmare that required an army of volunteers, as shown in the poster at right

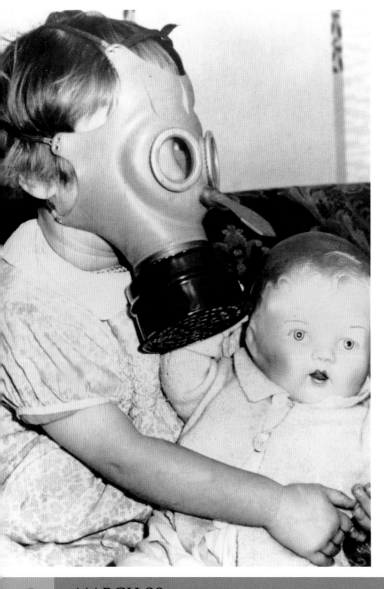

followed by a proclamation required by the existing Neutrality Act. And I trust that in the days to come our neutrality can be made a true neutrality.

It is of the utmost importance that the people of this country, with the best information in the world, think things through. The most dangerous enemies of American peace are those who, without well-rounded information on the whole broad subject of the past, present and future, undertake to speak with assumed authority, to talk in terms of glittering generalities, to give to the nation assurances or prophecies which are of little present or future value.

I myself cannot and do not prophesy the course of events abroad—and the reason is that because I have of necessity such a complete picture of what is going on in every part of the world, that I do not dare to do so. And the other reason is that I think it is honest for me to be honest with the people of the United States.

1939

MARCH 29
As German aggression threatens Poland, Britain and France agree to support the Poles

AUGUST 23
German Foreign Minister Joachim von Ribbentrop and his Soviet counterpart, Molotov, sign a Nazi-Soviet nonaggression treaty

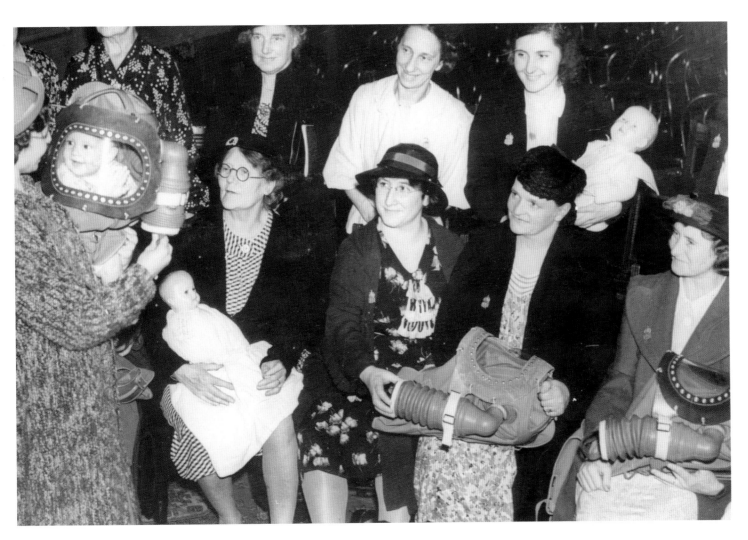

A special gas helmet was supplied for children under two years of age; the mothers above are shown how to use it. It was not uncommon to see groups of children, like the ones shown at right, being evacuated by train to the countryside, their gas masks in cardboard boxes hanging around their neck

I cannot prophesy the immediate economic effect of this new war on our nation but I do say that no American has the moral right to profiteer at the expense either of his fellow citizens or of the men, women and children who are living and dying in the midst of a war in Europe.

Some things we do know. Most of us in the United States believe in spiritual values. Most of us, regardless of what church we belong to, believe in the spirit of the New Testament—a great teaching which opposes itself to the use of force, of armed force, of marching armies and falling bombs. The overwhelming masses of our people seek peace—peace at home, and the kind of peace in other lands which will not jeopardize our peace at home.

AUGUST 25

Britain and Poland sign a formal pledge of mutual assistance

SEPTEMBER 1

Hitler invades Poland

1939

A group of children, above left, wait to join the throng of evacuees; air-raid shelters, like the one shown above, sprang up in gardens and backyards all over Britain

We have certain ideas and certain ideals of national safety and we must act to preserve that safety today and to preserve the safety of our children in future years.

That safety is and will be bound up with the safety of the Western Hemisphere and of the seas adjacent thereto. We seek to keep war from our own firesides by keeping war from coming to the Americas. For that we have historic precedent that goes back to the days of the administration of President George Washington. It is serious enough and tragic enough to every American family in every state in the Union to live in a world that is torn by wars on other continents. And those wars today affect every American home. It is our national duty to use every effort to keep those wars out of the Americas.

And at this time let me make the simple plea that partisanship and selfishness be adjourned; and that national unity be the thought that underlies all others.

This nation will remain a neutral nation, but I cannot ask that every American remain neutral in thought as well. Even a neutral has a right to take account of the facts. Even a neutral cannot be asked to close his mind or close his conscience. I have said not once but many times that I have seen war and that I hate war. I say that again and again.

I hope the United States will keep out of this war. I believe that it will. And I give you assurances and reassurance that every effort of your government will be directed toward that end. As long as it remains within my power to prevent, there will be no blackout of peace in the United States.

But for the Americans in Europe the blackout of peace was already in force. In the summer of 1939, 18-year-old

1939

SEPTEMBER 3

Britain and France declare war on Germany; later that afternoon they are joined by Australia, India and New Zealand

SEPTEMBER 3

Winston Churchill joins Chamberlain's cabinet as First Lord of the Admiralty

student James Goodson had come to Europe to perfect his French at the Sorbonne in Paris and visit relatives in England. On September 2, 1939, heading back to the United States and his university course, he was one of 300 Americans among the 1,103 passengers boarding the 13,500-ton SS *Athenia* at Liverpool. Just off the Hebrides, west of the Scottish mainland, the *Athenia* was spotted by the German submarine U-30, whose commander decided the liner was an armored cruiser.

We listened to Chamberlain's speech on the radio at eleven o'clock that morning and it was seven o'clock that evening that we were torpedoed. One hit amidships and one aft and almost immediately the midships area was flooded. I was on deck when it happened, immediately went to the hatches where the explosion had come up through the middle of the ship and looked down and saw the water shooshing around.

The ship immediately went dark. Then they put on emergency searchlights and, as I looked down to where the dining rooms had been and the companionways, here was this water shooshing around. The boat had lurched to one side and here were men, women and children floundering around in the water. There were a number of members of the *Athenia*'s crew and I said, "Come on, let's go down and rescue these people."

And strangely enough, as in the British Navy, so in the British Merchant Navy apparently, amazing to me as an American, very few of the crew of the *Athenia* could swim. So I went down into this water and was passing women and children and anybody I could help up to the crew, who were at the top and they had let ropes down.

It was a dramatic experience, particularly towards the end, when the ship had lurched even further, and the lights had gone out. I felt I should see if there were people trapped in the passageways in this main section. That was very dramatic, the dead bodies that were swooshing around in the water. I think the whole thing changed my attitude. I was plunged into the whole war thing, if you like, within a few minutes.

A Norwegian tanker picked up Goodson and took him to Galway in the Irish Republic, and from there he returned to Glasgow in Scotland. For this homesick American, war had started 27 months early. For the 93 passengers and 19 crew who perished, it was already over.

German tanks rumble across open countryside in Poland

SEPTEMBER 3

U.S. President Franklin Delano Roosevelt addresses the American people in his Fireside Chat radio broadcast, announcing that the United States will issue a proclamation of neutrality

SEPTEMBER 26

Issue of gas masks to British civilians commences

"Damn!" I exclaimed to Erwin. "The entire British Army went under here!" Erwin shook his head vigorously. "On the contrary! A miracle took place here!"

LUFTWAFFE SERVICEMAN
BERNT ENGELMAN
On visiting the Dunkirk beaches

CHAPTER TWO

THE FALL OF FRANCE

Within a week of Neville Chamberlain's declaration of war, the first elements of the British Expeditionary Force (BEF) disembarked in France, and the rest of the British Commonwealth declared war on Germany.

Percy Beaton, a 20-year-old north London watchmaker-cum-sapper, was serving with the Royal Engineers.

> They cheered us when the coach left Bethnal Green. The people there turned out in the thousands. Nobody thought about the war. They thought, "Oh it's going to pass over."

It did not. The invasion of Poland was to be followed by the German turn to the West. The word *Blitzkrieg* was entering the world's vocabulary.

By early October, the Poles had ceased fighting. As 1939 ended, the BEF was on the French and Belgian frontier, where, together with its French and Belgian allies, it sat and waited out the "phony war."

The BEF was commanded by a hero of World War I, Lord Gort, who answered to a vacillating French Army high command and to the varying queries of Britain's Secretary of War, Leslie Hore-Belisha. Percy Beaton's company moved from Cherbourg to Dieppe to Le Tréport.

> We were given a very large hotel which had to be converted into a hospital. There was a big marble staircase and I was washing this down with water. Down the stairs came Lord Gort and Hore-Belisha and a load of dignitaries. I said to them: "Mind out where you're going. You're making my bloody stairs dirty. I've just cleaned them." I was severely reprimanded by a young subaltern. He said: "Don't you know who you're talking to?" I said: "I haven't a bloody clue and I couldn't care less. Look at my stairs!"

Nurse Josephine Pearce had moved on from organizing evacuees. Born in France of English parents, she had arrived in Paris by the end of 1939 on her way to join Ambulance Unit 282, with the French Army in Alsace.

> The atmosphere in Paris was not the Paris I knew. There was something . . . I remember going to visit a great friend of mine in a top-floor flat in the Avenue Bosquet. But I remember her friend saying to me in French, "They talk of peace my dear, what peace? We've been sold." *Nous sommes vendus.* And it didn't register too much at the time. But when I eventually got up to Sarreguemines where the unit was, and inundated with questions from the nurses, I remember them asking me: "Was Paris behaving itself?" And at first I thought, "What do they mean?" I realized what they meant because we'd been at war for three months. And they were behaving as though there was no war. They were doing nothing, nothing to protect the people, nothing to protect themselves. And that was what Madame meant. We're sold. *Nous sommes vendus.*

On April 8, 1940, the Royal Navy mined Norwegian waters to prevent iron ore movement to Germany. On the 9th, the Germans launched an invasion of Norway, taking Denmark en route. In mid-April, British forces landed in Norway, but the campaign went badly and Allied forces were evacuated from Norway by early June. Back in the British House of Commons, the debate on Norway on May 7 and 8 found Chamberlain deserted by

At left, Canadian troops embark for France as part of the Expeditionary Force. Above, German troops make camp somewhere in Poland

At right, a father and daughter injured when the Germans bombed a residential area of Warsaw share a stretcher at an aid station. On the previous pages, a young German soldier wearing a British helmet acquired at Dunkirk. In the background, wrecked Allied equipment litters the Dunkirk beaches

SEPTEMBER 21

Head of Germany's Department of Security, Reinhard Heydrich, architect of the "Final Solution" for the extermination of the Jews, announces that all Jews in Poland are to be imprisoned in ghettos

SEPTEMBER 27

The Polish Army surrenders to the Germans in Warsaw

1939

many of his own supporters. On May 10, Winston Churchill became prime minister. On that day, too, the Germans invaded Holland and Belgium. The phony war was over.

Edward Davies-Scourfield was a 22-year-old officer with the King's Royal Rifle Corps which had been raised nearly two centuries earlier as the 60th Foot, known as the 60th Royal American Regiment. He was still in England when the news of the German attack came through.

> A feeling of excitement quivered through the battalion. This was coupled with an anxiety that we might not be there to take any part in the war, that the war would be won by some glorious Battle of the Marne counterattack and the whole thing would collapse and we would never even have got there.

The Wehrmacht used massed tanks, the Luftwaffe provided aircraft—including terrifying Stuka dive-bombers—in a coordinated, mechanized attack. By then Percy Beaton's company, based in the Broglie Woods near Rouen, had been detailed to blow up river bridges to stem the German advance.

> We saw a plane coming along and it was one of the Junkers type, I expect it was a Junkers 88. And as he came towards us we all cringed against the river bank. The rear

German paratroops land near Narvik, Norway, in April 1940

Winston Churchill became British prime minister on May 10, when Neville Chamberlain resigned

1939

OCTOBER 3

A neutral zone extending up to 600 miles off the coast of the American continent is established at a meeting in Panama attended by 21 countries of the Americas—within 3 days the Germans sink British merchant ship *Stonegate* inside the U.S. zone

OCTOBER 7

British Expeditionary Force of 158,000 men completes its crossing from England to France

gunner was like you see in magazines, a chap with a leather helmet on and goggles and white scarf slung around his neck. And he's sitting in the back of the plane with his gun there and he could have killed the lot of us—just one swing of his gun. Instead of that he just waved.

On May 10, 21-year-old William Harding, a Royal Artillery NCO, was based in Arras. When the *Blitzkrieg* began, his battery first advanced to the River Scarpe and then attempted to reposition. But a human tide was sweeping over the unit.

> The roads were absolutely jammed solid with civilians of all ages. The old people I shall never forget; some of them must have been in their 80s with huge bundles on their backs bowed right over walking along these hot roads. There were mothers pulling prams piled up with their belongings, little children hanging on their skirts crying, many were carrying babies. They were just trudging along in the heat, virtually worn out. We all responded straight away, all the lads rummaged in their pockets, and they started making loads of tea with what water we had and dishing it out to these poor unfortunate people.
>
> Then there was a terrible uproar, planes, there were flights of bombers coming over, low dive-bombing Stukas. Everybody was hopping mad, raving mad at seeing these refugees getting treated like this. There is nothing that infuriates a man more. It was just a blaze of fire. There were Brens firing, there was everything firing and there were these planes diving down with machine guns going and bombs going off, women screaming, kids screaming. It is just something you can never imagine but it's a thing you can't forget.

In World War I the Allies had stood against the German army on the Western Front for more than four years. In 1940, German General Heinz Guderian took 10 days to arrive on the French coast at Abbeville on May 20. This split France—and Allied forces—in two, with the Belgians, some of the French and the bulk of the British in the north.

For William Harding, the retreat from Arras brought him to Calais where an outnumbered British force and 800 French soldiers and sailors were under attack from the 10th Panzer Division and waves of Luftwaffe bombers.

Driven from their homes by intense fighting, the refugees shown above top clogged the roads, causing problems for the Allies and slowing the retreat into Dunkirk. Above, the alliance between Britain and France was promoted by the topical news magazine Picture Post, *showing French soldiers in training*

OCTOBER 18

The Soviet Union invades Estonia and shortly thereafter Latvia and Lithuania, as the Soviets move to secure the Baltic and gain access to ice-free harbors

NOVEMBER 4

The Neutrality Act is passed by the U.S. government, allowing the United States to supply Britain and France with arms and equipment

1939

Just as they had done during World War I, the Women's Land Army, shown at left, stepped in to provide farm labor, freeing male workers to fight. On the opposite page, rescued troops watch blazing oil installations at Dunkirk

Out at sea until May 20, there was assistance from four British, one French, and one Polish destroyer.

> They were constantly, non-stop, firing their shells. They were our artillery. At one stage I counted 80 Stukas. When I got to 80 I just stopped counting. The sky seemed full of them. Nine of the Stukas veered off to the ship that was nearest to us. And the ship immediately put up smoke. I saw the first Stuka dive into the smoke and there was an enormous explosion and a sheet of red flame through the smoke and the Stuka following disappeared as well. The other seven just wheeled round and went back over Calais and dropped their bombs.
>
> The smoke cleared and I fully expected to see some form of ship out there but there was nothing, nothing at all, no wreckage or anything. But the other ships never stopped their broadsiding. They carried on as if nothing had happened at all.

Edward Davies-Scourfield and the 2nd Battalion of the KRRC only arrived from Dover in Calais on Thursday, May 23, and became part of the defense of the town. But by midday Saturday the outlook was grim.

> A number of German light planes, Fiesler Storchs, flew suddenly quite low over our positions . . . dropping leaflets. It was all in French and it was telling us that we were in a hopeless position. We would be given one hour when there would be a complete ceasefire on the German side during which we were to collect ourselves together and march down the road to Kirkelle on the outskirts of town, without weapons and with our hands above our heads.
>
> This was a marvelous thing for us because we knew then we'd got a whole hour when we were not going to be fired upon. And we could get our food up and our ammunition up and go round and make sure the wounded had all evacuated. And sure enough exactly on the hour down came the artillery fire.
>
> Well, it was a pretty ghastly afternoon. The Germans pressed their attacks very strongly before they were repulsed. The whole of the citadel of Calais was totally in flames. Buildings were burning everywhere.
>
> The night was bad. High-level bombing, spasmodic artillery fire. We were all getting extremely tired and the strain was beginning to tell.

But by Sunday afternoon Davies-Scourfield was in the open, looking for survivors of his decimated platoon, surrounded by Germans.

> They hit me in the arm, a few seconds later through the ribs, which winded me rather and made a nasty hole I discovered in my back where it came out. And the third shot hit me across the head which more or less knocked me out. That was the end of the battle as far as I was

1939

NOVEMBER 8

Hitler cuts short an address to a Nazi gathering in Munich, narrowly escaping assassination when a bomb blast destroys the building

DECEMBER 23

The first Canadian troops arrive in Britain

concerned. The Germans came right through our positions that evening. I found it intensely painful to move at all. As the night wore on the Germans took no notice of me lying there. They didn't stick a bayonet in me and they didn't do anything for me. They were busy, and it began to rain. I did after a bit out of sheer necessity crawl or slide along very slowly. There was a little hut and I lay down there, and I passed out. I was woken by a German soldier just looking around. I gave him the most terrible fright because I moved. But I was treated with great chivalry.

That evening, from Washington, D.C., Franklin Roosevelt gave one of his Fireside Chats to the American people.

Tonight over the once peaceful roads of Belgium and France millions are now moving, running from their homes to escape bombs and shells and fire and machine-gunning, without shelter, and almost wholly without food. They stumble on, knowing not where the end of the road will be....

There are many among us who in the past closed their eyes to events abroad—because they believed in utter good faith what some of their fellow Americans told them—that what was taking place in Europe was none of our business; that no matter what happened over there, the United States could always pursue its peaceful and unique course in the world....To those who would not admit the possibility of the approaching storm—to all of them the past two weeks have meant the shattering of many illusions. They have

lost the illusion that we are remote and isolated and, therefore, secure against the dangers from which no other land is free. In some quarters, with this rude awakening has come fear, fear bordering on panic.

It is said that we are defenseless. It is whispered by some that, only by abandoning our freedom, our ideals, our way of life, can we build our defenses adequately, can we match the strength of the aggressors. I did not share those illusions. I do not share these fears.

The epic battle for Calais—and the battle for Boulogne (which fell on May 25)—helped the evacuation from Dunkirk, which began on May 27, the day Calais fell. The BEF and many other Allied units began to withdraw within a perimeter around Dunkirk. Outside it, on May 23, von Rundstedt—on Hitler's authority— had ordered his armor to halt, leaving the Allied enclave to the attention of the Luftwaffe. The expectation in

JANUARY 8

Food rationing is introduced in Britain with weekly allowances for butter or lard (4 ozs), sugar (12 ozs), raw bacon or ham (4 ozs), eggs (2) and cooked bacon or ham (3.5 ozs). Meat will be rationed within two months

MARCH 12

Russo-Finnish Treaty is signed, ending three months of fighting. Finland had 70,000 casualties, 25,000 killed; the Soviets 400,000 casualties, 200,000 killed

1940

Britain was that of the hundreds of thousands of British, Belgian, Canadian, Czechoslovak, Polish and French soldiers, maybe 45,000 could be saved.

Across the English Channel, in Portsmouth, 25-year-old Elizabeth Quayle of the Women's Auxiliary Air Force was on liaison duties, running the one phone line into Dunkirk.

> A few miles away a disaster was unfolding. I'm rather ashamed to say it put the fear of God into me! Because every time you came on duty, we knew where the Huns were, we had maps with pins in, and they seemed to be advancing very fast. The Dunkirk crisis itself was unbelievable.
>
> Dunkirk was full of people mostly who had walked, not in any form of order. They had just got there as fast as they could. Some had hitched lifts wherever possible. There were a lot of refugees coming in. It had been bombed. We knew that a lot of the troops were sheltering in the buildings along the shore. We had no idea they were going to be rescued, it seemed the whole army was going to be bottled up there and the whole army was going to be captured.

Twenty-one-year-old Royal Engineer officer Allan Younger was among those at Dunkirk.

> To the west end of Dunkirk somebody had set fire to some oil storage tanks and a vast plume of smoke was coming out of this. Now by good luck that plume of smoke was being blown exactly along the beach. Therefore if the German aircraft – which were the main danger then – did come below the plume of smoke they were very low and everyone would fire at them and many got shot down. So all they could do was toss bombs through the plume of smoke and they couldn't really see what they were firing at.

But Winston Churchill had demanded that Sir Hugh Dowding, Commander-in-Chief of Fighter Command, commit more planes to the struggle in France against the Luftwaffe. It was a haphazard and costly operation, and Dowding began to fear that he would lose the ability to defend Great Britain with the losses the RAF was incurring across the Channel. At Dunkirk the survival of armies that could, one day, fight again, was at stake. The troops were subjected to continuous bombardment, and many felt that they had been let down by the RAF.

The sands near Dunkirk—thousands of troops queued for hour after hour on the beach and in the water, waiting to be rescued

1940

MARCH 20

Édouard Daladier resigns as prime minister of France and is replaced by Paul Reynaud

APRIL 8

Germany invades Norway—three days later the Royal Navy sinks eight German destroyers in the Battle of Narvik. Within a week, Allied troops will land in Norway

At left, Tony Bartley was a Spitfire pilot with 92 Squadron during the Dunkirk evacuations. Immediately after Dunkirk, Canadian soldiers newly arrived in Britain, like the ones shown below, would stand as the only properly organized fighting force ready to defend the English coast

Tony Bartley was a Spitfire pilot over Dunkirk. You saw a multitude of little craft. And there were naval ships shooting at everything, and lots of little boats came over. And the troops were just pouring down, going into the water, swimming out to the boats.

Hugh Dundas, a 19-year-old Spitfire pilot, watched the progress of that "great pall of smoke."

It came up and spread out and then leveled off and went down the Channel for a distance of 75–100 miles. Underneath that there was a lot of haze and general mayhem. It was altogether a very confusing scene, cloud, smoke. I think that's one of the reasons why perhaps the army had the impression that the Royal Air Force wasn't there half the time, because there was no control. We were outside the range of our own radar. We just had to go there. All the time one was playing a game of blindman's buff.

Somebody looking back at it from an historical perspective who wasn't there imagines the coast of France, and Dunkirk, and a clear summer sky and lots of things on the beach and the sea and perhaps a little cloud here and there. It wasn't like that at all.

Operation Dynamo, the evacuation from Dunkirk, involved hundreds of vessels from Royal Navy warships

MAY 10

British Prime Minister Neville Chamberlain resigns and is replaced by Winston Churchill

MAY 10

German *Blitzkrieg* (lightning war) is launched against Holland, Belgium, Luxembourg and France

1940

through paddle steamers to motorboats and yachts. One of the boats was the *Massey Shaw*, a shallow-draft firefighting ship based on the River Thames in London. Thirty-year-old Francis Codd of the Auxiliary Fire Brigade was a member of the crew.

> We'd had lunch on a fine sunny day. And suddenly the bell went to assemble us all. I suppose we were about 70 or 80 of us, and the station officer said, "A message from Lambeth Headquarters. The *Massey Shaw* is going to Dunkirk."
>
> We'd no idea what would be the duties of the *Massey Shaw*. We imagined of course that it would be fighting fires. "Now, I want a crew," he said, "which will be under the skipper of the *Massey Shaw* with the engine crew of regulars. And I want about half a dozen Auxiliary volunteers." There was a tiny second of hesitation. And then as one man we all stepped forward. He didn't know what to do because he'd got to choose about six out of about 70 people.
>
> We left Ramsgate in the afternoon. The sea was like a

The evacuation from Dunkirk, shown above, code-named Operation Dynamo, was to last for almost a week and involve over 860 vessels. In England, a patriotic public profile was presented by prominent women such as Lady Edwina Mountbatten (standing at right), London County Commissioner for the Red Cross

1940

MAY 15

Holland surrenders to the Germans; the British, French and Belgian armies retreat in the face of overwhelmingly superior German forces

MAY 28

Belgium capitulates and Operation Dynamo, the evacuation of Allied troops from Dunkirk, commences

In wartime Britain, key workers such as the telephone operators, at left, learned to do their jobs wearing gas masks. Above, packed onto the deck of a ship, weary British troops arrive from Dunkirk, relieved to be home at last

millpond. Quite exceptional. After an hour or so the first thing we could see was a black column of smoke, visible perhaps from 10 miles away. We thought perhaps the whole of Dunkirk was alight and burning. As we got closer we could see that it was an oil fire. Then we could see the outline of the coast and then from about a mile away, still no airplanes, no bombs, no menace; then we could see it was a flat beach, a sandy beach. And then we saw the silhouette of houses against this sky; not a continuous line of buildings but breaks in the buildings.

I thought I could see a wrecked small craft and then a bigger craft. Gradually we could see dark shapes against the sand and then we saw that there were hundreds, thousands of people on this sand and stretching up to the line of houses. But mainly we noticed that there were columns of men stretching down to the sea and into the sea. We didn't really understand what this was at first. And then it suddenly occurred to us that these were columns of men waiting to be picked up.

JUNE 2

Allied forces are evacuated from Norway

JUNE 3

Royal Navy destroyer H.M.S. *Shakiri* is the last evacuation ship to leave Dunkirk. Over 860 vessels, from pleasure boats and tugs to cross-Channel ferries and warships, were involved in evacuating over 330,000 Allied servicemen

1940

The skipper of the *Massey Shaw* was quite rightly very apprehensive that the props would get tangled up with the lines and debris that was in the water nearer the shore. Although we had a very shallow draft it seemed to be a high risk. In fact the props did get jammed. And we had to jump out of the boat, switch off the engines of course, free the propeller from tangled rope. So we decided it would be fatal to go too far in. Although we could have gone into probably three or four feet of water we stayed in about six feet of water some 50 yards further back than we could have been.

One of our auxiliaries, Shiner Wright, was a good swimmer. And he went from the *Massey Shaw* some 50 to 100 yards to a wrecked boat which was right inshore in about two or three feet of water. He swam with what we called the grass line which is a rope that floats on water. And he tied it to the wreck so that we had a fixed line into shallow water.

They got a rowing boat that would hold a very few people, a light rowing boat, and worked it along the line pulling hand over hand. Whoever was in charge of the column of men lined up near the shore end of the line detailed six men into the rowing boat to pull along the line till they reached the *Massey Shaw*, climb out on board and send their rowing boat back. I think we took aboard 36 soldiers out of the water that night. And when we were full there was nothing more we could do. We upped anchor and set course for Ramsgate.

The Dunkirk evacuation ended on June 4. Some 224,585 British Commonwealth and 112,546 French and Belgian soldiers had been rescued. By late June more than half a million men in total had been evacuated from France. Soon after the last Allied troops had left Dunkirk, two young off-duty Luftwaffe members arrived on the beach. They were friends, anti-Nazis, and deeply depressed by Hitler's triumph. One of them was Bernt Engelman.

On the beaches and in the dunes north of Dunkirk thousands of light and heavy weapons lay in the sands, along with munitions crates, field kitchens, scattered cans of rations and innumerable wrecks of British army trucks.

"Damn!" I exclaimed to Erwin. "The entire British army went under here!"

Erwin shook his head vigorously. "On the contrary! A miracle took place here! If the German tanks and Stukas and navy had managed to surround the British here, shooting most of them, and taking the rest prisoner, then England wouldn't have any trained soldiers left. Instead the British seem to have rescued them all— and a lot of Frenchmen too. Adolf can say goodbye to his *Blitzkrieg* against England...."

On June 22, France surrendered. France signed an

1940

JUNE 10

Italy declares war on Britain and France. Canada declares war on Italy

JUNE 14

German troops enter Paris

armistice with Germany, and Marshal Pétain set up his collaborationist government in Vichy. Elizabeth Quayle, from her job in French liaison, heard the news early:

> I was extremely upset, because it never occurred to me that we would survive. I thought we were defeated and frankly thought we would surrender and sue for peace.

Evacuation from other ports continued after Dunkirk—as did the fighting. And even after the fall of France, units were still making their way back to England. Josephine Pearce's situation had become desperate. She had been in Alsace, attached to the French Fourth Army. Then her 26-strong ambulance unit 282 headed south.

> France was just one mass of different regiments, different generals, hither and thither, none knowing what the other was doing. And it wasn't until we got into the Champagne territory that we began to realize that we were retreating. Sometimes we got proper instructions, and when we got to where we were told to go, they had gone. And it was constantly so. We were going to set up a hospital there. They'd gone. Till in the end we found no one and we realized we were on our own.
>
> Then came the terrible day when the armistice was announced. And then we were the enemy. And if it hadn't been for the medical orderlies, medical students, staying with us, and the médecin chef Dr. Gosset staying with us, as long as they did, I think we would have been taken prisoner. They stayed with us as far into the south of France as they could possibly stay. And in that way we managed to get petrol, until came the day when we were siphoning petrol from one car, one van or one lorry into the next car, all the time saying "But where are our own soldiers? Where is our air force? Why aren't they here?"
>
> After the armistice, we knew that we were the enemy. And the most dreadful thing to us was that as we passed through villages, they would throw flowers at us thinking we were the British, coming to save them. That was the state that France was in. Nobody knew what was happening at all.
>
> You felt so futile when you saw a granny hugging a baby that was absolutely dead, sitting on top of a cart piled up with furniture and being machine-gunned. And the baby had got the bullet. And the granny swaying backwards and forwards with the baby, holding it to protect it. And she didn't know she was protecting a dead baby. One saw so much that was utterly unbelievable.

Sleeping in barns and ditches, the 26 women made their way toward Bordeaux and, via the Royal Navy and a passenger ship, back to England.

Nineteen-year-old Roland Beamont had flown a Hurricane with 87 Squadron in France and Belgium.

> We who'd been in the French battle came home convinced that there was only one thing that was going to stop the enemy crossing the Channel and that would be us. We could see that coming all the way through the summer. By July and August it was building up to a fury. We knew absolutely that there was just one front line holding. It had to be us that did it.

Marshal Pétain, pictured at right, surrendered France to the Germans and set up a puppet government in Vichy. On the opposite page, Allied equipment is being examined by curious German soldiers in the aftermath of Dunkirk

JUNE 16

Paul Reynaud resigns as prime minister of France and is replaced by Marshal Henri Philippe Pétain, who immediately sues for peace with Germany

JUNE 22

An armistice is signed between France and Germany in the same railway carriage used for the signing of the 1918 armistice after World War I

1940

. . . we shall fight on the beaches, we shall fight on the landing grounds, we shall fight in the fields and in the streets . . . we shall never surrender . . . .

PRIME MINISTER WINSTON CHURCHILL
House of Commons
June 1940

CHAPTER THREE

BRITAIN UNDER SIEGE

At the end of May 1940, a debate took place within the British Cabinet on which the future of the world hinged. Foreign Secretary Lord Halifax urged his colleagues to consider a negotiated peace with Hitler. It was a reasonable position. France was about to fall to Germany, most of the rest of Europe had gone, or was going, the same way.

Hitler had expressed his admiration for the British Empire, and there was the likelihood that Britain would be allowed to retain its colonies, although Germany's former colonies—taken away in 1918—would have to be handed back. Germany would also have to be allowed a free hand in Eastern Europe. To fight on seemed . . . unreasonable. This was a common view, one held by Joseph Kennedy, U.S. ambassador to Great Britain, even before the war had broken out.

The young student James Goodson had heard the pessimistic view of the outcome of the war expressed in London in the summer of 1939.

> Our ambassador informed most of us Americans that we should immediately make plans to get back to the States because there was going to be a war, which England, of course, would lose.

But the new prime minister, backed by his predecessor Chamberlain, rejected Halifax's proposal. On June 4, 1940, 65-year-old Winston Churchill addressed the House of Commons.

> Even though large tracts of Europe and many old and famous states have fallen or may fall into the grip of the Gestapo and all the odious apparatus of Nazi rule, we shall not flag or fail. We shall go on to the end, we shall fight in France, we shall fight on the seas and oceans, we shall fight with growing confidence and growing strength in the air, we shall defend our island, whatever the cost may be. We shall fight on the beaches, we shall fight on the landing grounds, we shall fight in the fields and in the streets, we shall fight in the hills; we shall never surrender, and even if, which I do not for a moment believe, this island or a large part of it were subjugated and starving, then our Empire beyond the seas, armed and guarded by the British Fleet, would carry on the struggle, until, in God's good time, the New World, with all its power and might, steps forth to the rescue and the liberation of the old.

British Foreign Secretary Lord Halifax (left)

On the previous pages, Winston Churchill at his desk. In the background, British boys salvage waste paper. Churchill, seen delivering a radio address below, knew that Britain's survival depended on massive aid from across the Atlantic

JUNE 22

In Canada, royal assent is given to the National Resources and Mobilization Act, allowing conscription to be introduced and stipulating that all males over the age of 16 must register for national service

JUNE 23

Hitler tours Paris

The Canadian Essex Scottish Regiment, above, leaves for England in August 1940. At left, a German propaganda poster promotes the Luftwaffe, "Our Air Force"

Refugees from across Europe had arrived in Britain to escape the terror and to join the struggle against it. Many German anti-Nazis were promptly interned on the Isle of Man. One of them was Dr. K. E. Hinrichsen.

> Once Dunkirk was over and it was a question of only defending Britain I think one thought "It will take a long time but Britain will win." Otherwise you could only commit suicide.

The evacuation of Britain's city dwellers, the vast majority of them children, to small towns and villages had begun before the war broke out. Around 1.5 million people moved in that first wartime autumn. During the phony war, many parents brought their children back, but events in 1940 triggered another wave of departures. Rich and poor, town and country, northerners and southerners were suddenly forced to face each other. The results were heartening, heartbreaking, farcical, tragic, and they sowed the seeds of post-war social revolution.

Eight-year-old Ernest Munson was a kid from West Ham in east London, who found himself among local kids in Timberscombe in rural Somerset.

> There was always a little bit of needle. But mostly we got on OK with them, children don't hold too much malice for anybody else. Several things got blamed on the evacuees. I can remember one incident; a hayrick caught fire and that was blamed on the evacuee boys.
>
> I can remember a group of us boys walking from the village, the house where I was billeted was just on the outskirts of the village. It was about three-quarters of a mile up a small narrow road and we was walking up there just after we'd been delivered to Somerset and one of the boys in his little Cockney

The end of the phony war brought about a new wave of evacuations, shown above. Clutching a bag of belongings and his gas mask, the little boy at left is distraught at having to leave his London home

accent said 'Innit funny round here?" he said. "There ain't no houses!"

And there weren't. There was the house that we was billeted in, 200 yards down the lane was the mill, an old mill, just above that was a chapel, and then you got back into the village again, but from where we were stood you could only see one or two houses! And that was strange. That was strange.

Many children were forced to make long journeys, but for four-year-old Marylebone-born Londoner Sylvia Townson, it was just a short trip to Buckinghamshire, west of the capital.

I remember getting off the train in High Wycombe and standing on the platform, being pushed into some kind of crocodile, and walking from the station in the middle of the road, again in a great column, and taken to a reception center, and people standing on the

JUNE 25

Canadian destroyer H.M.C.S. *Fraser* collides with British cruiser H.M.S. *Calcutta* and sinks in the Bay of Biscay while evacuating troops from France. Forty-seven of the Canadian crew die along with 13 British sailors

JUNE 27

Japanese troops invade part of Hong Kong

Evacuees like these boys from Lowestoft in East Anglia had "luggage labels" on their clothing in case they got lost en route

The arrival of inner-city children to rural areas was not always as harmonious as the photograph below suggests. Surrounded by suitcases, the little girl below right is being evacuated from Chatham in southeast England

JUNE 28
Italian Governor-General of Libya, Marshal Balbo, dies when his plane is shot down by his own anti-aircraft guns over Tobruk

JUNE 28
The Pope offers to mediate between the British, Germans and Italians

1940

DER FÜHRER GROSS DEUTSCHLANDS

pavements. I wasn't sure what they were saying at the time, I wasn't taking very much notice at that age. I was probably more aware of the people walking with me. But my mother did tell me afterwards that people were shouting quite a lot of abuse, calling us foreigners and refugees. They probably didn't want a great influx of Londoners into somewhere as suburban and select as High Wycombe in those days. So I think it wasn't very pleasant for the people arriving there.

Lilias Woolven, then age 12, was living in Hull and then evacuated to Scarborough.

I thought it was a great joke. You get into these school stories and you think "Oh it's just like a boarding school." We were evacuated to a hotel, the Astoria, which overlooked the Italian Gardens at Scarborough. They wouldn't do it now, but there were two girls to a bed and we were six in a bedroom.

There was an alternative to staying in Great Britain. Through the Children's Overseas Reception Board

Mothers put on a brave face below as they watch their children depart on evacuation trains at London's Waterloo Station. German propaganda posters like the one at left promoted Hitler's dynamic, heroic image

JUNE 28

In America, Congress passes the Alien Registration Act, under which all foreign nationals must register and be fingerprinted. It is also now illegal to call for the overthrow of the U.S. government

JUNE 28

Charles de Gaulle is recognized by Britain as leader of the Free French

evacuees were sent to America, Canada, South Africa and Australasia. Thirty-year-old Beatrice Wright was an American who had married a British Conservative MP, but, with the war, she had sent her two children, age seven and five, to stay with her family on Long Island.

> They were there with my uncle and aunt together with the most wonderful nanny we had, who was a member of the family, she was so remarkable. She went with them— we had no qualms as to their well-being. They were with family, who we knew and loved, and a nanny we absolutely trusted and they started their schooling in America.
>
> For us it was much easier than it was for other people.

Ten-year-old Colin Ryder-Richardson, then living in Wales, was being sent as a private evacuee to the United States and a wartime home in New York. The chosen ship was the 11,000-ton *City of Benares*. On September 13, 1940, Ryder-Richardson was one of the 90 children among the 199 passengers and 209 crew who set sail from Liverpool as part of Convoy OB-213 for Montreal. By then the German U-boat fleet had moved into new bases in Brittany and was ranging far out into the Atlantic. Four days and 600 miles out into the ocean, the Royal Navy escort was withdrawn. Within hours U-48 fired a torpedo at the British ship shortly after the 10-year-old had gone to bed.

> There was a very loud bang and almost immediately a smell of, presumably cordite or something like that, it was an unmistakable smell. There were a lot of shouts so I immediately knew what was happening and I had a slight problem because I was in my pyjamas—my pink pyjamas—and I hadn't got my lifejacket but I immediately put it on, as I got out of bed, put on my slippers and then I had a dressing gown and now I had a problem. Did I put the dressing gown under the lifejacket or on top of the lifejacket? It wouldn't go over the top of the lifejacket and things were beginning to happen rather fast. I thought I mustn't panic, on the other hand I must think these things through rationally.

Ryder-Richardson made his way to the assembly station. There was no panic on the stricken ship, despite a force-10 gale. *City of Benares*'s elderly nurse took him under her wing and they boarded a lifeboat—which promptly took water, immersing and numbing him up to his chest. Paradoxically, the waterlogging prevented

The liner City of Benares, *at top, prior to its fateful voyage across the Atlantic. At bottom, one of the lifeboats from* City of Benares *with some of the survivors*

that lifeboat from capsizing—the fate suffered by many of the others. In appalling weather many of the ship's crew were lost. As the night wore on, other survivors, either clinging to the boat or inside it, perished from the freezing weather and from choking in oil. Ryder-Richardson held on to the old nurse and was befriended by John Day, a 59-year-old professor of economics at Montreal's McGill University:

> He was gently suggesting to me that I should release the ship's nurse, as in his view she was dead, and I was so cold that really I couldn't really move my arms and legs. I was holding on for my life, holding on to her, and I really didn't want to let go of her because I felt that I would then lose whatever resource that I had in my arms but it then became apparent to me that she was dying, and possibly was dead, and I still couldn't let go of her. I just

felt that any minute we might be rescued and there might be the possibility of life within her and it seemed to be so—there was no need to let go of her—it would be cruel to let go of her. She was a person, even though she was patently dead and her mouth was open.

They said, "Come on, Colin let go of her, let go of her" and I just couldn't do it. Eventually the storm solved the problem and she was swept away. We were getting fewer and fewer in numbers. There was a young man, a student, an Englishman as far as I know, who said he wanted something to eat or drink and he started drinking the seawater and everybody was telling him—the other people were telling him "No," in between the waves, because it was very difficult to talk. The waves were just flowing over you. He was insistent on it and the next minute he jumped from the relative safety of the lifeboat into the sea.

After 20 hours Colin Ryder-Richardson, described as a "wisp of a Welsh boy" in the Toronto *Globe & Mail*, was rescued, one of 14 survivors from the 38 originally in his lifeboat. Among the 258 people from the ship who died, 77 were children. The loss of the *Benares* was the end of overseas evacuation. Children and adults faced the

Roadside signposts like the ones above were removed to confuse the enemy in the event of invasion

Shortages of all sorts made recycling a priority. The Scouts at left are collecting paper salvage. On the opposite page, roadblocks and barricades to be manned by the Home Guard were put in place ready for the invasion

JULY 1

German forces invade Jersey, bringing all of the Channel Islands under German control—the only part of the British Isles to be conquered by Hitler

JULY 1

Allied shipping sunk by German U-boats in the Atlantic now totals 900,000 tons for the first six months of the year

bombs—and the threat of invasion which dominated the summer of 1940—together. In June the family of RAF fighter pilot Hugh Dundas was living in Yorkshire.

> Even there, far away from the Channel, there were constant preparations taking place then. People cutting down trees and putting them in fields and taking all the signs down in the little by-roads and all roads. There was a real feeling in the country that invasion was likely. After all, we'd seen what had happened in Poland and France and Holland and Belgium. There wasn't much doubt about what we were up to in anybody's mind.

For 18-year-old Nancy Bazin, a teacher in Exmouth, England, fear of invasion meant bizarre maneuvers.

> We were told that we had to mobilize all our civilian force in Exmouth to resist the invasion that was likely to come across the Channel at any time. Our local battalion of Devons who were organizing this, were going round with microphones and loudspeakers, calling us to come to the beach with spades and shovels, anything we could lay our hands on. We were told to dig, and we dug a trench in the sand, and we were, at the same time as digging, and getting blisters on our hands, and working for hours on this, we were looking out to sea expecting to see these flotillas of German invading troops come. On this whole two-mile stretch of beach we were digging this trench, and it was so obviously hopeless because, with the wind and the rain and the high tide, all our work would disappear. But we did it, in this extraordinary way, believing that somehow we were defending . . .

In the wake of the Dunkirk evacuation, for a time the only properly equipped and organized military group defending Great Britain was the Canadian Army's First Division. Meanwhile, in May 1940, the British set up

JULY 2

The Luftwaffe launches its first daylight raid against British mainland targets

JULY 2

A British passenger ship, *Arandora Star* en route to Canada carrying 1,500 German and Italian prisoners of war, is sunk by a German U-boat

1940

the Local Defence Volunteers. By July it had become the Home Guard and its tasks were to man roadblocks, watch out for German paratroopers, and carry out acts of sabotage to delay the invaders. As the threat of invasion grew, people like 45-year-old Harold Gower, a World War I veteran, became the backbone of the new

Originally recruited as Local Defence Volunteers (LDV), the soldiers above became the Home Guard in 1940. The British Army had lost so much equipment in France that Canadian troops, like these talking to War Minister Anthony Eden, were vital to Britain's defense

organization. He was a Home Guard musketry training officer in Amersham, west of London.

> Except for a few in Amersham, in the villages they were just a bunch of chaps. Although some of them had been in the forces before they didn't seem to me to know anything. I don't think they knew which end of a gun the bullet came out of. They took a helluva lot of training. They were a mixture of ages, reserved occupations most of them, that is to say they were farm laborers or whatever. We didn't have plans for blowing up bridges because we had no explosives of any sort. Only Molotov cocktails and that sort of thing.

In 1940 John Graham was a 17-year-old, and he joined the Isle of Wight battalion of the Home Guard in the south of England near Southampton.

> My company commander was Sir Ralph Gore who lived at Bembridge, who was a great yachtsman. My platoon commander was Tom Love, who became the local publican. And they made me a lance corporal although I was the youngest member on the strength of having got certificate A in the Cheltenham College Officer Training Unit. And we spent some very happy months there.

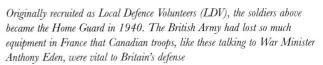

JULY 2

Canadian destroyer *St. Laurent* rescues 857 survivors from the *Arandora Star*

JULY 2

The Bank of Canada in Montreal receives delivery of £30 million in gold and £200 million from the Bank of England for safekeeping

Two Home Guard members practice with a Vickers machine gun on a Surrey village green

European statesmen exiled in London included Free French leader General Charles de Gaulle, above left, and leader of the Polish Government in exile General Wladyslaw Sikorski, above

In May 1940, with the catastrophic loss of weapons by the British in France, President Roosevelt had 500,000 rifles, 129 million rounds of ammunition and 80,000 machine guns sent to Britain. John Graham's battalion was among the beneficiaries.

> We had American P14 rifles, 50 rounds of ammunition, a civilian gas mask, a leather belt, leather gaiters, boots and a bayonet. We went on duty as a section every fifth night, for which we got one and threepence to cover the cost of the sandwiches. I've said I was the youngest member of the platoon. The oldest chap, Chichester—sergeant—had been in the Boer War. He was the best shot of the lot of us. As far as I remember the section consisted of a chap called Smith, a gentleman of leisure who'd only got one arm—he'd lost the other one in the First World War, and a chap called Allen, the local electrician, who was therefore in a reserved occupation, Henley the baker's boy, who had TB, and my particular colleague with whom I always did stag—went on sentry duty—was Mick Curran. And Mick Curran had been a stoker at the Battle of Jutland in the Royal Navy. And a most amusing colleague but he suffered terribly from wind.
>
> And we used to go on duty together—used to do stag—in a field of cows behind Nodes Fort. And of course from our vantage point we could see Portsmouth and Southampton and even London on a clear night being bombed. But with the noise of the bombing and Mick Curran's wind we didn't get a great deal of sleep.

Just back from rescuing soldiers on *Massey Shaw* at Dunkirk, Francis Codd encountered the Home Guard.

JULY 3

Following earlier seizures of French vessels, the Royal Navy takes over all French navy warships anchored in British south coast ports, encountering some armed resistance from the French

JULY 3

The Royal Navy opens fire on the French fleet in Algeria to stop the ships falling into German hands. Over 1,000 French servicemen are killed

1940

An idealized English countryside became part of Britain's domestic propaganda war

Although Home Guard units like the one below trained enthusiastically, they knew that if the Germans landed they stood little chance. On the opposite page, the British were actively recruiting women for work on the production lines far earlier in the war than the Germans

JULY 4

In Africa, the Italians launch the latest in a series of air raids against Alexandria in Egypt, and Italian troops attack British forces on the Sudanese border

JULY 5

President Roosevelt bans the shipment of strategic materials from the U.S. to Japan

I remember I was wearing the reefer jacket of the Auxiliary fireman and the dark trousers. I had an open neck white tennis shirt and my cap. Now I was extremely sunburnt. And my hair being fair always bleaches completely, almost white, and was a bit long and unruly.

When I got to Sandwich on my way back to Ramsgate—Sandwich is a place I've known since a child and has always been one of my favorite towns—and I thought, well, I must have a walk round in the hour I'd got to wait between buses, walk round the town and have a look at the churches. And there was one big churchyard. I'm not sure it isn't called St. Clements and a particularly fine church. So I walked towards it. And stood in the churchyard looking up at the tower, the old flint tower, and admiring it on this calm beautiful summer evening, and suddenly I was pounced on by two enormous men. They didn't seem to be hurting me. But their obvious enmity towards me was a bit offputting. And they were feeling for guns. Anyway they frisked me, the only time I think in my life I have ever been frisked. And they looked in my pockets for something incriminating.

They said, "We've had a lot of German spies here, you know. And we're not satisfied."

So I said, "Well, I'm not a German spy."

They said, "Well we think you might be. You look German."

So I said, "I don't." I said, "This is my standard uniform. I've been to Dunkirk."

They said, "Well, that's your story. Come along to the police station."

Well, that was the first I'd heard of the Home Guard in action. And they were just enthusiastic local Sandwich Home Guard people, thought they had trapped a German descended on them by parachute and out to take all sorts of notes about church towers and points of advantage for troops due to arrive just after me. I could see the comic side. And of course I didn't really treat it seriously. And I was two hours before I was driven back by the police in a police car in state, back to our headquarters in Ramsgate. Rumor of course had reached them by then from London because they'd been alerted by then that Codd of the River Service had been arrested in Ramsgate for spying.

WOMEN OF BRITAIN
COME INTO THE FACTORIES
ASK AT ANY EMPLOYMENT EXCHANGE FOR ADVICE AND FULL DETAILS

Back on the Isle of Wight, John Graham thought that his battalion was rather proud of itself.

Although we had minimal equipment and very little training and were pretty senile or juvenile, we had a good spirit and it was our territory. We felt the Germans if they came would be at a disadvantage initially, I mean either seasick or parachuted or something. We did at least know the fields and the hedges and everything else. And we'd put up a good show for about half a day. And that would be the end of us. But they never came.

JULY 8

The Metropolitan Police in London, traditionally unarmed, are to carry firearms when guarding sensitive or vulnerable targets

JULY 9

Tea rationing of two ounces a week per person is introduced in Britain

1940

Wartime Fashions

[T]he fashion world, forever in a state of dramatic and permanent a change as any other facet of life during World War II.

In the 1930s, what the fashionable woman in Britain wore depended largely on her social status. Haute couture was for the upper class while the emerging middle class shopped at quality department stores where clothes would be made to measure or expertly altered to fit. Working-class people bought from less expensive shops or market stalls, more often than not depending on hand-me-downs or second-hand items.

Although the class system in the U.S. was less overt, the social elite still looked to London or Paris, with the "English" look of King Edward VIII and the chic masculine style of Wallis Simpson providing inspiration. The sophistication of American mass manufacture, however, meant that good-quality, affordable and fashionable clothing was far more widely available. This, ultimately, would have a major influence on popular fashion on both sides of the Atlantic after the war.

Utility style—high heels were restricted to two inches

Clothes rationing was introduced in Britain on June 1, 1941. Each adult was allocated 66 coupons per year and to buy a man's suit, for example, whatever the price being paid, required 22 coupons. Shoes were rationed to one new leather pair per year, although for many

their first completely new pair of shoes would be those issued to them by the quartermaster when they enlisted.

Further to conserve vital supplies, the British government introduced the Utility Scheme, official manufacturing restrictions covering everything from the number of pleats in ladies' skirts to the width of collars, seams and even belts. Ornamentation in the form of embroidery or leather or fur trims was also banned.

With materials of all kinds diverted to the war effort, shortages became commonplace. Silk stockings were soon in short supply and nylons, introduced in America prewar, were not widely available in Britain until after the war. Nevertheless, a girl must look her best, and for a small fee women could have their legs painted to look as if they were stocking-clad. Many achieved the same effect by using cocoa powder or gravy browning. Sadly, the homemade alternative could easily be ruined by a shower of rain!

While the wardrobes of the wealthy were often extensive enough to weather the storm, others were encouraged to "Make-do and Mend," altering or repairing any kind of garment before attempting to buy new. For working-class women this had always been second nature, and most already

Go through your wardrobe

Make-do and Mend

possessed the needlework skills to help them extend the life of their families' clothes.

Women's magazines offered endless tips and advice on how to effect repairs, and department stores offered previously unheard-of services to transform men's pants into women's skirts or evening dresses into work clothes. Since blackout curtains now had to be hung at the windows, old curtain fabric was often reused as dress material.

Shoes were the only item rationed in the United States, the allocation being two new leather pairs per year, but restrictions like those in Britain were placed on manufacturers. This led to similar fashion styles on both sides of the Atlantic, with women's clothing adopting an austere, military look. Similarities in fashion trends in the United States and Britain had flourished in any case, influenced by Hollywood stars such as Rita Hayworth, Lana Turner and Lauren Bacall. While the more extravagant costumes seen on-screen were totally impractical, hairstyles were often achievable and an obvious way for fashion-starved women to recapture some essential femininity. Unfortunately, hair styling products such as setting lotion also became scarce, although resourceful young women again resorted to homemade

Models pose in Berkertex utility dresses designed by top couturier Norman Hartnell

remedies such as sugared water in an attempt to achieve the same effect.

The American influence grew ever stronger with the end of the war, and a more casual sporty look began to dominate women's fashion for everyday wear. The mass manufacture of affordable clothing and changing social attitudes would come to mean that many of the prewar attitudes to fashion in Britain now became distinctly unfashionable.

That's not to say that haute couture and more formal wear were gone. Far from it. The "New Look" of the late 1940s, attributed mainly to Christian Dior, was an obvious reaction to the constraints of the war years. With its full skirts, pinched waists and elegant jackets, the New Look was flamboyantly feminine and, despite the ongoing rationing in Britain, it was a most definite statement that the war was now a thing of the past.

Unthinkable before the war, this blouse and dungarees were ideal for work wear and used up very few ration coupons

Nobody ever said, "What happens if we lose the Battle
of Britain?" None of us ever thought, it never even
crossed our minds, that we would lose.

92 SQUADRON SPITFIRE PILOT
TONY BARTLEY

CHAPTER FOUR

WAR IN THE AIR

The air war over Britain in 1940 would be different from any encounter the Luftwaffe had previously faced. The Royal Air Force (RAF) was fighting a desperate defense over its homeland. Its pilots included many foreign nationals, some of whom came from countries already overrun by the Nazis. The German fliers were operating at the limit of their range. It was a conflict between two major industrial powers and, for the first time, the Germans did not have the technological upper hand. Britain's unique air defense system utilized a top-secret chain of radar stations directing state-of-the-art fighter planes to intercept the enemy and, although the Germans enjoyed numerical superiority, the Allies had yet another secret ace up their sleeve. . . .

Dallas-born William Ash was regarded as a wild radical by his friends at the University of Texas. Most of the people he knew sympathized with the British struggle against Nazi Germany, but the 22-year-old took it further. He set off for Canada and enlisted in the Royal Canadian Air Force (RCAF).

I know some other Americans who did come over early. But for many of them as much as the question what the war was about, was the fact that they really wanted the excitement. With me, it was rather the other way around. The first thing as far as I was concerned was my absolute horror at the kind of things that the Nazis were doing in Germany, the invasions of Czechoslovakia and Poland and other countries. The Canadians were very strongly committed and absolutely a hundred percent with their British brothers. And the Canadians showed this great hospitality to all of us who enlisted in

JULY 9

A flight of 12 British Blenheim bombers attacks Stavanger in Norway and 8 of the planes are shot down

JULY 9

Canadian Prime Minister Mackenzie King, at a meeting of the Cabinet War Committee, approves a study into the uses and effects of germ warfare

Almost 20 percent of the 3,000 pilots who flew in the Battle of Britain were foreign nationals. On the previous pages: a Spitfire and a Hurricane soar through the sky over southern England. In the background, a female factory worker rivets the fuel tank on a Spitfire in production

Despite an initial reluctance by the military to put women in uniform, a recruitment drive was soon under way, as shown by the poster on the opposite page. Below left, women age 21 or over were eventually required to register for industrial call-up. At right, American Spitfire pilots relax between sorties

I was very upset. I said, "I am afraid I've lost everything on the *Athenia*. I don't think I can afford seven shillings and sixpence a day."

He said, "We pay you."

I thought the English are lovable fools. To be able to fly a Spitfire and be paid for it was really something extraordinary.

The two Americans were far from the only non-British fliers on the Allied side in the Battle of Britain. Fliers came from Poland, the Irish Republic, Belgium, Canada, Jamaica, Czechoslovakia, the future Israel, Australasia, France, Newfoundland, South Africa, Southern Rhodesia (Zimbabwe)—and the United States. In 1940 Tony Bartley, the son of an Irish lawyer, was a 21-year-old Spitfire pilot with 92 Squadron:

If one had a slight weakness in some area then somebody from Australia or New Zealand or something, they compensated for it. Mostly Commonwealth but we had Czechs and Poles who were very brave and we had a Frenchman in our squadron who joined the Battle of Britain; together it made an absolutely indestructible team because everybody's morale was compensated by the others. And the whole thing, put together, was undefeatable.

the forces. When I enlisted at that stage it meant losing my American citizenship. Because you swore allegiance to the King. Later on they devised a way in which Americans coming up and enlisting in Canada could pledge obedience to the King and retain their citizenship. But I lost mine.

Rescued from the sea after being torpedoed on the SS *Athenia*, New Yorker James Goodson came across an RAF recruiting station in Glasgow.

I asked if an American could join their RAF. They found out eventually that, yes, they could but since they had to swear their allegiance to the King of England, they would automatically lose their citizenship.

They found out at the recruiting station that I had had some experience of flying, and immediately said I could join the RAF.

They said: "Of course, there is the question of pay. It is seven shillings and sixpence ($1.50) a day to start with."

JULY 10

Military targets in southern England are bombed by the Luftwaffe, with 12 German planes shot down for the loss of 3 RAF fighters—the Battle of Britain is now underway

JULY 10

President Roosevelt requests almost $5 billion from Congress for military expenditures

1940

One thousand West Indian RAF recruits arrive in Britain to play their part in the war. At left, an unconfirmed "kill" is chalked up below the cockpit of a Spitfire; later it will be confirmed and painted on

JULY 10

Canadian merchant ship *Waterloo* is attacked by German aircraft and sunk in the North Sea off Great Yarmouth

JULY 11

In France, Marshal Pétain proclaims himself head of state of the French Republic

Major repairs and servicing had to be carried out in record time to keep the fighter squadrons airworthy. At right, the Hurricane was a more rugged aircraft than the Spitfire, and many pilots regarded it as a more stable gun platform

Nobody ever said, what happens if we lose the Battle of Britain? None of us ever thought, it never even crossed our minds, that we would lose.

Two fighter aircraft came to symbolize British hopes of survival, the Hawker Hurricane and the Supermarine Spitfire. A few years earlier, from a senior post in the British Air Ministry, Frederick Winterbotham had watched with fascination the Spitfire's development.

The Spitfire had been designed by this man down in Southampton (R. J. Mitchell) who had been designing the Schneider Trophy airplanes before. He had really studied the flight of birds, he was a very brilliant man. The Air Staff were asked down to see the test flight of the first Spitfire, and some of my friends from the Air Ministry went down, and they were so excited about this

airplane. All through the Air Ministry it was terribly secret. Nobody had to know anything about it, but it really looked as if we were going to have something which would match up to anything that the Germans could build.

The Spitfire had first entered service in August 1938. The Hurricane had entered service in 1937. Roland Beamont flew it from 1939.

I particularly wanted to fly the Hurricane. The Spitfire always looked like a beautiful and elegant airplane but I felt that the Hurricane was somehow more rugged.

Hugh Dundas flew the Spitfire.

It was a lovely airplane to fly. The only thing was, at that stage, that we still had canvas or fabric ailerons. It wasn't until the beginning of 1941 that we got metal ailerons,

13 JULY

Hitler announces that his air offensive against Britain will begin on August 5

JULY 14

Bastille Day in France is declared a "Day of Meditation" while in London, de Gaulle and the Free French lay wreaths at the Cenotaph

1940

which made a tremendous difference to the handling of the Spitfires at the high speed of a dive. They'd had certain other shortcomings from an operational point of view. We didn't have rear-view mirrors. One of the first things we did after our first one or two engagements at Dunkirk was to go down to the local motor agency and get rear view mirrors and have them screwed on to the top of our windscreens.

William Ash's training planes in Canada had included the Fairey Battle light bomber. The Spitfire was something else.

It was absolutely delightful from the beginning. I remember the first Spitfire I saw close to and having flown Battles it seemed so small and so beautifully made, it had such a shape. I used to think of it as being a kind of Platonic ideal of what an airplane ought to look like.

James Goodson:

The Hurricane we all loved. It was a very steady plane. It could take quite a beating. It was a gentlemanly plane. It was very good defensively because it could out-turn the German planes. It was a very steady gun platform. I think most pilots when they switched from Hurricanes to Spits, were disappointed in the Spit. They'd heard so much about it but it was very difficult to land because it

A recruitment poster aimed at French Canadians.
At left, the Spitfire had no equal in experienced hands, despite being more demanding to fly than the Hurricane

JULY 15

W.M.L. Fiske, one of the first Americans to volunteer for service with the RAF, is badly injured when his damaged plane burns on landing—he dies two days later, becoming the first American in uniform to be killed in Europe in WWII

JULY 16

Hitler sets out his plans for Operation Sea Lion—the invasion of Britain—but does not set a date

was so sensitive. With the Hurricane you could be hamfisted but it would still land. With the Spitfire, you moved that stick just a fraction of an inch, and the thing would immediately respond. Therefore you could always tell a pilot who had just gone on to Spits from Hurricanes by the way he landed, the thing was bouncing up and down. And when it landed it was on one wheel then the other, and ballooning up and coming down again because he was over-controlling. But once you got used to the Spitfire you loved it. It became part of you. It was like pulling on a tight pair of jeans. It was a delight to fly.

Tony Bartley:

The Spitfire was probably the finest combat aircraft. The Germans had the Messerschmitt Bf 109 and they had other things. They had the Focke-Wulf 190 which was a desperately good airplane. But the Spitfire started with 1200 horsepower Rolls-Royce Merlin engine, which was a marvelous engine, and the final one in the same airframe was 2400 horsepower. The Focke-Wulf in 1942 was a better airplane than a Mark V Spitfire. And the 109E was better than a Mark V. But finally the Spitfire, with only adding a small bit on the frame, I think it was about another nine or ten inches or something,

In 1940 the Messerschmitt Bf 109 shown at right was the Luftwaffe's premier fighter, and its pilots almost invariably had more extensive training and experience than their RAF counterparts. Above, British statesman Anthony Eden visits troops re-equipping and retraining in northern England

JULY 17

Increasing RAF night bombing of German targets leads to the formation of Luftwaffe night fighter squadrons

JULY 19

Addressing the Reichstag in Berlin, Hitler makes what he describes as a "final appeal to common sense" to Great Britain

1940

encompassed twice the horsepower. And it was the best airplane.

Alongside the comparative qualities of the aircraft, there was the issue of pilot skill, as James Goodson argued:

> What makes a pilot is experience and unfortunately at the beginning of the war most of our pilots were shot down before they had time to gain that experience. The Germans had far more experience and they were better.

Roland Beamont stressed morale and confidence:

> The way the affairs of Fighter Command were carried on there was always present the tacit assumption that you had better equipment and were better trained and were altogether a more capable chap than the opposition were going to be. There wasn't any foreboding about it, one didn't feel scared of the enemy. It's odd this, because we had every right to be scared of them, particularly the experienced ones from the Spanish war.

Before World War II the idea that "the bomber will always get through" had become widely accepted. The British scientist Robert Watson-Watt disagreed. On February 12, 1935, in an experiment using a BBC transmitter at Daventry, he employed radio energy to detect an approaching RAF bomber. In 1936, he became head of the new Bawdsey research station near Felixstowe, Suffolk,

1940

JULY 19
President Roosevelt signs a Two Ocean Navy Expansion Act outlining a plan for hundreds of new ships and thousands of naval aircraft

JULY 22
The Special Operations Executive (SOE) is created in Britain to train and infiltrate agents into occupied Europe

to explore the use of radio direction finding (RDF), as radar was misleadingly labeled. By 1938 a coastal chain of radar stations was under construction. By 1940 a system in advance of anything in the world was operational.

Roland Beamont:

> The RDF that had been established, with brilliant foresight, just before the war did provide, in the area roughly from, I suppose, Portland Bill round to the north of the Thames Estuary something like 100 to 120 miles, warning of aircraft flying into our airspace at altitudes above 15,000 feet. This gave sufficient warning of the formation and the progress of any enemy bomber raids to be given to our fighter squadrons to get them up into position to intercept, rather than flying wildly round the sky hoping to meet up with something.

Women, at left, working on a brand-new Hurricane. Above right, WAAFs plot aircraft movements in the Operations Room of RAF Fighter Command's 10 Group, Box, near Colerne in Wiltshire. On the opposite page, the Focke-Wulf 190, introduced in 1942, became the Luftwaffe's finest single-seater fighter plane

> The basic plan on all the big intercepts was that the Hurricanes were vectored against the bomber streams and the Spitfires were directed immediately to the higher altitudes to intercept the escorting fighters.
>
> Radar was probably the key to enabling us to win.

From the 21 Chain Home radar stations, information on approaching enemy aircraft was sent to Fighter Command headquarters at Bentley Priory in Stanmore, then to the four Fighter Group HQs covering England, and from there to individual fighter bases. But in 1940, the RAF had a severe shortage of manpower, mechanics, fitters, construction workers and staff to operate the new radar system. Despite initial resistance, recruits to the Women's Auxiliary Air Force (WAAF) began to supplement, and then replace, men.

Before the war, 21 year-old Diana Pitt Parsons had been studying art. By 1940 she was training as a radar operator.

> You have a transmitter station which sends out a signal which hits the aircraft and the signal comes back to the reception area, and you have a means of calibrating the distance, finding the distance in between, which you then display on a display unit. So you can judge how far away the airplane is and you have, in those days, a pretty rough idea of its height and its azimuthal position. It was a complicated business. A lot of the girls

JULY 23

The Local Defence Volunteers in Britain are renamed the Home Guard with a force of almost 1.5 million men

JULY 23

The British Chancellor announces his latest war budget, with tax increases including a penny extra on a pint of beer

1940

An ATS woman, above, uses a telescope to identify incoming aircraft at an anti-aircraft gun site. Below, WAAF and RAF personnel at work in a radar station

in radar had been to boarding schools. They chose those girls of that background. And I always insist that, after a girls' boarding school, anything'd be quite blissful. I mean, being in the WAAF was freedom after knowing what a girls' school could be like.

In the late 1930s, Anne Duncan, after completing art school, had ambitions to become a dress designer. But with the threat of war in 1939 she decided to become a military nurse. She was turned down, so in late 1939 she joined the WAAF, and the 23-year-old trained as a plotter in Leighton Buzzard.

It was three weeks' training. We were billeted in a beautiful country house and taken by bus each day. The first day I remember going into it we were absolutely fascinated because it was all covered in netting with camouflage over the top. We couldn't think why, but we realized then that it must be something very secret. There was a table with the map of England on it and the whole of the map was marked out in a grid. The man on the other end of the telephone, when he was reporting things coming in, he'd give you, as far as I remember, two letters and four numbers and from

that we put down a little round disc, like a tiddly-wink. Then a few minutes later there would be another one, that would be a bit further on and you could see the course gradually building up of something coming in. You plotted everything. Everything came in over their radar tubes. We manned the things 24 hours a day. We used to be talking [by telephone] to these men who were sitting on these outstations, "Yes, they're coming now, there are so many, now we can see them. . . ." Then one day I was on, I was connected with the station at Ventnor on the Isle of Wight, and they saw these aircraft coming for them. They were being attacked while I was actually talking to them. They were badly—I think several people were killed, the station was quite badly damaged.

In spring 1940, Rosemary Horstmann was a 19-year-old WAAF plotter at RAF Filton.

We sat round, or stood round, a large map table of the area, in the operations room. And with the aid of long sticks, like billiard cues, we pushed little symbols around on this table, showing enemy aircraft coming in, our aircraft going up to intercept them, and that sort of thing. We were hooked up by headphones to Observer Corps stations, and the Observer Corps people would telephone in to us with information about plots. There might be an unidentified something or other, and they would give us a grid reference, and we would put a little symbol onto that grid reference, and gradually the information would be built up.

JULY 24

Estimates from the Red Cross put the number of refugees in Vichy France at 5.5 million

JULY 25

The evacuation of women and children from Gibraltar is ordered

American-born entertainer Josephine Baker, right, in the uniform of the Free French. Below, a Canadian airman with boxes containing carrier pigeons used by downed bomber crews to send emergency signals

In 1940 19-year-old Jean Mills agreed to accompany her mother on a day's shopping in London's West End. At Harrods, she encountered an armed forces recruiting drive and ended up being sent to Leighton Buzzard as a WAAF trainee before being posted to RAF Duxford, where she found herself working in the operations room:

> It was really dominated by a large table which was a map. In the case of Fighter Command operations, it was the whole of the British Isles, but on individual fighter stations and groups it was more or less their area, with a slight overlap. This was a map with a grid like you would get on an Ordnance Survey of large squares and each large square was divided into 100 smaller ones, 10 by 10, so it was possible to get a metric reading on that map. It was like a graph and the plots came over to you as a metric reading like that, with a direction. It came over like Northwest B for Bertie—that would be the name of the large square, the configuration of it and then it would be, say, one-nine-two-three, 1923, 20 at 10, which would be 20 aircraft at 10,000 feet.

From working as a plotter Rosemary Horstmann moved on to Hawkinge in Kent as a member of Y Service, which monitored the radio conversations between Luftwaffe pilots.

JULY 25

The United States cuts back on oil exports, causing further tension with Japan

JULY 31

The German Army's plans for the invasion of Great Britain, much criticized by the German Navy, are discussed with Hitler and it is clear that the operation can begin no earlier than September 15

1940

We had to be taught how to operate the receivers, how to search the band until we picked up some conversation or other, and how to tune in carefully. I still find myself doing this when I'm using the radio. Most people would just sort of switch it on, and just tune in like that. I still find myself searching backwards and forwards over the station, because I was taught to do it in 1940.

The 30,000-strong Observer Corps, the radar chain and radio monitoring provided a web of information which could be fed to Anti-Aircraft Command and Fighter Command, headed by Air Chief Marshal Sir Hugh Dowding. But at the very core of British defense—and at the heart of Allied strategy throughout the war—was the secret of Ultra, only revealed in the 1970s. This was intelligence gathered by the breaking of "unbreakable" German encyphered messages. The decoded signals traffic was invaluable during the Battle of Britain and in making preparations against Operation Sea Lion— Hitler's planned invasion of Britain.

Between 1929 and 1945, Frederick Winterbotham

1940

AUGUST 1
Since May, 1,200 fighter aircraft have been produced in Britain, substantially narrowing the gap between the RAF and Luftwaffe operational strengths

AUGUST 1
Hitler updates his plan for the invasion of Britain in Directive 17 with a target date of September 19–26 and orders the destruction of the RAF and British aircraft industry

New planes were delivered from the factory to the airfield by Air Transport Auxiliary pilots like the ones shown at left—American Ralph Canning, Canadian A.V. Laursen, American Ken Kleaver, an unknown Spaniard and American Earl Ortman. On the opposite page: as soon as they landed, undamaged fighters were refueled, rearmed and made ready for the next sortie

Hitler's orders for the invasion of England, shown at right below, detail the areas of coastline where three different assault groups would land

obvious because the whole of the rearrangement came through on the air.

This was the beginning of Sealion. It wasn't until the actual Battle of Britain had started that we got the orders from Göring through to his squadrons that now they were going to conquer Britain and that the Führer had given permission and that Operation Sealion would be undertaken. And we started getting all the movements of the German troops up to the coast and we got the installation in Holland of a number of what they called "air loading points," where an airplane could come in, and rather like railway platforms, there would be two platforms either side of it, so that it could be reloaded with troops or equipment in a matter of minutes, and then turned round and off again. And the invasion was obviously to be on these lines, parachute drops and an immense amount of equipment dropped by air, and all the time the German Air Force would be bombing behind—the whole plan of the invasion was there.

served with the Air Staff Department, Secret Intelligence Service. Throughout the war Winterbotham controlled the Ultra decoding and utilization of the German Enigma codes from Hut Three in Bletchley, center of the decrypting operation.

One had to be able to get information quickly to Dowding, and I had a direct line from Hut Three to Fighter Command, and that was taken by a WAAF at the other end who had that sole job. They had two or three of them at the job of taking the Ultra signals. So Dowding was right on the ball. He knew exactly what was happening, because you would sometimes get the advance notice of a big raid on a certain target with some hours to spare. We knew, more or less, what the strength of the Luftwaffe was. But we didn't know exactly how they were going to be placed, but we got the positions from Ultra of all the Luftwaffe, all their units, wherever they happened to be, and the air fleets, with old Kesselring in command of one of them. Some of them were still up in Holland, and others stretched right down to Brittany, and the functions of each of their squadrons became quite

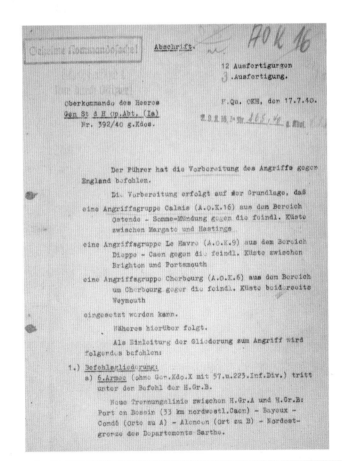

FIGHTERS OF THE BATTLE OF BRITAIN

Although the Battle of Britain was primarily, from the British side, a defensive action against the waves of German bombers bent on destroying the country's defenses, infrastructure, and civilian morale, it was dominated by the fighters of both sides. Three airplanes—the Hawker Hurricane, the Supermarine Spitfire, and the Messerschmitt Bf 109—proved to be exceptional aircraft, and developed versions of the two latter types were to continue in service with air forces around the world until well into the 1960s.

In all, four Fighter Command squadrons that took part in the Battle of Britain had strong Canadian links, in each case reflected in their squadron badges. No. 73 Squadron (badge: an heraldic dog with a maple leaf on it) flew Hurricane Mk Is. No. 92 (Spitfire Mk I; badge: a cobra entwining a sprig of maple leaf), had been a Canadian unit during World War I and took part in the last stages of the battle from September. No. 242 (Hurricane Mk I; badge: a moose's head) served in the battle from mid-June. No. 401 (Hurricane Mk I; badge: a Rocky Mountain sheep's head) began as No. 1 Squadron, RCAF, and brought its own Hurricanes from Canada, arriving at its first base in Britain on June 21 and taking part in the battle through to October.

THE HAWKER HURRICANE

The lion's share of the victory in the Battle of Britain belonged to the Hurricane, which accounted for twice as many enemy aircraft as any other type and went on to fight in more campaigns and in more theaters than any other aircraft of World War II. By the time it was taken out of service in 1946, more than 14,500 had been built. It may have lacked the glamorous image of the Spitfire, but the RAF's first monoplane fighter proved to be a war winner.

The robust Hawker Hurricane, although slower than the Spitfire, could survive extensive battle damage

THE SUPERMARINE SPITFIRE

Designed by Supermarine's R. J. Mitchell to meet the same Air Ministry specification for an eight-gun monoplane fighter as the Hawker Hurricane, the first Spitfires entered service with the RAF in 1938. Of monocoque construction and powered by the same Rolls-Royce Merlin engine as the Hurricane—and many other Allied aircraft, including the Lancaster bomber and the American P51 Mustang—the Spitfire proved to be fast, maneuverable, and exceptionally agile in the thin air of higher altitudes. As development progressed, the type ran to more than 30 marks, and was to stay in RAF service until the late 1950s. Hugely admired, it remains one of the most handsome aircraft ever designed.

The badge of No. 92 Squadron

Nationalities of Royal Air Force and Fleet Air Arm pilots engaged in the Battle of Britain:	
U.K.—RAF	2,365 (397 k.i.a.)
U.K.—FAA	56 (9 k.i.a.)
Polish	141 (29 k.i.a.)
New Zealand	103 (14 k.i.a.)
Canadian	90 (20 k.i.a.)
Czech	86 (8 k.i.a.)
Belgian	29 (6 k.i.a.)
South African	21 (9 k.i.a.)
Australian	21 (14 k.i.a.)
Free French	13 (0 k.i.a.)
Irish	9 (0 k.i.a.)
U.S.	7 (1 k.i.a.)
Southern Rhodesian	2 (0 k.i.a.)
Jamaican	1 (0 k.i.a.)
Palestinian	1 (0 k.i.a.)
Total pilots: 2,945	**Total k.i.a.: 507**

Canadian Spitfire with its maple leaf badge

Around 35,000 Me109 fighters were built, some post-war variants even being fitted with Rolls-Royce Merlin engines

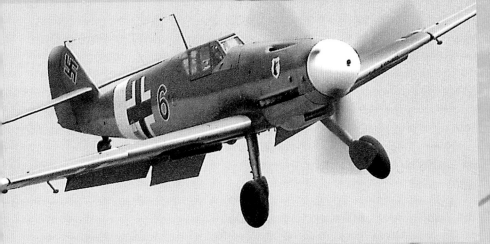

THE MESSERSCHMITT Bf 109 'EMIL'

Developed from the smaller Messerchmitt 108, the 109 entered Luftwaffe service in time to serve with the Condor Legion against Republican forces in the Spanish Civil War, 1936–39. Fast, maneuverable and, unlike the British fighters it opposed in 1940, armed with cannon, it proved less agile than the Spitfire and Hurricane and was outclassed in some respects by the latter. Nevertheless, it remains one of the world's great fighter aircraft, and developed models were to stay in service with European and South American air forces until well into the 1960s.

You knew the fate of civilization was being decided 15,000 feet above your head in a world of sun, wind and sky.

AMERICAN JOURNALIST VIRGINIA COWLES

CHAPTER FIVE

BATTLE AND BLITZ

There is no real consensus about when the Battle of Britain actually started, but on July 16, 1940, Hitler ordered plans for the invasion of Britain to be drawn up and on August 6, Luftwaffe leader Hermann Göring proposed a plan to destroy Fighter Command in four days. Two days later the Luftwaffe ineffectively attacked British radar stations.

Thanks in part to Ultra decryption, the British were able to work out how the Germans intended to achieve the air superiority they needed as a prelude to invasion. Ultra helped with strategy. Radar-focused tactics and the RAF's combination of modern fighters and dedicated pilots confronted the Luftwaffe with its first serious challenge. And civilian morale, expected by many to crack, did not.

The Germans never understood the full significance of the British radar defenses, although on August 12 and 13, the Luftwaffe launched a string of attacks on radar stations and RAF bases.

Jean Mills was a plotter at Duxford.

We could hear the crackling voices of the pilots come back and although we had headsets on and the work was quite intensive we used to manage to ease one earphone off so we could hear what was going on and then we could listen out for "Tally-ho," which meant they'd sighted the enemy and then you could hear them talking to each other, like "look out blue two bandits to your right" which seemed to bring it right into the room. There was an indescribable tension about the whole thing. When there was something going on the atmosphere was electric.

On August 15, Roland Beamont was flying a Hurricane out of Exeter with 87 Squadron.

My squadron was scrambled about four o'clock in the afternoon to intercept what was described by the controller as "100-plus heading north from

Hurricane pilot Roland Beamont

A chain of coastal radar aerials like the one shown at left gave England its eyes in the sky. On the previous pages, scanning the skies for enemy intruders at an antiaircraft gun site (inset). In the background, bomb damage around St. Paul's Cathedral, London

AUGUST 3

Italian forces advance into British Somaliland in Africa

AUGUST 5

The German government declares that all citizens must be able to prove their ancestry back to 1800 to qualify for a mandatory Certificate of Racial Purity

Florence Edgar inspects a Rolls-Royce Merlin engine destined to power a Hurricane or Spitfire. The bombing of England was not one-sided, however. By 1941 fliers like Flight Lieutenant D. A. Boards, below, were heading for Germany in the new four-engined Stirling

Cherbourg." We were vectored to Portland. We climbed out to Portland as quickly as we could and as we started heading south over Weymouth at about 15,000 feet the controller was saying, "Your 100-plus is now 150-plus, 20 miles south of Portland Bill heading northeast."

We continued on our course. We had about nine airplanes that day. We were pulling our harness straps tight and turning on the gun sight. . . .then the controller said, "Bandits now 20 miles ahead of you, you should see them directly ahead."

Almost immediately the clear sky ahead started to turn into a mass of little black dots. It could only really be described as a beehive. . . .Our CO continued to lead us straight towards it. I just had time to think "I wonder what sort of tactic he's going to employ?" While I thought that, it was quite apparent he wasn't going to do anything. He bored straight on into the middle of this lot until we seemed to be going into the biggest formation of airplanes you ever saw. Then his voice came on the radio and he said, "Target ahead, come on chaps, let's surround them."

Just nine of us.

At the beginning of the last week in August, the first bombs fell on central London. A couple of days later, RAF Bomber Command hit Berlin, having earlier bombed Milan and Turin. Both sides produced

AUGUST 5

The Mayor of Montreal is arrested and sent to prison in Ontario's Camp Petawawa

AUGUST 8

British Intelligence officer Wing Commander Winterbotham discovers the plans of Reichsmarshall Hermann Göring (head of the Luftwaffe) for the air offensive against Britain and alerts Air Marshal Dowding

1940

A WAAF radar operator monitors incoming aircraft on her screen

Marketing heroism: Pictures like the ones shown below projected the image of "the few" worldwide. Pilot Officer Keith Gillam, below left, was only 19 years old when he failed to return from combat over the English Channel in August 1940. Below right, pilots stand by for scramble at Rosemary Horstmann's base in Hawkinge, Kent

inaccurate figures of each other's losses but, while the British assumed (wrongly) that the Luftwaffe had plenty of aircraft left, the Germans assumed (wrongly) the opposite about Fighter Command. Göring was told at the beginning of September that Fighter Command had 100 planes left when it had more than 700. Fighter Command was also being resupplied at a greater rate than the Luftwaffe.

American James Goodson arrived back from flight training in Canada to join 43 Squadron at Tangmere.

Even at the worst time of the Battle of Britain, I don't think the thought ever entered our heads that Germany would win the war. My memories of those days are the jokes, the fun in the mess, the camaraderie. If people were frightened or tired or neurotic or disillusioned and despondent there was an unwritten

AUGUST 8

British army pay is increased by sixpence a day with a private now earning 17 shillings and sixpence (less than $3) a week

AUGUST 10

Aldertag—"Eagle Day"—when Göring's air offensive against Britain was due to commence, is postponed because of bad weather

Farm labor for women of the Land Army was seldom as joyful as the propaganda photograph shown at right implies. Propaganda could even incorporate haircuts, below right, into the war effort.

law in Fighter Command, you did anything rather than show that. Probably those that were cracking the jokes the most, who were making silly pranks, schoolboy pranks in the Mess, they were probably the ones most frightened but they never showed it.

Rosemary Horstmann was based with the WAAF at Hawkinge, Kent, at the center of the battle.

There was a general feeling of elation. It was frightening, it was worrying, we used to see our own aircraft shot down, we would see German aircraft shot down, we would see parachutes opening over the countryside. But there was always the feeling that we were jolly well going to win, a great sense of the gallant boys in blue arriving at dawn, you know. It was really rather like knights in armor on their trusty steeds. Their Spitfires and their Hurricanes.

Vera Holdstock was an 18-year-old member of the Women's Land Army. Her Italian father, head waiter at London's Savoy Hotel, had become a British citizen in the wake of Mussolini's conquest of Abyssinia four years earlier. In 1940, Vera was on a farm near Tenterden, Kent, with a friend from a German-English background. Above her head the battle went on.

We used to stand open-mouthed and watch it all. One night one of the sheds on the farm was caught alight by incendiary bombs. I think the Germans were just going back over the Channel and they just unloaded their bombs on the way back. We had some blue

Ground crews prepare the aircraft for takeoff as the two Canadian pilots at right sprint to their Hurricanes. Below, British Spitfire ace and Wing Commander "Johnny" Johnson notched up 38 "kills" and spent much of the war flying with Canadian squadrons

Persian cats in this shed and they were burned to death. They were quite expensive cats. That was our only bombing. After that the local station master said to Robert Nickells, the farmer I was working for, "It's those two girls you've got on your farm, one half-Italian and one half-German, they're spies." He was quite sure.

Tony Bartley was flying out of Biggin Hill where, on August 30, in the most costly attack on an air base during the battle, 39 personnel were killed and 25 injured.

You went to your dispersal hut half an hour before dawn and when the tannoy said scramble, you scrambled. You went up and you fought all day long until the sun went down. Whether it be three, four, five missions a day—you just fought and fought and fought. At the end of the day we used to get off the airfield, because they used to bomb us at night, so we used to go down to the White Hart at Brasted and drink beer.

In the month of August, 1,075 civilians had been killed, including 392 women and 136 children, and the casualty toll was mounting all over the country. In Southampton on August 13, bombers hit a warehouse in the eastern docks. Eight-year-old Eric Hill had been out with his mother.

We were in the bottom half of Southampton when the air-raid sirens blew and we had to dive for cover underneath All Saints Church. . . . I remember we were in the air-raid shelter for three to four hours until we

1940

AUGUST 14

The RAF flies over 700 fighter sorties and downs 45 Luftwaffe aircraft

AUGUST 15

The Luftwaffe deploys in force with over 2,000 sorties over England and the RAF responds by deploying all three of its fighter groups for the first time

got the all clear to come out. . . .when we came out the high street was running with melted margarine and butter because they'd hit the cold storage. My mother and most of the women—because it was wartime—they were just grabbing handfuls of this butter and trying to ram it into whatever they could so we could have butter or margarine.

On September 4, Hitler ordered the Luftwaffe to focus on cities. Three days later, on Saturday afternoon, three waves of bombers hit London, killing 448 civilians and injuring 1,600. The raids continued all night. The Battle of Britain was not over, but the nighttime Blitz had begun. In retrospect, the following seven days, culminating in the big raids of Sunday, September 15, were to prove decisive. Frederick Winterbotham in Hut Three at Bletchley noted:

For the final day raids on London Göring ordered practically the whole of the bombers that were left in France to come over and bomb London. It was a *coup de grâce*, because if he couldn't down the Air Force, he'd down the population. And we got good advance information about that.

Churchill was told about it, and he went down to the headquarters of 11 Group. He didn't go to Fighter Command where Dowding was. He went down to number 11 Group, to Keith Park's, to watch this battle. And Dowding had collected every fighter airplane left in Britain. They completely shocked the vast German air fleet that was coming over, and they just turned round and fled and dropped their bombs.

The Ultra which came from Göring really almost burnt the paper. They were to turn round, refuel

A Civil Defence Warden surveys bomb damage in London's Holborn district at right. Above, Luftwaffe Chief Hermann Göring claimed he could destroy the RAF in just four days

AUGUST 16

Luftwaffe bombers continue to attack military sites in southeastern England while RAF bombers attack the Fiat manufacturing plant in Turin

AUGUST 18

The first German bomber is brought down over London while RAF bases at Kenley and Tangmere as well as other airfields are badly damaged

1940

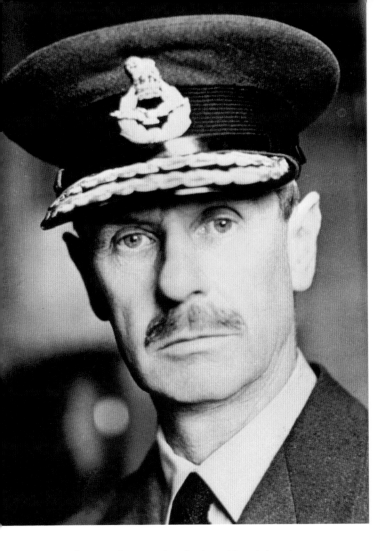

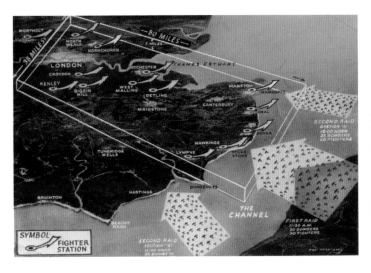

The diagram above illustrates the Luftwaffe's two great raids against southern England on September 15, 1940. At left, Air Chief Marshal Sir Hugh "Stuffy" Dowding, head of Fighter Command

their airplanes and go back and bomb London. Churchill.... seeing the enormous formations that were coming over on the radar and the plotting.... turned to Keith Park and said, "What reserves have you got?"

Keith Park said, "Perhaps you'd better ask the Commander-in-Chief, Sir." So the Commander-in-Chief was telephoned at Stanmore and asked "What reserves have you got?" And Dowding's remark, "I have no reserves, sir, every airplane is in the sky."

They [the Germans] came back on that evening, they didn't even get as far as London. They just turned round and fled again, and that was the end of daylight raiding in England.

From September 7 to 15, the Luftwaffe lost 199 bombers and 99 fighters, the RAF 120 fighters. The air superiority needed for the Germans to launch an invasion had not been won. The tactics of the New Zealander Keith Park at 11 Group had been vindicated, and so had the strategy of Sir Hugh "Stuffy" Dowding.

Elizabeth Quayle:

We all admired Stuffy, our Stuffy, enormously. We had great loyalty to him. I think you might call it affection, he built up a tremendous—well it's an old-fashioned word—esprit de corps amongst us. He was a gentleman.

It was in the months, and years, after the defeat of the Luftwaffe that the measure of what had been achieved in what became known as the Battle of Britain was realized. In autumn 1940, however, for the people of the British Isles, the threat of invasion remained. But Frederick Winterbotham, with access to Ultra, knew that if Hitler didn't invade by mid-September, Sea Lion was off.

We got this signal from Hitler giving permission to dismantle the air loading bays in Holland. That signal I sent straight through to Churchill, and it went to the Chiefs of Staff.

Churchill ordered a conference. Among those present were Major-General Hastings Ismay, Churchill's link with the Chiefs of Staff, Air Chief Marshal Sir Cyril Newall and Sir Stewart Menzies, head of Secret Intelligence Services. Winterbotham was asked what he felt the signal meant.

I pointed out that if these loading bays were dismantled it meant that they would not have their proper air support and that in fact Hitler had given up the idea of invasion. So Churchill looked at me, and then he turned to Chief of Air Staff. "May I have your views?" he said to Cyril Newall, and Newall said, "That is entirely our view. With the dismantling of this, the invasion is off."

AUGUST 20

Churchill broadcasts his inspirational tribute to the RAF pilots fighting the Battle of Britain: "Never in the field of human conflict was so much owed by so many to so few"

AUGUST 24

Several civilians are killed when a German bomber offloads over central London

And Churchill sat back and smiled, and pulled out a big cigar and lit it.

In autumn 1940, Jean Mills was working in the operations room at RAF Duxford, near Cambridge.

We were on duty one night and it had been fairly quiet. That's the thing, there were periods of absolute inactivity when you had to do something to keep yourself from being bored. Suddenly we looked, and one girl stood up and put a plot way out in the North Sea. In no time at all there was a whole row of plots coming, and then the sergeant of the watch conferred with the commanding officer and they removed all the individual plots and put a long stretch of cardboard, covering several hundred miles. It was a 300-plus mile front of bombers coming.

The Battle of Britain was conflict in light. The Blitz was in darkness, illuminated by fire. The Luftwaffe escalated the nighttime raids which had begun in summer 1940 and went on to produce a winter of horror, death, demoralization—and heroism. The losses of the Luftwaffe were negligible, since at night Spitfires and Hurricanes were almost useless. The Observer Corps could see little, inland radar was minimal, and initially the

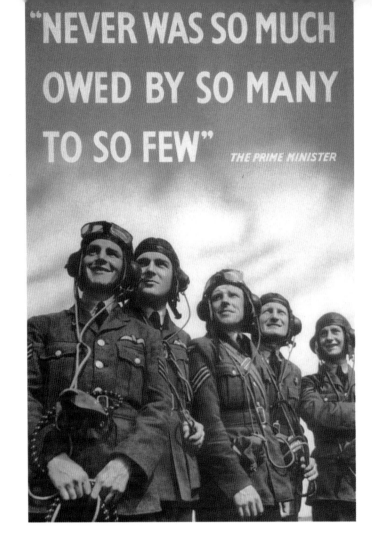

"NEVER WAS SO MUCH OWED BY SO MANY TO SO FEW" THE PRIME MINISTER

Winston Churchill's famous quote praising the RAF after the Battle of Britain adorns a propaganda poster. At left, crowds gather around a German Heinkel bomber forced to crash land in northeast England after being attacked by RAF fighters

AUGUST 25

In retaliation for the raid on London, RAF bombers attack Berlin. Earlier in the year, Reichmarschall Göring had declared in a broadcast: "If a single British bomb falls on Berlin, you may call me "Mayer." On the morning after the raid, the name Mayer is seen scrawled on buildings and vehicles all over Berlin

1940

Canadian Spitfires at right patrol the skies above southeast England. Below, St. Paul's Cathedral in London stands proud amid the ruins of war

RAF's night-fighter squadrons largely relied on an inadequate converted bomber, the Bristol Blenheim.

On August 18, 1940, 27-year-old William Gregory was the navigator with Pilot Officer Rhodes, flying a Blenheim out of Digby and Wellingore, in Lincolnshire.

> We were scrambled this night and the ground, the sector, used to come to you over the air and say we have a plot that is near you. Well this night they told us there was a plot given by the Observer Corps very near to where we were. I was in the gun turret looking round and I didn't see anything. We came out of a cloud at about 10,000 feet and immediately behind us came this German aircraft, with its cockpit light on, a Heinkel 111. I didn't know who was the most scared, the pilot or the gunner in the Heinkel, or me but I pressed the trigger first—100 rounds into the cockpit, and it started to flame and it came underneath and Rhodes finished it off.

Such success was a rarity. The raids built up as the winter progressed. At the end of December 1940, 136 bombers attacked the City of London. That night a reporter on a national daily, the *News Chronicle*, 35-year-old Stanley Baron, went to investigate. It was just after the all clear had sounded.

> I decided to walk round London. It was on fire. All the buildings round St. Paul's were on fire. Whenever one looked up the narrow alleys of the city you saw what it really looked like. I think I described it at the time as red snowstorms. Great showers of sparks were coming from the burning buildings. And you would see the silhouette sometimes of the firemen. And I remember particularly the silhouette of the firemen at the Guildhall on a high water tower and his jet illumined by the flames from the building.

> What struck me most about that night was the extraordinary beauty of it. It sounds fantastic. But it really was a very beautiful scene. The colors were fantastic. St. Paul's itself—the dome of St. Paul's—was to be seen against a background of yellow and green and red with great billows of smoke coming across it. Before the war I had walked around most of the City.

1940

AUGUST 27

The Luftwaffe raids 21 British cities

AUGUST 31

In two weeks the RAF and Luftwaffe have lost a combined total of 800 aircraft with the balance slightly in the RAF's favor

Coventry Cathedral was destroyed in a shattering raid on the city in November 1940

> I loved the City, and I knew its buildings. And there I was, simply watching the whole thing burn....

On the night of November 14, more than 400 Luftwaffe bombers destroyed the English midlands city of Coventry. London and Coventry were to suffer severely, but the Luftwaffe also paid nocturnal visits to Birmingham, Bristol, Sheffield, Portsmouth, Plymouth, Manchester, Belfast, Glasgow, Cardiff, Swansea and even neutral Dublin, by accident. For eight-year-old Eric Hill, the real Blitz came to Southampton that November.

> All we could see was the town ablaze, you could just see the glow, we knew that Southampton was really getting hammered. And then there was an incident just before my father got called up. There was no air-raid siren blown that night, but you could tell the different sound of the airplanes' engines. You knew the Dornier had a sort of gnawing, groaning sort of effect.
>
> My father rushed in and threw my mother and me underneath the kitchen table and we heard an almighty explosion. It was a land mine on a parachute, it landed in the next road and killed several families....

By March 1941 the few RAF night-fighter squadrons were re-equipping with the rugged and efficient Bristol Beaufighter. William Gregory was a Beaufighter navigator and radar operator with pilot Ken Davidson, still flying out of Digby and Wellingore.

> We were on patrol one night when the ground came through to say Liverpool was getting blitzed. When we arrived you could see the glow of the fires through the clouds, and we were at about 10 to 15,000 feet. I switched on the radar and found a contact so we closed in. It was a Dornier 17, and just as this chap Davidson was about to shoot it down, our starboard wing was shot off by ack-ack. I bailed out and landed on a little place next to Lime Street, Liverpool, and he landed inland some place.
>
> I was on the roof of this house for about 10 minutes when a ladder came up to the eaves and a chap came up the ladder with a gun. I said, "Thank God you can get me off." And I was fastened on to a chimney pot I had held on to.
>
> And he said, "You bloody German, you can speak as good English as we." And he said, "When you get on the ground you'll find that out."

SEPTEMBER 4

Hitler declares his intention to reduce London to rubble and to raze other British cities to the ground in response to RAF attacks on Germany

SEPTEMBER 5

The Luftwaffe drops 60 tons of bombs on London

The equipment operated by the ATS girls at left calculated the height and range of incoming aircraft, information which was then passed to the antiaircraft gun team below

So they started to put the boot in when I eventually got down. They had every right, when you saw the fires that were going on. Eventually a police chap came up and took me to the police station.

Across Britain a defense of sorts against bombers was provided by the Anderson Shelter, named after Home Secretary Sir John Anderson, who had put together the scheme for the two-bunk corrugated steel garden shelters. In north London the family of Elizabeth Harris had their own early-warning system for departure to the shelter.

We had a cat who used to tell us before it arrived that an enemy plane was on its way, before we heard it. The cat would scurry from the side entrance, up the garden, and down into the shelter. And we'd hear in a very short time. We'd be scuttling across the ground to follow the cat.

In London, safer still as a shelter, if excessively communal for some, was its underground railway, the Tube. The government attempted to block its use by the public, but soon abandoned that folly. Elizabeth Quayle took the train.

When you came back at night on the underground, the entire underground, only the bit, the 18 inches or maybe two foot near the rail were left, and all the rest were rows of people with their belongings, cats and dogs and children. They were as good-tempered as it was possible to be. Looking back on it everyone was much more friendly, you would have thought nothing of leaving your bags or your suitcase there, nobody would have taken anything.

The Blitz went on into the early summer of 1941. At the beginning of May, Liverpool was bombed every night for a week and 16-year-old Dorothy Hont was a witness to the raids.

Your life rotated around the sirens. You'd go to work and you'd close the shop early or come home a little bit earlier have a fast tea, get yourself into something warm, gather little bits of specials that you wanted to save, down to the shelter and that was it. And we used to knit in the shelter or play cards or guessing games or just

SEPTEMBER 7

London is attacked by more than 900 German aircraft

SEPTEMBER 12

More than 1,000 German vessels berthed in French, Dutch, and Belgian ports in preparation for the invasion of Britain are attacked by the RAF with 80 invasion barges sunk in Ostend

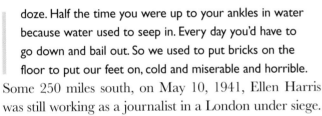

Above left, survival amid the devastation thanks to an Anderson shelter. Above, firemen struggle to control a massive blaze in a London street

doze. Half the time you were up to your ankles in water because water used to seep in. Every day you'd have to go down and bail out. So we used to put bricks on the floor to put our feet on, cold and miserable and horrible. Some 250 miles south, on May 10, 1941, Ellen Harris was still working as a journalist in a London under siege.

It was the night London was set afire. And I'd been in a dugout under Liberty's in Regent Street. I left early enough, quite early that morning because I was to be on duty, to get home, wash and change and get back on duty in Fleet Street by eight o'clock. It's a good long distance from Oxford Circus to where I lived in Islington and I was walking over hose pipes, dozens and dozens. No bus could have run, there were hose pipes everywhere, and the firemen fighting the blazes still.

And I was walking down from Bloomsbury past Lincoln's Inn. And a man, almost in tears, stopped me and said, "What are we going to do? We can't go on like this, we've got to seek peace. We can't go on in this way."

And I said to him, "Do you realize that you're playing right into Hitler's hands? This is just what he's setting out to do. If he can do this to you to get you into this state and you come here and you start on

me and I join in with you and I go up the road and tell somebody and you do the same to somebody else. Now," I said, "you'd get people in the state of mind and their morale goes."

I said, "What you've got to do is to remember you're in the front line as if you were in the trenches in the last war." I said: "This is what I'm telling myself all the time, this is my war effort. And this is your war effort. . . ."

But continuing that journey home, I came up past Sadlers Wells theater and opposite Sadlers Wells was a row of little, old Victorian houses with the iron railings round them. Well, the whole lot—what wasn't down to the ground had got all the insides out. I saw people moving children's prams which they'd filled with little things they'd rescued from their homes. . . . no tears, nothing whatsoever, just the firmness, we'll rescue what we can. What got me into tears was a birdcage still hanging in the window and a little dead canary. Now can you understand that? I just burst into tears going up the road. I thought, "This is terrible."

SEPTEMBER 15

On the day that the RAF scrambles all its fighters for the first time, the Germans lose 56 aircraft compared to British losses of 26, signaling the failure of the Luftwaffe to gain control of the skies and casting the invasion of Britain into severe doubt. Nowadays, this is known in Britain as "The Battle of Britain Day"

1940

We must be the great arsenal of democracy. For us this is an emergency as serious as war itself.

PRESIDENT FRANKLIN D. ROOSEVELT
December 29, 1940

CHAPTER SIX

AMERICA PREPARES FOR WAR

In January 1940, it was widely assumed that Franklin Roosevelt would be ending his final presidential term—and the U.S. Army was smaller than that of Holland. By summer most of continental Europe—Holland included—had fallen to the Nazis. A Gallup Poll, taken in the wake of the fall of France, asked Americans whether keeping out of the war was more important than helping Great Britain; 62 percent of those polled said it was. But there were other ties, other memories. . . .

When the war in Europe began, New Yorker Steve Weiss was 14 years old.

> Living in Brooklyn, it was easy to get down to the Narrows, the entrance to New York Harbor, and see ships like the *Normandie* and the *Queen Elizabeth* and the *Queen Mary*—these ships just beautiful, stream-lined, big—being escorted by tugboats and fireboats spraying water. It was just a marvelous sight. I would go over to the North River and I would see all these glorious-looking ships lined up, pier after pier, and with it the excitement of what it would be like to travel across the ocean to Europe.

Europe held a certain fascination, but remained for many Americans a place to be avoided.

The 1917—18 U.S. excursion into World War I had cost 50,000 GI lives; the "war to end wars" had not lived up to its claim. Yet the war had not stayed in Europe; it had come home to America. As Steve Weiss recalls:

> My father had been in World War I as an infantry soldier in France. He had been wounded and gassed in 1918, and he would regale me with stories about trench warfare. He had to recuperate from his wounds and, being gassed in Tours, he had a relationship with a French nurse that carried into our home. There was a photograph of her on the chest of drawers in my parents' bedroom. Yvonne became a member of the family. Her presence was felt.

President Roosevelt signs the Conscription Bill in October 1940. Roosevelt was returned for a third term as president in November of that year. Draftees, opposite, arrive for their physical examination at the U.S. induction center on Governors Island, New York City harbor, in September 1941

On the previous pages, women work on a B-17 bomber. In the background, a new B-17 is maneuvered onto its parking stand at an airfield in England

1940

SEPTEMBER 17

Hitler announces the postponement of his proposed invasion of England

SEPTEMBER 21

Though civilians have been using London Underground stations as shelters since the bombing raids began, the British government grants official permission for this practice to continue

For skeptics, U.S. intervention appeared at best an error, at worst a fraud. Burton Stein was 10, a Chicagoan from a Russian-Jewish background.

> I was a very young boy and the war didn't really have much of an impact. It was part of the newsreel world. It all seemed very distant and very strange. The people we knew most closely were other Jews and other immigrants. They felt very strongly against Hitler either because he persecuted people, or because he was occupying their old land. So there was a great deal of sympathy for the Allied cause and certainly a great willingness to see the war expanded and American participation in it.

Roosevelt was building up U.S. arms expenditure and in July 1940, he accepted the Democratic Party's nomination to run for an unprecedented third term. In September, a deal with the British promised old U.S. Navy destroyers for the Royal Navy in return for bases in the West Indies and Newfoundland. That month, too, the first peacetime draft in U.S. history became law. In November, Roosevelt won a third landslide. By that time Gallup results showed, post-Battle of Britain, that 60 percent of Americans thought helping Great Britain was more important than keeping out of the war. On December 29, Roosevelt delivered one of his "fireside chats" to the American people. It concluded:

> We must be the great arsenal of democracy. For us this is an emergency as serious as war itself. We must apply ourselves to our task with the same resolution, the same sense of urgency, the same spirit of patriotism and sacrifice as we would show were we at war. We have furnished the British great material support and we will furnish far more in the future. There will be no "bottlenecks" in our determination to aid Great Britain. No dictator, no combination of dictators, will weaken that determination.

It was not just equipment. A trickle of Americans—men and women—was making the Atlantic crossing. One of these was 31-year-old Gilman Warne from Montclair, New Jersey, who enrolled in the British Air Transport Auxiliary, which played a vital role in ferrying aircraft from factories and airfields to front line RAF squadrons.

> December 7, 1940, that's when I first signed up for membership of the ATA. The Battle of Britain had ended a few months before that, but the war was still very much going on and we knew what we were getting into. We also had to put up with some feelings here among certain elements in this country who are traditionally anti-British. The Irish-Americans, the Jewish-Americans at that time, the Germans of course, the Italians were euphoric about Mussolini and what he was doing. My family doctor was very annoyed with me because I was going over to help the British. He was a first-generation American-Italian.

Opinion crystallized around the issues of isolation from the European war, or intervention. Isolationism was represented by the America First Committee, while the Committee to Defend America by Aiding the Allies stood for intervention. Both had been formed in the spring of 1940. The AFC was chaired by the head of the Sears Roebuck mail-order company; its supporters included two future presidents—the young John F. Kennedy and Gerald R. Ford, as well as the country's most famous aviator, Charles Lindbergh.

SEPTEMBER 22

The RAF launches another bombing raid on Berlin

SEPTEMBER 27

Germany, Italy and Japan sign a tripartite pact. Although Japan is still technically neutral, the agreement divides Europe and Asia into proposed "spheres of influence" among the three countries

1940

Lindbergh advocated "the maintenance of armed forces sufficient to defend this hemisphere from attack by any combination of foreign powers." He spoke to the AFC on April 23, 1941, in New York.

> France has now been defeated, and despite the propaganda and confusion of recent months, it is now obvious that England is losing the war. I believe this is realized even by the British government. But they have one last desperate plan remaining: They hope that they may be able to persuade us to send another American expeditionary force to Europe and to share with England militarily, as well as financially, the fiasco of this war. . . . I have been forced to the conclusion that we cannot win this war for England, regardless of how much assistance we send. I ask you to look at the map of Europe today and see if you can suggest any way in which we could win this war if we entered it. Suppose we had a large army in America, trained and equipped. Where would we send it to fight? The campaigns of the war show only too clearly how difficult it is to force a landing or to maintain an Army, on a hostile coast.

> Suppose we took our navy from the Pacific and used it to convoy British shipping. That would not win the war for England. It would, at best, permit her to exist under the constant bombing of the German air fleet. Suppose we had an air force that we could send to Europe. Where could it operate? Some of our squadrons might be based in the British Isles, but it is physically impossible to base enough aircraft in the British Isles alone to equal in strength the aircraft that can be based on the continent of Europe. . . .

The AFC had plenty of mainstream support, and until June 1941, and the Nazi invasion of the Soviet Union, much of the left backed nonintervention. The young Burton Stein observed some support for the Nazis.

> There were those people on Hitler's side in Chicago and particularly in Milwaukee, in Wisconsin. We used to go up there in the summertime when there was the American Bund—which was American Nazis—so we were aware of fascists in the United States. This was another reason for supporting the war. There were also people that, for other reasons politically, I would have heard from my elders, would be suspect.

SEPTEMBER 30

The Luftwaffe delivers a final daylight raid on England. During September, London was bombarded with over 14,500 tons of high-explosive bombs and incendiaries

OCTOBER 1

After the Battle of Britain, the Luftwaffe's series of nighttime raids known as the "Blitz" puts a far greater strain on British ground defenses and civil defense

It was not just that they were against resisting fascism, but they were also for anti-black legislation and a whole lot of other things that looked bad in social terms. The *Chicago Tribune* was a conservative and an isolationist newspaper; it was against being in the war. The other newspapers took basically the supportive role of Roosevelt, Lend-Lease, and sympathy for the Allied cause. The radio people were similar.

Roosevelt's Secretary for the Interior, Harold Ickes, speaking in New York on May 18, 1941, argued that defeat for Great Britain would spell disaster for the United States.

We would be alone in the world, facing an unscrupulous military economic bloc that would dominate all of Europe, all of Africa, most of Asia, and perhaps even Russia and South America. Even to do that, we would have to spend most of our national income on tanks and guns and planes and ships. Nor would this be all. We would have to live perpetually as an armed camp, maintaining a huge standing army, a gigantic air force, two vast navies. And we could

not do this without endangering our freedom, our democracy, our way of life. Perhaps such is the America "they"—the wavers of the future—foresee. Perhaps such is the America that a certain aviator, with his contempt for democracy, would prefer. Perhaps such is the America that a certain senator desires. Perhaps such is the America that a certain mail-order executive longs for. But a perpetually militarized, isolated and impoverished America is not the America that our fathers came here to build. It is not the America that has been the dream and the hope of countless generations in all parts of the world. It is not the America that one hundred and thirty million of us would care to live in.

The fight for Britain is in its crucial stages. We must give the British everything we have. And by everything, I mean everything needed to beat the life out of our common enemy. . . .

. . . We must greet with raucous laughter the corroding arguments of our appeasers and fascists. They doubt democracy. We affirm it triumphantly so

On the opposite page, 800 members of the fascist German-American Bund joined a 1938 parade through New York

Senator Burton Wheeler of Montana and Colonel Charles Lindbergh salute the American flag at a rally in 1940

OCTOBER 6

Hitler orders his army into Romania to protect the oil fields, a vital source of fuel for his military forces

OCTOBER 7

Berlin is subjected to its heaviest raid by the RAF, when 30 Wellington and 12 Whitley bombers offload 50 tons of high-explosive bombs on the German capital

1940

LICK THEM *over there!*

COME ON CANADA !

that all the world may hear: "Here in America we have something so worth living for that it is worth dying for!"

On August 23, 1939, the Soviet Union and Nazi Germany had signed a nonaggression pact. But on June 22, 1941, the Nazis invaded the Soviet Union. The movie house provided a curious logic for Burton Stein:

It seemed perfectly reasonable to watch the newsreels on how what was, one week before, impossible from the point of view of the newsreels— Reds who were not only bad in terms of being Bolsheviks, but were also bad in having done a deal with Hitler, were now fighting in the good fight and on the right side. In a week the whole thing could shift. That struck me as slightly amazing—that things could change so easily, but as a young person, it seemed to me that's the way the world was.

Few expected the Soviet Union to survive long, particularly after initial Nazi successes. But Roosevelt announced that aid would be sent. It proved to be a turning point. In the previous six months, the President had defined the "four essential human freedoms" in his State of the Union Address (freedom of

Factory worker Veronica Foster, known as "The Bren Gun Girl," is shown at left with a finished Bren gun at the John Inglis & Co. factory in Toronto. Above left, if only crossing the Atlantic had been as easy as this Canadian propaganda poster suggests

At right, dummy explosives are being used by women training for armament manufacture at the Royal Ordnance Factory. The head scarfs and overalls, as well as special cosmetics and creams, were used to protect them from exposure to chemicals. Above right, a U.S. propaganda poster features Franklin Roosevelt's "four essential human freedoms"

speech and expression, freedom of every person to worship God in his own way, freedom from want, freedom from fear); enacted the Lend-Lease act to aid Great Britain, and increased the U.S. Navy's involvement in convoy protection in the Western hemisphere. By 1941, the 32-year-old Hollywood film star Douglas Fairbanks, Jr. had been commissioned into the U.S. Naval Reserve.

> I went to sea as a very very junior-grade lieutenant, which is the only thing I could get at my age and training, in the summer of 1941. It was on destroyers. The U.S. Navy was what you might say at war, although the U.S. government was not. President Roosevelt had declared about two-thirds or three-quarters of the Atlantic as being a neutrality zone. And so American ships were joining with Canadian and British ships in escorting convoys across the Atlantic. And so we had several engagements with U-boats and several of our ships were sunk in battles with U-boats—but it was not considered actual war by the government of the United States.

At the outbreak of war in 1939, Canada's armed forces were nearly nonexistent. Its fleet comprised just six destroyers and four minesweepers.

OURS...to fight for

Freedom of Speech

Freedom of Worship

Freedom from Want

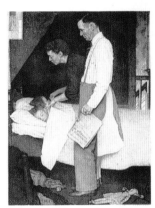

Freedom from Fear

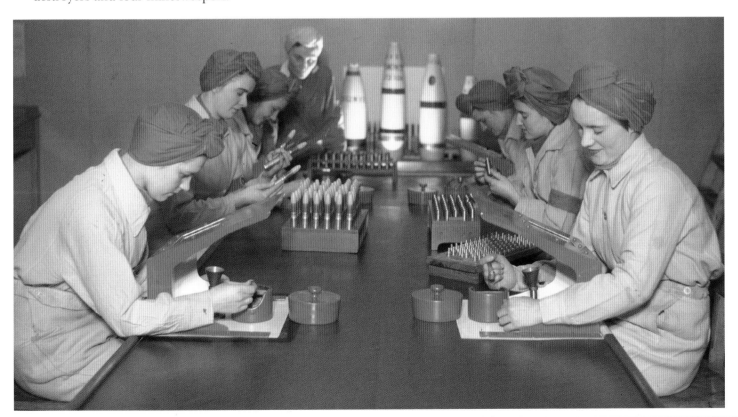

OCTOBER 15

With the focus now on night bombing, Göring's main targets are aircraft manufacturing plants, the Midlands industrial region, and London

OCTOBER 18

The French Vichy government removes all Jews from public office and high-level positions in commerce and industry

1940

Canada had hardly more than 4,000 regular soldiers, its air force had 3,000 men and less than 40 combat-ready aircraft. All was to change. The first Canadian soldiers arrived in Great Britain in December 1939. By mid-1941, the Royal Canadian Navy (RCN) had taken over convoy escort around Newfoundland. In Canada, the British Commonwealth Air Training Plan had begun to turn out air crew. By the end of 1945, the total had passed 130,000. Five years earlier, the first graduates included the Texan William Ash:

> I had never flown, I had no flying experience at all. I did my elementary flying at Windsor, Ontario, and my service flying at Kingston. There was great hospitality shown to those of us who came up into Canada and enlisted in their forces by the Canadian people. They were very strongly committed, absolutely a hundred percent with their British brothers.

By the end of 1940, William Ash had arrived in Britain. He was initially posted to Digby, in Lincolnshire, on the east coast of England.

> They were forming a new Canadian fighter squadron, 411. For the next four or five weeks we were just becoming fully operational. It was the first all-Canadian fighter station entirely staffed by Canadians, although there was another American who, like me,

1940

OCTOBER 22

On its first Atlantic convoy mission, RCN destroyer *Margaree* is involved in a collision with a freighter, and 140 seamen die

OCTOBER 23

Hitler crosses Europe in an armored train to meet Spanish dictator Francisco Franco, but fails to persuade him to join in the war against Britain

had enlisted in the RCAF, Don Blakesley. The other squadrons were Canadian also—there was 411, there was also 412.

If we were doing sweeps over France, we used to fly down to some aerodrome in the south, refuel and then fly on. The Canadian prime minister, Mackenzie King, visited Digby, and it just happened that on that morning we'd been on a sweep. We had been escorting some Boston light bombers. And on the way back somebody in my squadron suddenly called to my section that we were being attacked. As I came out of my 180-degree turn, there was an Me109 diving down, blowing me to the right. And I managed to swing around behind it and at about, I guess 150-200 yards, got in a couple of good bursts and saw that I was hitting it. But by this time I was being attacked myself and had to break away—and lost one person out of my section. I only claimed a damaged Messerschmitt 109—it may have gone down, I didn't wait and see—but Mackenzie King was congratulating me on this victory over France.

There had been plenty of communication between President Roosevelt and Winston Churchill, but the two men had not met for 23 years—and the prime minister had forgotten even that.

At left, Texan pilot William Ash is congratulated on his victory by Canadian Prime Minister Mackenzie King. Above left, British airmen enjoy a party thrown for them by their hosts during a training course in Florida

A British air crew in Florida relax by their U.S. Army Air Force Stearman PT-17 training aircraft. Above right, Roosevelt and Churchill aboard the British battleship H.M.S. Prince of Wales *for their Atlantic conference*

OCTOBER 24
Hitler meets with Marshal Pétain in Montoire, France, only to be told that the French people were not yet ready to go to war with Britain

OCTOBER 25
The British Air Ministry announces training and deployment of airmen from Poland, France, Holland, Belgium, and Czechoslovakia, as well as Australia, New Zealand, the West Indies, Ireland, Canada, and the U.S.

1940

At left, a British worker making armored waistcoats for airmen. Below, Britain's future Queen, Princess Elizabeth, in uniform as a member of the Auxiliary Territorial Service (ATS)

On the opposite page, Land Army girls saw larch poles for use as pit props in coal mines

Early in 1941, moves were made for a meeting. At the end of July, the new Royal Navy battleship *Prince of Wales*, back from its encounter with the German battleship *Bismarck*, was at anchor at the Scapa Flow naval base north of the Scottish mainland. Lieutenant Colin McMullen was a young gunnery officer on *Prince of Wales*:

> Various buzzes went round the ship; there was complete secrecy as to what was going to occur. Finally a destroyer came alongside. There on the bridge was Winston and the three chiefs of staff. We realized that we were embarked on a most important mission.

Prince of Wales was taking Churchill across the Atlantic to meet Roosevelt, and McMullen has distinct memories of the trip:

> Winston spent a lot of his time on the bridge smoking a cigar. He'd stub it out on an ashtray. You'd immediately see a sailor pinch the remains as a trophy. We finally arrived in Placentia Bay in Newfoundland where the American squadron was. We had this marvelous church service on board, the

combined American and British sailors on the quarterdeck. I had the privilege of having to take charge of the parade. I wasn't sure what the American orders were for taking caps off, but we managed. Roosevelt was very interested in ships. We had the backs of the turrets open. The captain asked me to accompany him. When we took Roosevelt round the upper deck in his wheelchair, he looked into the backs of the turrets. He knew an awful lot about naval ships. Then he went down to the wardroom where he answered all sorts of questions.

During the encounter with *Bismarck*, *Prince of Wales* had almost, accidentally, opened fire on a United States coastguard cutter, *Modoc*. Roosevelt's reaction on hearing the story endeared him to the British naval crew, as McMullen recalls:

We told him the story. He remarked, "Gee, if you'd have sunk that ship, I would have found it very difficult to explain to the great American public." It was quite interesting. We thought he was the most splendid chap. He was very easy to talk to.

Food shortages and rationing in Britain seemed a world away when Churchill hosted a party on board for the assembled dignitaries, as McMullen describes the occasion:

During the visit of the president, our prime minister, Winston, gave a lunch party in the wardroom of *Prince of Wales* which was attended by the First Sea Lord, Admiral Pound, the Vice Chief of the Air Staff, who was Air Chief Marshal Freeman, and the Chief of the General Staff, CIGS, who was General John Dill. It was a great success. Among the American guests was Admiral King, who was the equivalent of our First Sea Lord. Admiral Stark also attended, who was going to be the American liaison officer in London. General Marshall, who was a very well known American soldier. Winston had various members of his staff, Professor Cherwell was one, Sir Alexander Cadogan was another. About 36 people attended the lunch. It was a splendid lunch—smoked salmon and caviar, turtle soup, roast grouse, I think out of season, coupe Jeanne d'Arc.

The prime minister was hoping that the U.S. would declare war. They did not. Instead, the president suggested a declaration of war aims, and what eventually emerged was the Atlantic Charter, the basis of the 1945 United Nations Declaration, and, in its respect for "the right of all peoples to choose the form of government under which they will live," indicated that the days of the British Empire were numbered.

They [the Russians] had hoped we would come as liberators from communism. They soon found out we didn't come as liberators but behaved rather—not so well.

GERMAN ARTILLERY OFFICER KARL GÜNTHER VON HASE
Speaking about Operation Barbarossa

CHAPTER SEVEN

BLOODY BATTLES, BITTER BARBAROSSA

On June 11, 1940, a week after the Dunkirk evacuation and as France was collapsing, Benito Mussolini's fascist Italy declared war on the Allies. The Mediterranean was the focus of the dictator's ambition to build a new Roman Empire, but the results were to prove disastrous for him at sea, in the Horn of Africa, and in Libya, despite vast numerical superiority over Commonwealth forces, mainly British, Indian, Australasian, and African.

With continental Europe occupied by Hitler's armies and Great Britain besieged, the land war was concentrated in North Africa and the Balkans, until Hitler's Operation Barbarossa unleashed unprecedented horror on the Soviet Union.

By February 1941 Major-General Sir Richard O'Connor's Western Desert Force had covered 350 miles of Libya in response to Mussolini's aggression in North Africa and captured 130,000 prisoners. Five hundred men were killed, 1,373 wounded. The good news boosted Britain's sagging morale, as O'Connor commented:

> It was a contribution to morale as much as anything else. And had we really been able to profit by it, it would've been much more important. We allowed the Germans to arrive, and we had all this terrible fighting in the desert that followed. But I think it did a great service to morale, the morale of the nation, who welcomed the first sign of victory, which really it was.

On the previous pages, German Grenadiers march past a Russian church. In the background, a German destroys a house with a flame thrower. Below, a Lockheed Hudson, the first American-built aircraft to see active service with the RAF, flies above the pyramids in Egypt

At right, a British soldier guarding Italian prisoners in Egypt. Below right, German Army motorcyclists bogged down on a muddy track in Greece

NOVEMBER 5

Franklin D. Roosevelt is re-elected, the first time any U.S. President has served for a third consecutive term

NOVEMBER 14

Coventry is devastated during a 10-hour attack by the Luftwaffe, resulting in 500 deaths, 865 casualties, and the destruction of the city's medieval cathedral

On July 31, 1940, the British were forced to attack the French fleet at Oran and Mers el-Kébir to disable it, and French naval forces in Alexandria were neutralized on July 4. But the Italian naval threat remained. A key base was Taranto.

On the night of November 11, 1940, 25-year-old Hugh Janvrin of the Fleet Air Arm was on the Royal Navy carrier *Illustrious*. He was part of a 21-plane, two-wave raid of 90-mph Swordfish biplanes on Taranto.

> We arrived over Taranto and dropped our flares at about eight thousand feet. We had a fair amount of ack-ack fire and most extraordinary things that looked like flaming onions. The flares were absolutely right for the torpedo aircraft, and the torpedo aircraft went down and they attacked in two sub-flights. The leader took his sub flight of three and went down and attacked and, he himself, he attacked a Cavour Class battleship, launched his torpedo, which hit and was shot down, immediately afterwards. We dive-bombed fuel tanks. And then we returned to the carrier.

A group of biplanes flying at sea level had torpedoed three battleships, hit a cruiser, and damaged the dockyard—for the loss of two Swordfish. The following day, the remnants of that Italian fleet fled to other bases.

Half a world away, Admiral Isoroku Yamamoto, commander of the Japanese Empire's Combined Fleet, studied the operation with interest. He saw a tactical similarity between Taranto and Pearl Harbor.

Four months later, at the battle of Cape Matapan, the Royal Navy's Admiral Cunningham effectively ended the threat of the Italian surface fleet. An Italian force heading toward Crete was pursued by Cunningham's battle fleet and, in the ensuing action on the night of March 28, 1941, the Royal Navy destroyed Italian cruisers *Fiume, Pola,* and *Zara,* as well as destroyers *Alfieri* and *Carducci,* with the loss of 2,300 Italian seamen.

On April 6, 1941, Operation Marita, a German-Hungarian-Italian invasion of Greece and Yugoslavia, was launched. Lance-Corporal Norman Norris was with the British forces in northern Greece:

> Within no time at all the whole of the Allied army, over 50,000 men, was in full retreat. The battle for Greece was an overwhelming air battle. The soldiers didn't really stand a chance.

On April 22, 1941, the Royal Navy began to evacuate, with some troops joining the garrison on Crete. Lance-Corporal Norris of the Royal Army Ordnance Corps found himself dug in at the Maleme road in the far west of Crete when the German airborne assault began on May 20.

> The days leading up to the 20th of May were pretty idyllic. The sun shone. There was oranges, fruit and good swimming, a lull in the battle. The Luftwaffe weren't really giving us a lot of trouble. Just the odd plane was coming over. The unfortunate thing about it is we had no equipment. What men stood up in was their equipment. Men were sharing a blanket and under the olive groves. Food was in short supply. Each day became heavier and heavier with aircraft. The olive groves were ploughed from 109s strafing. Then on May 20, approximately 8:00 a.m., after a tremendous bombardment, we looked out to sea and saw these gliders being towed in very low over the water. People were saying, "But they don't have any propellers." ... And over came the Junkers 52s which I believe each had about 16 paratroopers.

NOVEMBER 16
In response to the attack on Coventry, the RAF launches assaults on a number of German and German-occupied cities

NOVEMBER 17
Air Marshal Sir Sholto Douglas replaces Dowding at RAF Fighter Command.

1940

Far from being confined to the factory floor, British women, like the one at left, were making their presence felt in all areas of industry

Taken from the Prince of Wales, *this, at right, is the last ever photograph of* H.M.S. Hood *as it went into action against the* Bismarck

Sailors, below, at a Fleet Air Arm shore base arm a Swordfish biplane with its torpedo

And these started to drop on the aerodrome. Some of them were coming down almost within 50 yards of where we were well dug in. We were inexperienced as we had no real form of training as infantry, but morale was pretty good.

Even though losses to the German paratroopers were colossal, the German High Command decided to make Maleme aerodrome the focal point. They poured men in to take the airfield, overwhelming the opposition. Once the German 5th Mountain Division had landed, the tide started to turn. The retreat was on. Lance-Corporal Norris recalls the route march:

Many thousands of men had been taken from Greece, deposited onto an island in the Mediterranean. At first they didn't really know where they were. They were led up in columns in the dark into olive groves. And that olive grove could have been anywhere in the world. The main evacuation was down from the Maleme Road down to Suda and then over the White Mountains to the south coast to a very tiny fishing port, Sphakia. Slowly we retreated down from the Maleme Road. But every inch of that way was strafed. Food was short. By the time we got to the middle of the island men were hungry, thirsty, their clothes and their footwear were really in an appalling state. The wounded were being carried. The road to Sphakia was

NOVEMBER 20

Birmingham and other Midlands towns and cities are subjected to nighttime attacks by the Luftwaffe

NOVEMBER 27

In a naval battle off Sardinia, the Italian fleet retreats from the Royal Navy force just a stony track which led across this hinterland of Crete, which was a pretty bleak place. Eventually men did reach Sphakia. The boats came in. A wonderful job the Navy did.

But the Royal Navy had been battered by Luftwaffe attacks. Nine ships were sunk, including the cruiser *Orion*. The evacuation of Crete—which carried 14,000 New Zealand, Australian and British soldiers back to Egypt—ended on May 30. Norris was one of around 5,000 left behind.

There was this bluff which overlooks the end of Crete, which drops into the Mediterranean where the Australians were still holding out. But on the morning of June 1, we were told we had to give in. And we would be taken prisoners of war. I witnessed an Australian soldier who got hold of one of these officers, and he shook him like a rat. He told him he was a fifth column bastard and "we are not going to give in." The morale of these men! They were hungry, they were tired, their boots were hanging off. And they were literally at the end of their tether. And yet that spirit was right there till the last.

The officer—a First World War veteran—calmed this young soldier down.

We were prisoners of war and then the long trek back to Suda began; the temperature rose to about 100 degrees Fahrenheit and these men were being rounded up to be taken back to the spot almost in which they had landed. We started up our main climb, a long file of about 5,000 men, going through hell. The Germans made no provision for water or for food.

On the very first night, the group I was in the Germans put in a field, which was surrounded by a dry stone wall. I had a Scottish friend who was a little bit more daring who said, "Shouldn't we get away?" pointing to the mountains, an awe-inspiring sight. We got over this dry stone wall and got out round the further end of the field, got up on the main road and started to walk. It was a beautiful black night, very black. The idea was to get away into the mountains. In the very early hours, we were walking along very carefully, not a sound, in the pitch black when suddenly a searchlight hit us with "Halt!" It was a roadblock put up by paratroopers.

Norris was marched through Chania en route to Suva Bay and Salonika.

The whole town lined the route. And they had bunches of grapes, apples, bread, cigarettes, tobacco. And as fast as they fought to give us—through the Germans who were also lining the route—they were being smashed back by rifle butts, but it didn't make any difference. The Cretans still surged forward and deposited these wonderful gifts.

On May 19, 1941, the world's most powerful and modern battleship, the *Bismarck*, set sail with the cruiser *Prinz Eugen* from the Baltic to threaten Atlantic convoys. On May 23, the great ship was spotted by British cruisers. On May 24, the *Bismarck* and the *Prinz Eugen* were engaged by a new, and not fully operational, battleship, the *Prince of Wales*, and the ship which had for a quarter of a century symbolized naval power, the battle cruiser *Hood*.

NOVEMBER 30

Southampton endures an intense Luftwaffe air raid lasting seven hours

DECEMBER 29

At least 10,000 firebombs are dropped by the Luftwaffe in a determined attempt to set fire to the city of London; large-scale fires blaze within parts of the city

1940

German prisoners of war at work in English fields

At right, sailors aboard a British destroyer prepare to launch torpedoes. Below right, Bismarck survivors arrive in Britain en route to POW camps

Lieutenant Colin McMullen was a gunnery officer on the *Prince of Wales*.

She was known as the "mighty *Hood*." We were the new boy but we felt perfectly confident that there was the mighty *Hood*. The ordinary person didn't realize that the *Hood* was very lacking in deck armor. She was very vulnerable to plunging fire. So we opened fire at the *Bismarck*. We never saw any of the *Hood*'s fall of shot. She only fired two or three salvoes. Suddenly the inside of our spotting top, it was like as if there was a sudden sunset. This was when that great ship, which we were following, blew up. At one moment we were full of confidence astern of the mighty *Hood*. Next moment, as a new, untried ship, we were facing the *Bismarck* and the *Prinz Eugen*. The *Prinz Eugen* hit us three times. I think the *Bismarck* hit us five times.

The *Prince of Wales* broke off. The loss of the *Hood* and its 1,400 sailors shocked the world. But the *Bismarck* had been damaged. The *Prinz Eugen* slipped away, leaving the battleship to head for the French port of Brest. The Royal Navy continued its shadowing, and on the night of May 24, launched an attack from the new aircraft carrier *Victorious*. Lieutenant-Commander William Garthwaite, who was flying a Swordfish, remembers the attack:

DECEMBER 29

President Roosevelt's "Arsenal of Democracy" speech is broadcast, with 76 percent of all radio listeners tuned in

DECEMBER 30

By the end of 1940, in spite of the heavy bombing endured by the United Kingdom, Hitler's strategy has failed to crush morale among civilians and the forces

MARCH 11

The Lend-Lease Act, under which the U.S. government agrees to provide equipment, matériel and services to countries fighting the Nazis, is passed in Washington

MARCH 13

Adolf Hitler announces his directive for the invasion of Russia, although the decision and plans are maintained as a well-kept secret

1941

At left, women of the Auxiliary Territorial Service (ATS) parade for inspection by the Queen

At right, firemen in Croydon make toys for distribution to children's nurseries

I was so intent on marveling what a wonderful sight the *Bismarck* was—something like 50,000 or more tons, simply going all out at about 30 knots or more, very sleek, beautiful design—that I hadn't realized that the two aircraft I was with were no longer with me. I dropped my torpedo at about 400 yards, which was very close indeed. And they sent all sorts of flak up. I don't think that the Germans could realize, could appreciate, that a Swordfish taking off with a torpedo and a full crew could only stagger off doing about 80 knots. They didn't realize how slow we were, nor did they realize how low we were. And those early torpedoes you couldn't drop from a height above 60 feet; we were down probably to about 40 feet. And the result was that their antiaircraft guns couldn't bear on us. They couldn't get them low enough, although they shot at us with their big guns and made great fountains in the water, which would have been tricky if we'd gone into them.

I dropped my fish and turned round to get the hell out of it. And my observer had a service camera and he took a photo of the explosion as the torpedo hit. Although hit, the ship sailed on—and then the Royal Navy lost contact with it. But around 10:15 a.m. on May 26, 1941, the pilot of an RAF Catalina flying boat of 209 squadron, 690 miles out from Brest, spotted a dark shape in the ocean. The pilot was Ensign Leonard "Tuck" Smith of the U.S. Navy Reserve, one of a group of U.S. servicemen assigned to the RAF as "special observers" to teach British pilots how to fly Catalinas.

The flying boat, captained by RAF Flying Officer Dennis Briggs, closed in, and from that dark shape a cascade of flak flew into the sky. It was the *Bismarck*. Smith recalled that he had "never been so scared in my life," but the German ship was back inside the Royal Navy's web.

From the aircraft carrier *Ark Royal*, 24-year-old Sub-Lieutenant Kenneth Pattisson made three sorties with other Swordfish. The second sealed the battleship's fate.

1941

APRIL 16

London is subjected to a heavy all-night attack, as 500 German aircraft drop around 100,000 bombs—a total of 440 tons—on the capital

MAY 8

Hamburg and Bremen are subjected to a nighttime attack by 359 RAF bombers

We climbed up 8,000 to 9,000 feet in cloud, in snow, in appalling flying conditions. During the run up I was hit by the flak. We turned and started our dive, came out at about 800 feet above the water. There was the *Bismarck* about a mile or so on our starboard beam. We made our attack down to 90 knots, 90 feet. We reckoned she was doing about 20 knots. I aimed well off over the bow, dropped the fish, turned hard downwind and jinked all over the sky. You could see all the guns firing at you in the tracer in green, red, orange, white, all coming towards you. As we turned away, my observer . . . he looked over the side of the aircraft astern and saw our torpedo running. Suddenly there were great eruptions of spray going up in the air. She was firing her main armament at us.

It was probably either the torpedo from Pattisson or from Lieutenant "Feather" Godfrey-Faussett that had jammed the *Bismarck*'s rudders. The ship was crippled, and Allied ships closed on her. Among them was the old battleship H.M.S. *Rodney*, which had been en route to Boston, Massachusetts, for a refit. Together with the new battleship *King George V*, the *Rodney* went into action early on May 27. Gunnery officer William Crawford was one of the *Rodney*'s crew.

We were steaming at full speed, there was a lot of vibration, there was a tremendous lot of spray. I opened fire entirely on a guessed range of I think it was 27,000 yards, and I think my third salvo certainly straddled the ship and I think probably got a hit on one of her turrets. *Bismarck* opened fire on us very

MAY 9
The Luftwaffe targets the East Midlands Rolls-Royce aircraft engine factory. Contrary to Radio Berlin reports, the factory remains untouched

MAY 10
In the final heavy mission of the Battle of Britain, London comes under attack from 550 Luftwaffe aircraft; 1,400 civilians are killed, 27 German aircraft are lost

soon after and her third salvo was extremely accurate, and straddled us. But after that she never came near us. We came in from 27,000 yards, finally to about 4,000 yards, and were pumping stuff into her pretty hard. She kept up a desultory fire for a long time, a very, very brave action. She was on fire in many places, lot of smoke. And you could see the shells crumping against her side. I thought, "Thank goodness she's gone," but she was the finest ship that I ever saw.

The *Bismarck* was an inferno. Twenty-year-old gun layer Herbert Gollop was on the cruiser *Dorsetshire*.

There was bodies all over the sea. So Captain Martin decided to try and rescue some of them. But there was a German submarine sighted, so unfortunately we had to leave many Germans. We felt very sorry afterwards for the Germans when they came on board. We all looked after them. It was a navy tradition, you always got on well with the enemy somehow or other. They were in a very bedraggled state, some with very little clothes on, some had oil all over them. One died. We buried him at sea and we managed to get a German flag. One of the survivors, he had a mouth organ and he played the German national anthem.

The struggles of the Greek and Yugoslav civilian populations, and of the Allied forces, against the Axis invasion helped delay by a few weeks what was arguably the most terrible event of World War II—Operation Barbarossa, the Nazi invasion of the Soviet Union. The Soviet dictator Joseph Stalin's espionage network had warned him, the Americans, thanks to a German anti-Nazi, warned him, and so did the British, relying on Ultra, the Allied intelligence system headquartered at Bletchley Park in London. Ultra's Frederick Winterbotham:

We knew to the day when the invasion was going to take place and we knew where most of the German forces were. Somebody used to make up a report which was handed to the Russian mission, giving an outline of what we knew, but in no case giving away that we got it from intercepted material. It was a summary of the information which we would have had from other sources, and telling the Russians what the Germans were trying to do. I don't think they believed a word of it.

German artillery officer Karl Günther von Hase assumed he was on exercises. On June 22, 1941, some 3.6 million Axis soldiers invaded the Soviet Union. Von Hase was one of them in Army Group Center.

MAY 10
Rudolf Hess secretly flies to Scotland with peace proposals guaranteeing Germany would respect the integrity of the British Empire if former German colonies were returned and Germany was granted a free hand in Europe

MAY 24
The world's most powerful battle cruiser, H.M.S. *Hood*, is sunk by Germany's 45,000-ton battleship *Bismarck*

At left, Red Army infantrymen march toward the front line past a row of T-34 tanks. Above, despite their state-of-the-art mechanized armor, much of the German Army relied on horse power

At right, German armor fords a river on the Eastern Front

first time in that war that we moved a step backwards.

The Russians had their fresh troops and their marvelous winter outfits. These troops from Siberia were much better than we, they were absolutely fresh and they were well armed and well clad. I, personally, think that this first winter did probably more damage, cost us more lives and also cost us a little bit of courage and our feeling of superiority than later, on other campaigns.

Our biggest enemy was the terrible cold. If you don't have any shelter and you have to fight this 42 degree minus. . . . We couldn't start sometimes our tanks, motorcars or trucks. We had to keep them running, which was very expensive with gasoline. We had huge material losses and we lost confidence in our material superiority.

This was our first experience with the Russian tank, the T-34. Our shells couldn't penetrate the T-34. In our division we had the old Czech tanks which we had taken over. We lost so many brave tank commanders and artillery men fighting the T-34.

We made great advances, and then came what the Russians call *Rasputitsa*—that means the rainy season— and we had already a feeling that not everything in Russia went with the same precision, went to plan. The enemy was much harder and did fight more bitterly than the enemy before in the west—with the exception of some areas where we were given a welcome with bread and cake and water. This was a time right at the beginning between the border and Vitebsk in White Russia—and others had the same experience in the Ukraine—they had hoped we would come as liberators from communism. They soon found out we didn't come as liberators but behaved rather . . . not so well.

And then came the big rains. The tanks couldn't go on and we were waiting for the winter, that it would freeze, and we could then restart the attack. Then came the winter with such a force—with 35-40 degrees minus— that fighting practically came to a standstill. It was the

The *Bismarck*, which Germany claimed was unsinkable, is sunk by the Royal Navy after a four-day pursuit

JUNE 22

Operation Barbarossa begins without any formal declaration of war, as German forces enter the Soviet Union in a surprise invasion

1941

THE SINKING OF *BISMARCK*

The thunder of the barrage hurling a fury of deadly fire at the frail-looking biplane made Oberbootsmann Kirchberg wince as he stood at his battle station by one of the *Bismarck*'s starboard four-inch antiaircraft guns. He barely heard the sound of the torpedo impact on the ship's armored hull, but he couldn't miss the tower of water it sent shooting skyward. At the same instant, the blast wave from the explosion swept up and across the deck, punching Kirchberg into the air as though he weighed

no more than the uniform he wore and smashing him helplessly against the ship's superstructure. Kirchberg died instantly, the first of more than 2,000 of his shipmates who would perish within the next 48 hours.

It was later announced over the ship's loudspeaker that the torpedo, from a British Swordfish biplane, had done no more than "scratch the paintwork." The officers and crew of the *Bismarck* had every reason to enjoy an attitude of such dismissive arrogance. Morale aboard the *Bismarck* was at an all-time high. This was the most advanced, heavily armed and heavily armored warship afloat. Few British ships came close to matching the *Bismarck*'s firepower. One was the *Hood* which, like the *Bismarck*, could hurl a shell weighing as much as a small car a distance of over 20 miles. Unlike the *Bismarck*, however, the *Hood*'s deck armor was one of its weak points.

That had been amply proven when the *Hood* and another British battleship, the H.M.S. *Prince of Wales,* had intercepted them earlier that morning. The *Bismarck* and *Prinz Eugen* had

concentrated their fire on the H.M.S. *Hood*. Within minutes, a hit from the *Bismarck* penetrated the *Hood*'s deck and detonated inside an ammunition store, causing a funnel of flame to soar into the sky. The explosion split the ship in two and the H.M.S. *Hood* sank within three or four minutes. Although the *Bismarck*'s crew had no way of knowing it at the time, only three of the *Hood*'s crew of over 1,400 survived.

The *Prince of Wales* was also hit and forced to withdraw, but not before her guns inflicted some telling damage on the *Bismarck*. There was, nevertheless, jubilation on board the German ship. They had sunk the pride of the British navy. It was announced that Hitler had awarded the gunnery officer, Fregattenkapitän Schneider, the Knight Insignia of the Iron Cross. Cigarettes, chocolate, and sausage were issued to the crew and there was much celebration.

The first and last operational cruise of the *Bismarck* had begun almost a week before at the occupied Polish port of Gdynia. Admiral Günther Lütjens, flush with success following a fruitful Atlantic cruise with the light battleships *Gneisenau* and *Scharnhorst*, which had accounted for over 116,000 tons of Allied shipping, was to lead Operation Rheinübung. This time, the *Gneisenau* and *Scharnhorst* were to join the *Bismarck* and *Prinz Eugen*. Had all four of the ships, plus their attendant escorts, actually sailed together, the outcome of Operation Rheinübung would have been markedly different. As it was, the *Scharnhorst* had to undergo boiler repairs and the *Gneisenau* had been badly damaged by a British torpedo bomber attack. The *Bismarck* and *Prinz Eugen* would sail alone.

Top: *A carrier-borne Fairey Swordfish torpedo bomber of the Fleet Air Arm*
Opposite: *Canadian Fleet Air Arm pilot Lieutenant R. I. W. Goddard from Toronto flew his Swordfish against* Bismarck
Below: K.M.S. Bismarck *in the North Sea, May 1941*

"The day we have longed for has at last arrived. . . ." Lütjens announced to the *Bismarck's* crew, "the moment when we can lead our proud ship towards the enemy. Our objective is commerce raiding in the Atlantic, imperiling England's existence. I give you the hunters' toast—Good Hunting and a Good Bag!"

Lütjens's orders were to avoid engaging enemy warships and make all haste to the Atlantic convoy routes. The action against the *Hood,* if unavoidable, had been a costly glory. The *Bismarck* was now short of fuel and in need of repair.

The British battleships *King George V, Rodney, Ramillies,* and *Renown,* as well as the carrier *Ark Royal* and a flotilla of destroyers, which included the Polish ship *Piorun,* were closing on the *Bismarck.* Lütjens realized that the enemy was not far away and that the *Bismarck* would be the main focus of their attentions.

"I have, therefore," he announced to the crew, "released the *Prinz Eugen. . .* to wage commerce war independently. She has managed to evade the enemy. We have received an order to head for a French harbor. The enemy will gather en route. In the morning or at night, we will have a fierce battle. The German nation is with you and we will fire until our barrels are aglow, and until the last shell has left its muzzle."

Further announcements to the *Bismarck's* crew led them to believe that, within a few hours, more than 80 aircraft would be coming to their rescue, that every U-boat in the area was converging on their location, that two ocean-going tugs were heading out to meet them, and that a tanker was bringing them badly needed fuel.

The mood among the crew was still good. They sang sea chanties and the "Bismarck hymn," but no help was to reach them, and the stress of being relentlessly hunted down was about to start taking its toll.

After a cat-and-mouse stalking game that lasted for two days, the *Bismarck* was attacked by a flight of Swordfish torpedo bombers from the H.M.S. *Ark Royal.* The resulting damage to the *Bismarck's* steering gear left

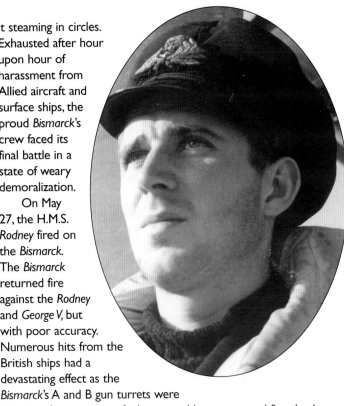

it steaming in circles. Exhausted after hour upon hour of harassment from Allied aircraft and surface ships, the proud *Bismarck's* crew faced its final battle in a state of weary demoralization.

On May 27, the H.M.S. *Rodney* fired on the *Bismarck.* The *Bismarck* returned fire against the *Rodney* and *George V,* but with poor accuracy. Numerous hits from the British ships had a devastating effect as the *Bismarck's* A and B gun turrets were put out of action, range-finders were blown away and fires broke out all over the ship.

The decks were awash with water and strewn with bodies torn apart by the explosions. Many areas of the ship were consumed by fire. Smoke and fumes from paint burning on the *Bismarck's* bulkheads suffocated or poisoned those unlucky enough to be caught in an enclosed area without a respirator. Many others drowned below decks when compartments were deliberately sealed and flooded in an effort to contain the fires. Panic set in among the crew and, according to a U.S. Navy intelligence report, one officer is said to have shot several crew members for disobeying orders, while other officers were reported to have committed suicide.

Crewmen sought shelter from the bombardment wherever they could, but overcrowding in the best-protected areas on deck led to many falling overboard into a sea inches thick with leaked oil. Many more were washed overboard when waves broke over the violently lurching ship, now listing by around 20 degrees.

Having absorbed almost one and a half hours of devastating fire, the *Bismarck* lay low in the water and heavily ablaze. Torpedoes from the cruiser H.M.S. *Dorsetshire* were intended to finish her off, but the final *coup de grâce* came from the Germans themselves when technicians still aboard the *Bismarck* scuttled her.

Only 115 from the *Bismarck's* crew of more than 2,200 survived.

Yesterday, December 7, 1941—a date which will live in infamy—the United States of America was suddenly and deliberately attacked by naval and air forces of the Empire of Japan.

PRESIDENT FRANKLIN D. ROOSEVELT
December 8, 1941

CHAPTER EIGHT

PEARL HARBOR

At 6:00 a.m. (Tokyo time) on November 26, 1941, the Imperial Japanese Navy's First Carrier Strike Force set off from the Kurile Islands off the north coast of Hokkaido. An unprecedented combination of maritime and air power, it comprised seven support ships, nine destroyers, two cruisers, two battleships, and, at its heart, six aircraft carriers.

Eleven days later, on December 7, soon after 6:00 a.m., Hawaii time, the strike force launched 183 warplanes from carriers 200 miles north of the island of Oahu, home to the U.S. Pacific Fleet's Pearl Harbor base. Within an hour a second wave of 167 aircraft had taken off.

At 6:53 a.m. on December 7, the destroyer U.S.S. *Ward* sank an unidentified midget submarine—one of five such Japanese vessels en route to Pearl Harbor. Minutes after 7:00 a.m., the *Ward* hit another midget submarine. At the Opana radar site, on the northern tip of Oahu, Private Joseph L. Lockard was monitoring the radar screen with Private George E. Elliott. Later, Lockard was to tell what happened.

> We were going to close down, but we figured that we might as well play around, because the truck had not come in yet to take us back for chow. So I was just checking the adjustments and was going to let Elliott operate them a while. He had not been in the outfit very long; he was a new man with us. I was going to let him operate. To me it looked like two main pulses. That is why I thought there was something wrong with the equipment, and I was checking to see if there was anything wrong. Apparently there was not.

> I showed it to Elliott. I fooled around some more trying to determine exactly whether it was something coming in or whether it was a defect in the equipment, and finally decided that it must be a flight of some sort. Since it was the only activity we had had that morning, I decided to plot it. Elliott plotted it. We picked it up at 136 miles.

When the largest echo that Lockard had ever seen got to 132 miles north, the two men reported what seemed to be a group of aircraft to the Fort Shafter information center, The officer at the center, extremely inexperienced,

On the previous pages, wrecked U.S. seaplanes burning in the wake of the Pearl Harbor attack. In the background, the sea is ablaze around the U.S.S. West Virginia, as a survivor is plucked from the water. U.S. war preparations began before Pearl Harbor. The scrap aluminum, below, in Times Square was part of an Office of Civilian Defense collection in July 1941. At right, the view from a Japanese plane during the attack on Pearl Harbor

JULY 19
America extends its protection of Atlantic convoys by basing aircraft and destroyers in Iceland

AUGUST 12
Berlin endures its heaviest raid to date as RAF aircraft drop 82 tons of bombs on the city

concluded that the echo was probably U.S. bombers.

By 7:40 a.m. Fleet commander Admiral Husband E. Kimmel had been told of the U.S.S. *Ward*'s activities. News of the radar sighting got no farther than Fort Shafter.

Lee Soucy, a *Utah* crewman and pharmacist, was on board when two torpedoes hit the *Utah*. The Japanese attack began close to 7:55 a.m.

I had just had breakfast and was looking out a porthole in sick bay when someone said, "What the hell are all those planes doing up there on a Sunday?"

Someone else said, "It must be those crazy marines. They'd be the only ones out maneuvering on a Sunday."

When I looked up in the sky, I saw five or six planes starting their descent. Then when the first bombs dropped on the hangars at Ford Island, I thought, "Those guys are missing us by a mile."

Even after I saw a huge fireball and cloud of black smoke rise from the hangars on Ford Island and heard explosions, it did not occur to me that these were enemy planes. It was too incredible. Simply beyond imagination.

As I watched the explosions, I felt the ship lurch. We didn't know it then, but we were being bombed and torpedoed by planes approaching from the opposite (port) side. The bugler and bosun's mate were on the fantail ready to raise the colors at 8 o'clock. In a matter of seconds, the bugler sounded General Quarters. I grabbed my first aid bag and headed for my battle station amidship. A number of the ship's tremors are vaguely imprinted in my mind, but I remember one jolt quite vividly. As I was running down the passageway toward my battle station, another torpedo or bomb hit and shook the ship severely. I was knocked off balance and through the log room door.

AUGUST 14

Winston Churchill and President Roosevelt hold a secret meeting and confirm a Western alliance with the signing of the Atlantic Charter

SEPTEMBER 11

President Roosevelt orders that any German or Italian ship in U.S. waters is to be attacked

1941

I got up a little dazed and immediately darted down the ladder below the armored deck. I forgot my first-aid kit.

By then the ship was already listing. There were a few men down below who looked dumbfounded and wondered out loud, "What's going on?" I felt around my shoulder in great alarm. No first-aid kit! Being out of uniform is one thing, but being at a battle station without proper equipment is more than embarrassing. Losing his first-aid kit was the least of his problems once Lee Soucy followed orders to abandon ship.

After a minute or two below the armored deck, we heard another bugle call, then the boatswain's whistle, followed by the boatswain's chant, "Abandon ship!"

We scampered up the ladder. As I raced toward the open side of the deck, an officer stood by a stack of life preservers and tossed the jackets at us as we ran by. When I reached the open deck, the ship was listing precipitously. I thought about the huge amount of ammunition we had on board and that it would surely blow up soon. I wanted to get away from the ship fast, so I discarded my life jacket. I didn't want a Mae West slowing me down. I ended up with my bottom sliding across and down the barnacle-encrusted bottom of the ship.

When the ship had jolted, I thought we had been hit by another bomb or torpedo, but the mooring lines snapped, which caused the 21,000-ton ship to jerk so violently as she keeled over.

Nevertheless, after I bobbed up to the surface of the water to get my bearings, I spotted a motor

SEPTEMBER 15

Rocket development at Peenemünde, on the Baltic coast, which had been previously suspended, is restarted by Hitler; work on the production of the V2 rocket is given priority over naval and aviation requirements

SEPTEMBER 19

Kiev falls to the Germans after six weeks of heavy fighting

Above, the U.S.S. Arizona *sank with the loss of over 1,100 crewmen. At left, Mayor Fiorello La Guardia watches New York air raid wardens in training*

launch with a coxswain fishing men out of the water with his boat hook. I started to swim toward the launch. After a few strokes, a hail of bullets hit the water a few feet in front of me in line with the launch. As the strafer banked, I noticed the big red insignias on his wing tips. Until then, I really had not known who attacked us. At some point, I had heard someone shout, "Where did those Germans come from?" I quickly decided that a boat full of men would be a more likely strafing target than a lone swimmer, so I changed course and hightailed it for Ford Island. I reached the beach exhausted, and as I tried to catch my breath, another pharmacist's mate,

Gordon Sumner, from the *Utah,* stumbled out of the water. I remember how elated I was to see him. There is no doubt in my mind that bewilderment, if not misery, loves company. I remember I felt guilty that I had not made any effort to recover my first-aid kit. Sumner had his wrapped around his shoulders.

While we both tried to get our wind back, a jeep came speeding by and came to a screeching halt. One of the two officers in the vehicle had spotted our Red Cross brassards and hailed us aboard. They took us to a two- or three-story concrete BOQ [bachelor officer's quarters] facing Battleship Row to set up an emergency treatment station for several oil-covered casualties strewn across the concrete floor. Most of them were from the capsized or flaming battleships. It did not take long to exhaust the supplies in Sumner's bag.

SEPTEMBER 24

Bombs planted by Russian secret agents begin to explode in buildings in Kiev occupied by the Germans

SEPTEMBER 28

Notices are posted all over Kiev ordering all Jews to assemble at a specified rendezvous within 24 hours

1941

A line officer came by to inquire how we were getting along. We told him that we had run out of everything and were in urgent need of bandages and some kind of solvent or alcohol to cleanse wounds. He turned to us and said,

"Alcohol? Alcohol?" he repeated. "Will whiskey do?"

Before we could mull it over, he took off and in a few minutes he returned and plunked a case of Scotch at our feet.

SEPTEMBER 28

A convoy of badly needed food and provisions arrives at the besieged island of Malta off the North African coast

SEPTEMBER 29

At a ravine known as Babi Yar, to the northwest of Kiev, the massacre of almost 34,000 Jews, Gypsies, psychiatric patients, Russian POWs, and other "dissidents" begins

At left, the crew of the U.S.S. California *abandons ship. Hawaiian women firefighters, above, direct their hose on one of the blazing ships at Pearl Harbor dockside*

Sixty-four crewmen died on the *Utah*. Meanwhile, Ruth Erickson, a nurse at the Naval Hospital at Pearl Harbor, was eating breakfast with friends.

We heard planes roaring overhead and we said, "The 'fly boys' are really busy at Ford Island this morning."

We didn't think too much about it, since the reserves were often there for weekend training.

We no sooner got those words out when we started to hear noises that were foreign to us.

I leaped out of my chair and dashed to the nearest window in the corridor. Right then there was a plane flying directly over the top of our quarters, a one-story structure. The rising sun under the wing of the plane denoted the enemy. Had I known the pilot, one could almost see his features around his goggles. He was obviously saving his ammunition for the ships. Just down the row, all the ships were sitting there—the *California*, the *Arizona*, the *Oklahoma*, and others.

OCTOBER 17

The American destroyer U.S.S. *Kearny* sinks after being torpedoed off the coast of Iceland, while on convoy duty; 11 lives are lost

OCTOBER 28

The German offensive against Moscow grinds to a halt in boggy terrain with freezing overnight temperatures

1941

My heart was racing, the telephone was ringing, the chief nurse, Gertrude Arnest, was saying, "Girls, get into your uniforms at once, this is the real thing."

I was in my room by that time, changing into uniform. It was getting dusky, almost like evening. Smoke was rising from burning ships.

It was all over by 9:45. The Japanese had lost 29 aircraft, a submarine, and five midget submarines. The United States lost 2,403 service personnel and civilians, with 1,748 wounded; two battleships and the battleship-cum-target ship *Utah* were lost; another six battleships were damaged but later returned to service; three light cruisers and three destroyers were damaged, 164 aircraft were destroyed, and 128 damaged.

The world had changed forever. Two wars—the conflict in Europe and the Mediterranean, and the war in China—had been fused together at Pearl Harbor with the Pacific war. Within 24 hours President Roosevelt spoke to the nation, calling December 7, 1941, "a date which will live in infamy."

What the president would label an "unprovoked and dastardly attack" had been a long time coming. Industrializing Japan had seen itself as boxed in by the British, French, and Dutch far-eastern empires and treated as a second-class citizen by America and Great Britain. Its own army and navy, by competing ferociously with each other, had created a militarized, militaristic state.

In 1931, the Japanese had seized the Chinese border province of Manchuria. On July 7, 1937, a Japanese attack on Chinese soldiers of the nationalist Kuomintang Government and civilians at the Marco Polo Bridge near Beijing detonated the Sino-Japanese war, the beginning of the global struggle. In December 1937, Japan's "rape of Nanking" shocked the world.

At that time Burton Stein was an 11-year-old in Chicago, watching the war unfold—at the movies.

1941

OCTOBER 31

The destroyer U.S.S. *Reuben James* is sunk by a U-boat with the loss of over 100 men

NOVEMBER 7

Despite worsening weather and improved German air defenses, British Bomber Command continues nightly air attacks, including a raid on Berlin by 169 RAF aircraft

That was very big in the newsreels—the rape of Nanking. Those things were a part of our consciousness, so that to the extent that there was an awareness about Japan and concern about it, it was really indirectly through the China connection. China was supposed to be our friend, and these people were offending a friend. And we were also aware that efforts had already occurred in which the United States was supporting the Kuomintang in various ways—volunteers and that sort of thing.

The Japanese war was a catastrophe for China and turned out to be a disaster for the Japanese economy. On September 27, 1940, Japan, Nazi Germany, and Fascist Italy signed their Tripartite Pact. President Roosevelt identified the alliance as a worldwide totalitarian threat. So there was more backing for Great Britain and renewed pressure on Japan. In the summer of 1940, in the wake of the fall of France, Japan had moved into the northern part of the French colony of Indochina to open another front against China.

The day after the Pearl Harbor attack, the owner of this store, right, in Oakland—a University of California graduate of Japanese descent—erected this notice on his shop front. Above left, the U.S.S. Maryland *alongside the capsized U.S.S.* Oklahoma *with the* West Virginia *burning in the background*

NOVEMBER 13

The British aircraft carrier *Ark Royal* is torpedoed by a U-boat while transporting aircraft to Malta. She sinks the next day

NOVEMBER 16

Canada's Royal Rifles and Winnipeg Grenadiers arrive to bolster the defense of Hong Kong

1941

"above and beyond the call of duty"

DORIE MILLER
Received the Navy Cross
at Pearl Harbor, May 27, 1942

Benny Gordon was a 17-year-old Memphis-born African-American living in Webster Groves, Missouri.

> We felt threatened. We felt that it would be better to try to get them before they got us. Everyone was anxious to try to defend the country, fight for democracy.

It wasn't just Pearl Harbor that was attacked on December 7. The Japanese also launched assaults on the British colonies of Malaya and Hong Kong, as well as Guam, Wake Island, and the Philippines. In the summer of 1941, General Douglas MacArthur was appointed U.S. Army Commander for the Far East, based in Manila. He led 110,000 Filipino soldiers and 30,000 U.S. personnel.

Within an hour of the start of the Pearl Harbor attack (2:00 a.m., December 8, Philippines time), MacArthur had been informed. So had Tom King, who was a repair officer, submarines, for the U.S. Asiatic Fleet based in Manila. King was on the *Canopus*, a submarine tender and repair ship.

But Japan needed petroleum and scrap metal from the United States to feed its Chinese war. In December 1940, America banned sales of raw materials and scrap iron to Japan. July 1941 saw an embargo on all shipments to Japan, including oil. The Japanese cast their eyes on the raw materials and oil available from French Indochina, the Dutch East Indies, and British-controlled Burma and Malaya.

While Secretary of State Cordell Hull was still negotiating with Japan's ambassador, Nomura Kichisaburo, the attack on Pearl Harbor was unfolding. The news broke across a disbelieving United States.

Seventeen-year-old Michael "Flip" Pallozola worked in a radio shop and was training in electronics.

> It was a Sunday afternoon in St. Louis. I was out with some of my friends, using streetcar trolley cars and I'd heard about it. I was thinking, the war had started, I'm gonna become involved with this whether I want to or not. And I felt training in electronics would certainly be beneficial to me and to whatever job I was doing.

We Can Do It!

WAR PRODUCTION CO-ORDINATING COMMITTEE

NOVEMBER 23

German forces approach within 35 miles of Moscow

NOVEMBER 30

Hamburg is targeted by 84 RAF bombers, which drop 138 tons of bombs on the city; the first successful use of air-to-surface-vessel radar in action is made by a Whitley bomber, which locates, bombs, and sinks U-206

Roosevelt delivers his "Day of Infamy" speech to Congress, calling for the declaration of war against Japan, December 8, 1941

At left, "Rosie the Riveter" became a national icon in an extensive U.S. propaganda campaign. Above left, Naval Mess Attendant 3rd Class Doris "Dorie" Miller wearing the Navy Cross in a U.S. propaganda poster. Miller was honored for rescuing wounded men and shooting down four enemy aircraft

I heard a man coming down the ladder from topside. My room was on the promenade deck, just under that ladder. I thought some drunken sailors were coming back. I thought Ferrall had come back drunk. I went out on deck.

He said: "Mr King, we are at war." And I said, "You're drunk." And he said, "We've just got this signal." It was "Japan has started hostilities. Govern yourself accordingly." That was war.

Four hours later, Dr. Paul Ashton, serving with the 12th Medical Regiment of the Philippines Scouts, was at home in Bataan. He had just gotten out of bed.

I was shaving with an electric razor and it was a hot morning, and your face would get wet and you would have to use a towel with the razor. I was listening to the radio. This announcement came over.

As soon as we heard the news, we got dressed and we got packed. I got all my civilian stuff and put it in a big trunk, and knew I would never see it again, and I never did. I put on my uniform and went down to my HQ behind the hospital. I never left there again until I evacuated the post, because there were all sorts of communications coming in—where are we going? What are we doing? There were all kinds of people who were getting jittery and firing at things, but nothing really happened until that night.

About three o clock in the morning I got up—I had slept there at the HQ. I heard something. Behind the hospital there was a big field and across there was the main road going into Fort McKinley, and there was a radar post across there.

DECEMBER 7

Taking the land and seaborne defenses completely by surprise, the Japanese bomb Pearl Harbor, Hawaii, which leads to the United States declaring war on Japan

DECEMBER 8

President Roosevelt makes his "Day of Infamy" speech to Congress

1941

PROPOSED MESSAGE TO THE CONGRESS

Yesterday, December 7, 1941, a date which will live in ~~world history~~ *infamy*

the United States of America was ~~simultaneously~~ *suddenly* and deliberately attacked

by naval and air forces of the Empire of Japan.

The United States was at the moment at peace with that nation and was

still in ~~continuing the~~ conversation with its Government and its Emperor looking

toward the maintenance of peace in the Pacific. Indeed, one hour after,

Japanese air squadrons had commenced bombing in *Oahu* ~~the Philippines~~

the Japanese Ambassador to the United States and his colleague delivered

to the Secretary of State a formal reply to a ~~former~~ *recent American* message. ~~from the~~

~~Secretary.~~ *While* This reply *stated* ~~contained a statement~~ that diplomatic negotiations

~~must be considered at an end~~ *it* contained no threat ~~and~~ *or* hint of *war or*

armed attack.

It will be recorded that the distance ~~of Hawaii, and especially~~ of

Hawaii from Japan make*s* it obvious that the attack *was* deliberately

or even weeks ~~planned many days~~ ago. During the intervening time the Japanese Govern-

ment has deliberately sought to deceive the United States by false

statements and expressions of hope for continued peace.

> I didn't know what it was, and it was a bunch of airplanes, just a hum, high over, and they took that radar post out of there like it had never existed.

Louise Kroeger was a Roman Catholic nun. She lived 5,000 feet up in the Philippine mountains, helping to run a school and preschool for children of the Igowant tribe. It was 8 o'clock in the morning.

> We were sitting at the breakfast table and the phone rang. I think it came from the Spanish fathers. No sooner had we been told then the planes were overhead. We went outside to cheer. We were convinced they would be American planes. What other planes would be there?
>
> We were screaming and cheering, then all of a sudden, we heard the bombs dropping, we saw them dropping, saw the explosions.

Just after midday, Japanese warplanes based in Formosa arrived over Clark Airfield. Madeline Ullom was an American officer and an army nurse at Sternberg Army Hospital in Manila. It was lunchtime and she was on duty.

> We just stepped out of the wards—our hospital was built on Spanish-type architecture, so it was a courtyard and nice green grass around. We saw all these planes. We were Americans—and we thought after all—we saw six formations coming over. They were beautiful planes. There were nine in each group and there was a total of 54 in the formation and they came over the city.
>
> We said, "Look at that, aren't they beautiful, aren't they gorgeous?" We thought it's great to be an American—"these are our planes, look how beautiful they are, look at the sun shining on them."
>
> All of a sudden, the bombs started to drop. We were stunned for a couple of minutes, we just couldn't do anything—sort of frozen. We couldn't believe our eyes that they weren't ours. Then we started hearing the crashes and noises that the bombs were dropping. Nichols Field is probably about two miles away. We saw flashes of light. People started saying, "Hit the dirt, hit the dirt!"
>
> Here we were in our nice white starched uniforms and caps. We hit the dirt.

Jesse White was a master sergeant in the Army Air Corps, serving with the 24th Pursuit Group at Clark Field.

> I was in the cockpit of my airplane. I looked up and I saw these bombers overhead and people were running for cover. I was running a pre-flight inspection, so I killed the engine, jumped out, and ran as fast as I could and jumped into a ditch just as the bombs were falling. I was lucky to make it to the ditch. Some of the men didn't. The plane was demolished by the first bomb. I was very lucky.

Above left, the typescript of Roosevelt's "Day of Infamy" speech with his handwritten corrections. At right, a worker at the Shasta Dam in California reads about the Japanese raid

---

1941

DECEMBER 8
Britain, Canada, and other Allied nations also declare war on Japan

DECEMBER 11
Hitler declares war on the United States; in response, the United States announces its own declarations of war against Germany and Italy

DECEMBER 25

Hong Kong is surrendered
to the Japanese

DECEMBER 31

The Soviet Union manages to hold its position on the Eastern Front at the end
of 1941, narrowly preventing German forces from taking Moscow

The President of the United States ordered me to break through the Japanese lines and proceed from Corregidor to Australia for the purpose, as I understand it, of organizing the American offensive against Japan, a primary objective of which is the relief of the Philippines. I came through, and I shall return.

GENERAL DOUGLAS MACARTHUR
Adelaide, Australia
March 1942

CHAPTER NINE

SHADOW OF THE RISING SUN

Pearl Harbor and the Philippines campaign were accompanied, in December 1941, by Japan's moves against the Dutch East Indies, as well as the fall of Wake and Guam, Hong Kong, and the invasions of Malaya and Singapore.

From the start of their campaign to the conquest of Bataan would take the Japanese just four months. It would be two and a half long years before General MacArthur could fulfill his promise to the people of the Philippines—"I shall return."

In an attempt to deter Tokyo from going to war, the British sent H.M.S. *Repulse* and H.M.S. *Prince of Wales* to the Far East. An aircraft carrier that was supposed to provide air cover for the battleships had run aground and never made the voyage. On December 2, 1941, almost a week before war was declared against the Japanese, Lieutenant Colin McMullen, a young gunnery officer, arrived in Singapore on the *Prince of Wales*.

> Before war was declared, there was an air-raid warning. The army searchlights came on. There were nine enemy bombers in perfect formation. We actually opened fire on them while we were sitting in the dry dock. The intelligence regarding the Japanese was absolutely terrible. One of the things we'd been told was that they couldn't fly at night because they couldn't see properly in the dark.

On December 8, the *Prince of Wales* and *Repulse,* along with one Australian and three British destroyers, put to sea to counter the Japanese attack on Malaya (Malaysia) and Thailand. On December 10, they were attacked by Japanese warplanes. Lieutenant McMullen goes on:

> The total attacking force was 85 enemy aircraft. They were very efficient. The *Repulse* was a couple of miles away. I can remember her capsizing, with the ship still going through the water. It might have been a model boat going over. But the thing which did the final damage to the *Prince of Wales* was the torpedo attack from twin-engined torpedo bombers, one of which put a vital blow into our port quarter somewhere near the propeller shaft. The ship took on a violent list to port. We had further hits and Captain Tennant gave the order to abandon ship.
>
> We finally capsized. I actually swam off the bridge. On surfacing, I got into a Carley float with about four sailors who were singing the "Volga Boat Song." The *Express* and the *Electra* picked up about three-quarters of our ship's company and about two-thirds of the *Repulse's.*

The loss of the two ships was another blow to the morale of Hong Kong. The British had considered that the defense of the colony—on the southern coast of China—would be virtually hopeless in the event of war. Yet in September 1941, to boost local morale, they had requested two infantry battalions from Canada.

On the previous pages, General Douglas MacArthur on a balcony in Manila. In the background, the Japanese naval ensign

Canadian troops march to their barracks on arrival in Hong Kong, below. At right, U.S. sailors lay wreaths on the graves of comrades killed at Pearl Harbor

They were sent two battalions in "need of refresher training"—the Royal Rifles of Canada and the Winnipeg Grenadiers. On October 27, 1,975 men sailed from Vancouver. William Allister, a signalman with the Winnipeg Grenadiers, wrote in his diary:

> The enemy we faced was made up of tough veterans seasoned by years of war in China. Our Canadian force was deemed adequate only for garrison duty. You couldn't compare us to the trained Canadian divisions in England. Neither of our battalions had trained in anticipation of battle, and to make things worse, many reinforcements sent to the two infantry units were raw recruits or little better.

Soon after the initial Japanese attack, on December 8, William Allister wrote:

> Wallie had to ride back and forth to the front lines. Said it's blood-curdling to hear the Japs' battle cries. They came charging right into the machine guns.
>
> Our men used their machine guns till the barrels were red-hot. The Japs went down like wheat and still they kept coming, climbing over hills of bodies.
>
> The pillboxes turned out to be deathtraps. The Japs climbed on the roofs and lobbed grenades down the air vents. Our guys set their guns up on the roofs after that and the hell with the pillboxes. The Indians loved it all. They'd hold their fingers down on the trigger and never stop, happy as hell. They wept when they were ordered to retreat.

By December 13, the defenders had withdrawn from Kowloon to Hong Kong island. Allister observed the chaos of retreat.

> Withdrawal sounded fine on paper, but it reckoned without the chaos of half a million Kowloon citizens scrambling to escape across the half-mile of water. Panic and hysteria swept the waterfront. Fifth columnists fired at soldiers and civilians alike. Boats, sampans, junks, ferries, jammed with terrified refugees, were pounded by bombs and sprayed with machine guns. Mobs looted

JANUARY 12

The Japanese capture Kuala Lumpur, capital of Malaya (Malaysia)

JANUARY 14

President Roosevelt issues an order requiring all aliens to register with the government

1942

JANUARY 15

Japanese troops advance into Burma

JANUARY 20

SS terror chief Reinhard Heydrich presents his plans for the extermination of all European Jews at the Wannsee Conference in Berlin

warehouses. Police fired into crowds. Soldiers destroyed vehicles and ammunition. Last-minute demolition squads blew up harbor installations. Our signals section were kept at our posts until the last day, the 12th, and then ordered to get away as best we could.

The island was subjected to sustained bombardment. On December 15, the Royal Rifles helped beat off an attempted Japanese landing. But the Japanese were back for good on the night of December 18. William Allister was at West Brigade headquarters at Wong Nei Chong Gap. He confided to his diary:

Our captain knew we'd be trapped. He left four men to keep communications going and told the rest of us to start hoofing it. Where to? Anywhere—any way. We stumbled through the dark and rain, challenged by nervous sentries, and got lost in the hills. Ended up in a wrecked car and tried to sleep till dawn. At the first gray light, firing started all around us. Couldn't find any Canadians, so we joined an English officer. Killed my first men. Three. I often wondered how I'd feel. I felt nothing. Just numb with fright. We were encircled and had to run in front of their machine guns to get away. I've never known such terror.

By the evening of Christmas Day, the colony's Governor had surrendered. It was the Canadian Army's World War II baptism of fire.

UNE INDISCRÉTION PEUT CAUSER UNE CATASTROPHE

1 LE SOLDAT À SA FIANCÉE: "NOTRE TRAIN PART DEMAIN SOIR"

2 LA JEUNE FILLE LE CONFIE À SON PÈRE

3 LE PÈRE EN PARLE AU CLUB: UN ESPION L'ENTEND

4 L'ESPION RENSEIGNE LE SABOTEUR

5 LE SABOTEUR FAIT SAUTER LE TRAIN

Japanese troops march inland from their beachhead in the Philippines in the photo at left. Above far left, Indian machine gunners in Burma. Above left, British troops rest in front of Budah La, Pagoda Hill, Burma

Japanese officers escort Lieutenant-General A. E. Percival (farthest from camera) and the British surrender party to their headquarters in Singapore. Above right, a Canadian propaganda poster warns about the dangers of loose talk

FEBRUARY 8

The Japanese land in Singapore

FEBRUARY 12

German light battleships *Scharnhorst* and *Gneisenau*, bottled up in Brest, France, for more than a year, make a successful dash for home up the English Channel, escorted by over 100 surface vessels and 170 aircraft

1942

Servicemen and women relax above at Mount Lavinia Beach, Ceylon (Sri Lanka); the island would later come under heavy attack from the Japanese. At left, servicemen on leave in Ceylon visit the Mahaveli Ganga River on elephants

At right, WAAFs inspect sari cloth while shopping in Ceylon. Far right, a Japanese soldier amid the ruins of Bataan

FEBRUARY 15

The British surrender Singapore to the Japanese

FEBRUARY 19

President Roosevelt signs an order forcing more than 100,000 Japanese-Americans into internment camps. The internees lose an estimated $400 million as their homes and property are confiscated

On January 11, 1942, the Malayan capital, Kuala Lumpur, fell to the Japanese. By January 31, British Commonwealth forces had withdrawn to Singapore on the tip of the Malayan Peninsula. On February 15, the British Commander-in-Chief at Singapore, Lieutenant-General Arthur Percival, surrendered. It was a catastrophe, and signaled the end of the British Empire in the East.

On March 1, 1942, Vice-Admiral Chiuchi Nagumo, commander of the Pearl Harbor carrier strike force, bombed Darwin, Australia. This was a turning point in Australian history. Its armed forces refocused on the Pacific war and alliance with the United States. With Singapore captured, the Japanese gained control of the Strait of Malacca between the Indian and Pacific oceans. Nagumo sailed into the Indian Ocean. Thanks to advance warning from RCAF Catalina pilot L. J. Birchall, the Japanese Navy's air raid on Colombo in Ceylon (Sri Lanka) met with fierce resistance.

But Nagumo's forces did lay waste to Allied merchant shipping. Opposing him was Admiral James Somerville's weaker British Eastern Fleet. Meanwhile, two British cruisers, the *Dorsetshire* and the *Cornwall* were sailing from Ceylon to rejoin the fleet. Herbert Gollop was on the *Dorsetshire:*

> On April 5th, 1942, in the morning, we sighted the Japanese shadowing aircraft on the horizon. Then we were met, at about one o'clock, by 54 Aichii dive bombers. By then I was an antiaircraft-gunner second class, with a Canadian midshipman in charge.
>
> Waves of three bombers attacked us. We couldn't see them very well because they came straight out of the sun. We were hit by about thirty bombs and we sank in a matter of ten minutes.

FEBRUARY 26

Japanese Canadians are ordered to be evacuated from Canada's west coast

MARCH 6

Rangoon in Burma is evacuated in the face of the Japanese advance

1942

One of the things I remember is a port-side four-inch gun. I leaned over and I said, "Why have you stopped firing? Get on, get that gun loaded, get firing!" One poor chap looked up and said: "How can we fire when we're crippled and all the crew's dead?" He was the only one left alive.

The order was given to abandon ship.

The ship's siren had got stuck, and it was just wailing away. As I stepped onto the port side, I put my foot on somebody and my foot went right into his body. I had to shake the intestines off my feet. Then I just walked down to the side of the ship.

The Japanese aircraft started machine-gunning us. They killed quite a few chaps just helpless in the sea. Some of them tried to dive under the water and get away from it. I turned round as I swam away and I always remember that the home that I'd dearly loved for the last four years was just going down to the bottom of the sea with all my possessions.

I thought: "Well, that's the end of my life, almost." I watched it go down, stern first, and it was the saddest sight of my life.

The *Cornwall* was sunk also in about ten minutes. We congregated together and a large part of the mast was there. About sixty or seventy of us got onto this mast. We took turns of about an hour to cling to the mast. It was very, very hot, a brilliant sun was shining. All persons dying, we put them outside the circle, so that if the sharks were going to attack anybody, they would take the dead bodies. After about eight or ten hours, we all got very, very thirsty. There was one cup of milk between about forty of us. There was one ship's biscuit between about six of us. The bosun's mate piped "Hands to Breakfast," which raised a good cheer and a laugh.

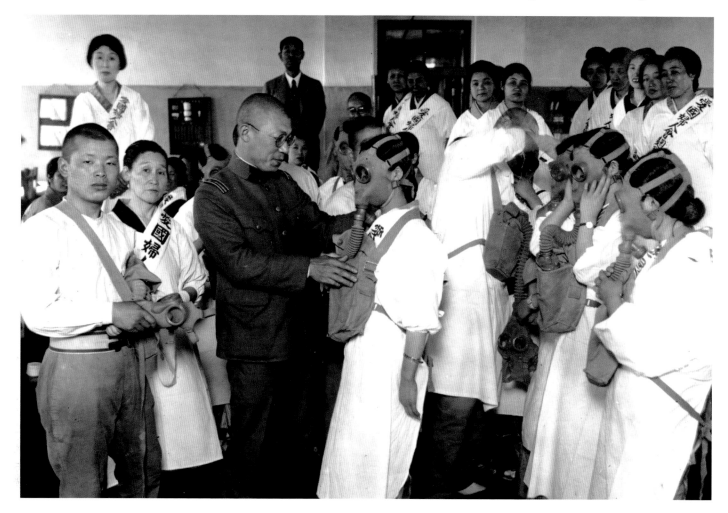

MARCH 9
100,000 Allied troops surrender to the Japanese in Java

MARCH 11
General Douglas MacArthur leaves the Philippines, assuring those left behind that "I shall return"

Indian women in the Auxiliary Territorial Service (ATS) on parade. Those wearing saris did not wear caps

Although they said they believed their cities could never be bombed, the women of the Ladies Patriotic League in Tokyo, shown below left, learn how to use gas masks. Below right, Mrs. Irma Lee McElroy finishes the paintwork on a U.S. fighter plane

> We were very cheerful, really, in the water. We started playing water polo one time, but they stopped us from doing that because we were told to conserve our energy.

On Easter Monday 1942, after around thirty hours, the survivors were rescued, having been spotted from the air.

On December 22, 1941, the Japanese had begun their major land offensive on Luzon in the Philippines. Roman Catholic nun Louise Kroeger's settlement fell just before Christmas.

> The really most remarkable thing was the poor, poor local tribesmen, the head hunters, were the ones who came across with things for us, whatever they dug from the ground. They risked their lives time and time again—at first they couldn't believe we were hungry. They never knew an American that was hungry.

U.S. commander MacArthur pulled his forces back into the Bataan Peninsula and the island fortress of Corregidor to avoid being caught in a Japanese pincer movement. The hope among many defenders was that U.S. forces would come to the islands' aid. Ruby Armbust was a dietitian at Manila's Sternberg General Hospital:

> I was convinced of rescue. We took the attitude "They can't do that to us, we're Americans." Cocky, but that is the way we all felt.

Not all. Dr. Paul Ashton was far more pragmatic:

> We had already been across that great void, the Pacific, on a ship. It took us 19 days to get there and it was going to take an awful long time, against resistance. We didn't believe for a moment there was going to be any relief.

In March 1942, President Roosevelt ordered General MacArthur to leave the Philippines and mastermind the entire Southwest Pacific campaign. This left Lieutenant-General Jonathan Wainwright in command. Nursing sister Madeline Ullom remembers:

Everybody liked Skinny Wainwright. General MacArthur was very hardworking, very serious, he worked his staff very hard; General Wainwright's leadership was altogether different. He knew that the end was coming and that we were all going to be caught there and possibly there was nothing to look forward to, really the only thing we had was ourselves. It wouldn't do much good to plan ahead because the Japanese were going to take over everything. A smile and a pleasant word was about all you had left.

Lieutenant Malcolm Champlin of the U.S. Navy was an aide to General Wainwright. One day in March 1942, he was with the general at the front in Bataan.

We pulled off the road in an area facing the Japanese. The Japanese artillery was coming right over the tops of the trees. There were sandbags facing the Japanese, there were foxholes. We all jumped into the foxholes except General Wainwright. He saw a captain he had known in Virginia—he was a sergeant then.

He went over and took this man by the arm: "How are you, Captain?" and he sat on the sandbags with his back to the Japanese. We were all in the foxholes. He was sitting there with his back to the enemy as the artillery projectiles were exploding right over our heads, coming right over the trees. We waited, and when they finished, the salvoes raked that road back and forth, and then we got back in the jeep.

I said, "General, I am a lieutenant in the Navy, I admit I do not understand your situation here. Do you realize, sir—which of course you do—that you are loved by your men, you are in command on

MARCH 27

RAF and volunteer American Flying Tiger airmen under retired U.S. aviator Claire Chennault are forced to quit Burma

MARCH 28

Allied commandos raid the French port of Saint-Nazaire, suffering heavy casualties but destroying the dock gates in an attempt to prevent its use by the German battleship *Tirpitz*

A powerful image of Old Glory—with a rousing message—on a U.S. propaganda poster

GIVE IT YOUR BEST!

Below left, Japanese troops celebrate the capture of an American artillery piece in Bataan

Bataan, you are risking your life, and I don't understand why. The men love you. They want you in command. They want you alive. Why do you expose yourself in the way you did a few minutes ago?"

He said, "Young man, you don't understand what we have to give to our men. A general in the Army of the United States does his best to give his men arms and ammunition, food, medicine, and recreation. We have none of those things. The men are starving. We are running out of ammunition. As you saw, they are dying. What can I give them? What can I do for my men? The only thing I can give them now is morale. My life is not worth as much as you think it is, I can give them morale and my presence on that front line is not the waste you think it is. When I sat on the sandbags, I did it deliberately. They want their general and they want to know he is here. I do that, and I do it for a good reason."

I said, "Thank you, God bless you, I understand."

One night, just before Bataan fell, Dr. Paul Ashton was at the front picking up casualties.

All night long the Japanese would get on their elbows and sneak across the river and climb up. In the morning, just at dawn, there's a second when it's dark and you can't see a thing, and then there's another second when it's light—and there's a Japanese. We've got foxholes dug all along and we're sleeping standing in them and didn't hear anything, and the Japanese have infiltrated right among us. You can see them when you shoot them, but then you realize, so you shot somebody, and then the Japanese see you shoot—so you get shot. After about a minute it's all over and everybody who's going to get killed gets killed.

Madeline Ullom was on Corregidor, confined to the extensive tunnels in the rock which served not only as MacArthur's and Wainwright's headquarters, but also as a hospital, mess hall and nurses' quarters. Medical staff could go for three days without seeing any daylight.

It was always good to see the blue sky and have the fresh air. Yes, it was real great. Towards the end, it was bombing almost constantly and the casualties, they were bringing them in all the time. I'm not a person who despairs. I don't believe in wringing my hands and saying how terrible things are. I was trained at Jefferson, in Philadelphia, which is a big hospital and in a big city. I was accustomed to dealing with a lot of people and a lot of stress situations, so you just take things for granted.

We knew the diesel fuel was getting low—we knew it was getting towards the end.

MARCH 29

The 1st Canadian Army, under A. G. L. McNaughton, is formed in Britain, with five divisions and two armored brigades

APRIL 8

Bataan falls to the Japanese

1942

Casualties would come in, all the fellows would tell you about what was happening. And it was just really tremendous, because they didn't complain. And they were so patient and they waited so well, and the only thing we could do while they were waiting was give them half a grain of morphine to reduce the pain until we could get to them.

Bataan fell to the Japanese on April 8. Some escaped to Corregidor, which held out until May 6. When Bataan fell, Dr. Paul Ashton was tending wounded prisoners:

I had 46 prisoners as chief of surgery, all badly wounded. We had picked them up, and when the Japanese commander came, I said, "We have prisoners of your people." They took all these people out—they'd had traction setups and casts and everything else—and they cut all the ropes, put them in big trucks and drove them off. They didn't take care of them. They said, "These people should have killed themselves." That was their attitude.

Approximately 60,000 Filipinos and 10,000 Americans, many malnourished and ravaged by disease, particularly malaria, were taken off by the Japanese on what became known as the Bataan Death March. The soldiers were clubbed, beaten, and, sometimes, murdered. Filipino deaths have been estimated at between 5,000 and 10,000. American deaths were probably in the high hundreds. The prisoners were marched 55 miles, then taken on by rail, before being marched a further eight miles to Camp O'Donnell. Dr. Ashton recalls:

There were some regular army sergeants, real tough monkeys—they were absolutely destroyed by the whole idea of this thing. Here is the U.S. Army, we have never been beaten, we've got everything, and all of a sudden they would realize they have been destroyed by a bunch of Japanese. Boy, their morale just keeled back. There was my own housemate, a West Point officer, a polo player, jumped off a bridge on the Death March. He said, "If it's going to be like

APRIL 9

British aircraft carrier H.M.S. *Hermes* is sunk when Japanese planes attack the port of Trincomalee in Ceylon

APRIL 15

King George VI awards the island of Malta the George Cross for the its people's courageous stand against the enemy

this, I don't want any of it." He had always been a good soldier, but when they come to a place where they realized, unavoidably, there was no help coming, and that the thing that they have always lived for, and lived in, and their great momma, the U.S. Army, was destroyed and could be destroyed, that was a blow they could not support.

By midsummer, at least 1,500 more Americans had died at Camp O'Donnell. The death toll among the Filipino prisoners would rise to more than 25,000. Primitive conditions and the lack of food and medicine meant that many died from malnutrition and disease. Many more were simply beaten to death by their captors.

Japanese soldiers pull down the American flag at Corregidor, below, following the U.S. surrender. At left, toughing it out in the Corregidor tunnels where first MacArthur and then Wainwright had their headquarters

American and Filipino prisoners heading for Camp O'Donnell, at right, after the fall of Bataan and Corregidor. Below right, the prisoners were brutally treated on what became known as the Bataan Death March

APRIL 18

Sixteen B-25 bombers under the command of Colonel James Doolittle take off from the aircraft carrier U.S.S. *Hornet* and bomb Tokyo

APRIL 24

In retaliation for the bombing of Lübeck, Hitler orders an attack on Exeter

1942

BEHIND BARBED WIRE

Long before the Pearl Harbor attack on December 7, 1941, American authorities had begun preparations for what looked increasingly like an inevitable conflict. Japan's aggressive expansion plans in the Pacific region and its deteriorating relationship with the United States made the gathering of certain information prudent. From the outbreak of war in Europe in 1939, lists of potentially dangerous enemy aliens were being compiled by U.S. government departments including the FBI, the Justice Department, the army's Military Intelligence Division, and the Office of Naval Intelligence.

> **There is no Japanese problem on the coast.**
> **There will be no armed uprising of Japanese.**
> *U.S. State Department Special Representative Curtis B. Munson, 1941*

The Japanese exodus began as soon as hostilities commenced, with every Japanese national who could heading for ports to catch a ship back to Japan

By November 1941, State Department Special Representative Curtis B. Munson had produced a report for President Roosevelt on the disposition and loyalty of Japanese Americans. Munson's report examined the attitudes of Issei, Nisei, and Kibei—Japanese born, and second- and third-generation Japanese Americans. Overall, Munson's conclusion was that the vast majority of those with Japanese ancestry in the United States posed no security threat. Any individuals who might have posed a

threat were already being monitored by the security services. In fact, Munson even went so far as to point out that, "The Japanese are hampered as saboteurs because of their easily recognized physical appearance."

Nevertheless, the 1930 and 1940 censuses were used to compile a list of the names and addresses of all alien and non-alien Japanese Americans in the country. Once America found itself at war, almost 750 Japanese Americans were immediately arrested by the FBI, along with scores of Japanese, German, and Italian nationals. This was a perfectly reasonable strategy to pursue. Much the same thing had already happened, after all, in England and other European states when war broke out there. Traumatic though it was for families where fathers or sons were removed from their homes by unsympathetic FBI agents, who would rifle through and confiscate family photo albums and other personal possessions looking for incriminating evidence, this was an unavoidable consequence of war.

Wartime paranoia partially explains why some of the Germans and Italians interned in the 50 or so camps set up around the United States may have been detained without sufficient justification. But those of German or Italian extraction were targeted quite specifically; there was always some kind of reason why they had fallen under suspicion. The fate awaiting the mass of Japanese Americans living on the western seaboard was even more sinister.

Fears that Japanese Americans could act as coast watchers reporting shipping movements to the enemy, spy on industrial or military installations, or cause mayhem as saboteurs led to a number of alarming measures being taken, the severity of which escalated with the passage of time.

Within three days of the declaration of war, the number of Japanese Americans detained by the FBI almost doubled. Restricted areas were established on the West Coast where those deemed "enemy aliens" had to obey a curfew and were only allowed to travel for the purpose of work—even then not more than five miles. Contraband was

> **A Jap's a Jap . . .**
> **It makes no difference if he's an American.**
> *General John L. DeWitt, Head of U.S. Western Defense Command, 1942*

Fearful of the soldiers, a Japanese-American boy waits with his mother to be "evacuated" from Los Angeles

confiscated—including firearms, hunting knives, binoculars, radios, cameras, and explosives that farmers often used to clear land.

With the signing of Executive Order 9066 in February 1942, restricted areas grew into "Military Areas" from which anyone could be deported as was "deemed necessary or desirable." Within a week the U.S. Navy evicted approximately 3,500 Japanese Americans, mostly employed in the fishing industry, from Terminal Island, a six-mile strip of land at the entrance to Los Angeles Harbor. Residents were given 48 hours to vacate. Modern-day carpetbaggers descended on bewildered housewives, many of whose husbands had already been arrested by the FBI. Unable to take all of their possessions with them, their household goods—refrigerators or even cars—were being snapped up at bargain prices. The day after the relocation deadline, Terminal Island was strewn with abandoned belongings.

The Farm Security Administration took responsibility for transferring ownership or tenancy of Japanese American farms, and the Federal Reserve Bank of San Francisco was appointed to handle property transactions. But the evictees rarely received fair value for their property, partly due to the fact that the number of evictees was rising alarmingly. Almost 120,000 people were forced to leave their homes in California, Washington, Oregon, and Arizona, taking with them only what they could carry.

They were transported to inland camps where they would spend the rest of the war living behind barbed wire. They farmed the land around the camps to produce their own food and were "hired out" to harvest vital crops, wherever manpower shortages demanded.

Conditions in the camps, run by the newly formed War Relocation Authority, were far from idyllic. Internees were outraged that some of them actually had relatives, even sons, training with the U.S. military. Indeed, over 100 Japanese-American soldiers refused to undergo combat training at Fort McClellan in Alabama until their families were released.

The regimes inside the camps were often extremely harsh, sometimes brutal, with suspicion and rivalries between different groups of internees and bitterness between prisoners and guards often erupting into violence. A number of prisoners were shot and killed by guards, reportedly "while trying to escape." The camps remained in existence until early 1946. Upon their release, internees who had suffered financial hardship because of the relocation policy were offered compensation of ten cents for every dollar lost—provided they could prove their losses.

In August 1988, President Ronald Reagan signed the Civil Liberties Act, providing a presidential apology and symbolic payments of $20,000 to internees, evacuees, and those of Japanese ancestry, whose liberty had been infringed or their property lost as a result of the U.S. government's relocation policy during World War II.

. . . they had two kids, a little boy who was nine and a sister who was twelve. They had never had butter in their life. They had never had a banana in their life. I had to teach their children how to peel 'em and eat 'em.

ORVILLE SCHLEF, U.S. ARMY
On visiting an English family's home

CHAPTER TEN

CROSSING THE GREAT DIVIDE

Great Britain not only became a fortress, a harbor, and an airfield, but also a social laboratory. It transmitted expertise such as jet engine and A-bomb research to the United States. It imported warriors—including West Indians, Australasians, Norwegians, Czechoslovakians, Belgians, Dutch, Poles, and French. And then there were the Canadians and the Americans.

Until mid-1943, when Canadian forces in Britain peaked at just over 200,000, they outnumbered those of the United States, but during the war, some three million American servicemen passed through Great Britain. Their culture, money, style, prejudices, and egalitarianism changed England—and themselves—forever.

Far from disembarking in Britain bursting with New World energy, the G.I.s tended to be queasy upon arrival. Flip Pallozola sailed from Providence, Rhode Island, in December 1942.

> The North Atlantic is rough. We were in a large convoy. We were on a very small Liberty ship, a cork in the ocean, 2,000 of us. Everybody was getting sick, it was horrible, smells. Nobody wanted to eat.

African-American soldier Benny Gordon had never seen a ship.

> It seemed to be several city blocks long and several city blocks wide. The journey was rough. You had more troops on the ship than you had bunks. Individuals got seasick, and it was really demeaning. Thank God that we were able to get there.

Canadian Army Private Albert Cunningham sailed from Halifax:

> It was in the winter. I was in a dining room. There was a stack of palliasses in the corner and at night you laid them down. If you wanted to go down to the toilet, you had to walk over 50 people to get in the corridor. You lay there at night and watched the cockroaches going up and down. I wasn't frightened. It was part of the adventure. We're going to England, that was the greatest target. God knows why. We landed at Liverpool. It had been bombed and the buildings were flattened. When you see pictures of Liverpool, you see pictures of a clock tower. Everybody rushed to the harbor side to have a look. The captain nearly went berserk. He was screaming "Everybody back!"

Newfoundlander Patrick Lewis, by then with the Canadian Army, landed at Gourock, Scotland, and set off on the train journey south.

It was foggy. We were waiting to get through Birmingham and all the girls were waving out of the windows of a factory. We were shouting to them. They were trying to shout to us. That was our first real contact with what, we were hoping, was going to be part of our future.

Lewis's next stop was the 80-year-old Warburg Barracks at Aldershot, Hampshire, in southern England.

That was quite a shock. We had very little heating. In the toilets and the washroom areas we had to stand on planks as the floors were always flooded.

On the previous pages, John Hartlage of Illinois, Edward Smith of Minnesota, and George Roberts of Virginia, somewhere in England. In the background, M-3 and M-4 tanks on exercise, Fort Knox, Kentucky, June 1942. Below left, one of the first contingents of Canadian troops to arrive in the U.K. in December 1939. U.S. troops parade, below, in a London park in 1942

What the Canadian Army in Britain faced for most of 1942 was inaction, terrible food, and primitive quarters.

We had no hot water. We had one bucket of coal a day. A lot of us slept in our clothes. Because we couldn't get warm, we took the windowsills down and burnt them. So we had to pay barrack damage. We weren't allowed to use electric irons. But when we saw what electricity was being wasted, we thought that was a lot of bunkum. One day, this civilian told us we had to stop using our irons. We were on the third floor of Warburg Barracks. They hung him over the side and told him that if he ever came back again, we'd drop him. We were paying the British government to come and fight for England. We didn't see him any more.

The first stop in England for U.S. 8th Army Air Force bombardier James Kirk was a new air base at Bovingdon, Hertfordshire.

APRIL 25

16-year-old Princess Elizabeth registers for war service

APRIL 26

U.S. sportswriters are advised by Associated Press to be sensitive to the war and not use words like "bombed" in baseball reports

1942

We walked into Hemel Hempstead, stopped in a pub, got a first look at English scenery, tried English beer and met some very nice English people. We asked for sandwiches in the pub and they didn't have any. Somebody disappeared and came back with a plate full of cheese and bread and butter. It was a man who lived next door to the pub. We didn't realize that this was his whole week's ration of cheese that he'd produced.

The Americans were joining a few fellow countrymen and women who had arrived pre-Pearl Harbor, like Texas fighter pilot William Ash, who was flying with the RCAF from a base near the capital.

I'd never seen London before and what impressed me was the courage and the good spirits and the unity of the people. When I was stationed at Hornchurch, I'd

Above left, the crew of the B-17 "I'll Get By"—within a month of this photograph's being taken, the plane was shot down and all but three of the crew were killed. At left, Canadian soldiers Private Darrich of Toronto and Sergeant Kriticos of Montreal help out at a children's party in Edmonton, London

At right, using the London Underground stations as air-raid shelters was eventually officially sanctioned by the authorities

APRIL 27

Over two-thirds of the Canadian people vote for conscription, although the government does not introduce it immediately

APRIL 27

The Office of Price Administration takes over the delivery of all new cars in the United States, allocating them by practical priority

be going back by Underground because it was only 40 minutes from the center of town to the aerodrome. When I'd go down to the Underground, and there'd be all these families just sleeping in these stations. And yet they were the cheeriest people you've ever seen. They'd all give you a big hello as I was going back to my station.

In this situation, England absolutely on its own, it was backs to the wall. And you have to have socialism. There has to be fairness for everybody. You're all in the war together, you're all sacrificing the same thing, your lives. And therefore there has to be equality of treatment. I know there was a black market, but I don't think it was ever all that extensive, really. And this impressed me terrifically.

Ration books were part of every British household's life, and rations varied. Yet rationing had virtues. Thanks to nutritionists, diets improved, and free or cheap milk was made available to mothers and children. Infant mortality fell, as did the incidence of a prewar scourge, tuberculosis. This, in 1944, was 20-year-old Glaswegian Catherine Niblock's situation:

I had two ration books, for my father, and my own. So that was your basic—you'd have a quarter pound of fat—that was two ounces for each adult—and half a pound of bacon, half a pound of sugar each. Fruit—that was unheard of. I believe they did better in the south of England because of the fruit crop there. I had no fruit during the war. And very, very little fresh vegetables.

British women were conscripted into industry and into the Women's Land Army. One recruit was Londoner Vera Holdstock. She went to work on a farm in southern England.

The only job that I did find unbearable was in the middle of winter, after we'd harvested the potatoes, they were put in big clamps. In January and February, when they started opening the clamps, we used to go out into an open field where these clamps were, and we used to have to wash the mud off the potatoes in cold water, and it really was unbearably cold.

Born in St. Louis, trained in California, Orville Schlef was posted to Chester, in northern England, to carry out U.S. Army administrative work. There, he became good friends with a local family.

I always arranged to take food along with me. I took the first butter—they had two kids, a little boy who was nine, a sister who was twelve. They had never had butter in their life. They had never had a banana in their life. I had to teach their children how to peel 'em and eat 'em. The little boy, Ron, he was ready to dive in and eat skin and all. They had one-dish meals but I was used to that. My family was very poor. Hash, a round of beef. The first Sunday it was rare roast beef. Each day it progressed. The roast was roasted over the open fire, heated up—by the time we got to the end of the week, it was well-done roast beef.

Young Englishwoman Prudence Portman's parents lived at Membury, which, in 1942, became the site of a USAAF base.

You invited an American into your home for supper, or would say, "Come and spend the evening with us and have a glass of homemade wine." They loved coming into English homes. They would nearly always bring something, such as a piece of bacon for boiling.

We thought their eating habits were odd. Piling everything on the plate and always eating with a fork. The English lay your knife and fork and you use it. They pushed the knife across the plate and finished the plate. Or they put jam on the plate—if you had a homemade jam, they'd put it on with something odd like fish. Queer to us, odd. But they were nice, very polite, always called my father "sir" and mother "ma'am"—a thing like that we had not been used to.

Flip Pallozola started touring the country.

APRIL 30

Silk stockings and sugar are rationed in New Zealand, soon to be followed by all clothes and shoes

MAY 1

British civilian casualties for April stand at almost 1,000 killed and the same number of wounded

Gathering the harvest beneath the wings of parked B-17 bombers. At left, shortages meant that few butchers were as well stocked as the one in this rationing propaganda shot

I bought a bicycle. I just went out to villages and met people. London was so full of G.I.s, you were just seeing the same kind of people all the time. When I got a seven-day leave, you could go on the trains and they didn't charge for any travel. So a couple of times I went up to Edinburgh and enjoyed that so much. There were about 100 pubs in this street below the castle and we were going to try to hit each one of them every night. We never did do it.

I met a very nice young lady there, Jasmine, and we became friends. I was a very naive young man. We had no sexual activities. It was just being enjoyable with each other.

Sex—or lack of it—plus nationality, race, drink, and money—or lack of it—blended with boredom, created a potentially explosive relationship among British, American, and Canadian soldiers. Mutual incomprehension could have the same effect. Patrick Lewis had grown up in Newfoundland with a belief in the Empire but was shocked at the attitude he found when he finally arrived in England.

When at home they played "God Save the King" at the end of the movie, everybody stood. In Aldershot, I was amazed to see people getting up and walking out while the National Anthem was being played. We looked on the Royal Family as the head of Great Britain and leader of the Commonwealth. Not everybody had that attitude.

MAY 4

Aircraft from the U.S.S. *Yorktown* attack a Japanese base at Tulagi in the Solomon Islands in the opening rounds of the Battle of the Coral Sea

MAY 6

Corregidor is finally surrendered to the Japanese. U.S. Lieutenant-General Wainwright becomes a POW along with 10,000 U.S. and Filipino personnel

1942

Flip Pallozola was not at all happy with his fellow Americans.

> We had a lot of obnoxious G.I.s! Their crudeness, the way they would talk to the English. They were blaming them for everything. They didn't want to be there, some of them, and they were blaming the English that this was going on.

Nor was African-American Benny Gordon:

> I was really surprised how the American white man, with his superiority complex, how he would treat his British counterparts, referring to them as Limeys: "They don't know what they're doing," they said. "We're just gonna have to take that over, because they're too slow."

Canadian Albert Cunningham had a wry view of the British Army.

We were a bit more casual. Everybody liked our uniforms. We had good-quality material, not coarse horrible stuff like the British.

In summer you had a uniform which was nice and light. I had two rounds of ammunition in each leg to hold my trousers down. Think of the weight of that! But you didn't think of that—it looked real sharp. The crease in your trousers was like a razor blade. You were always pressing your trousers.

MAY 7

A Japanese invasion force heading for Port Moresby in Papua New Guinea is intercepted by a U.S. Navy task force in the Coral Sea

MAY 7

The Battle of the Coral Sea is the first ever naval air battle—carrier versus carrier—with no surface ships actually firing on each other

Americans and Russians make friends, above, at a Christmas party in London, 1942. At left, a less informal shot from the same party

Far left, a Canadian sergeant teaches a member of the unofficial Women's Home Defence Unit how to use a rifle

American servicemen (and woman) playing pinball at Rainbow Corner, the American Red Cross club for U.S. troops in London. The machines were free and cigarettes could be won for high scores

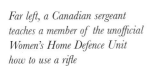

MAY 8

The Japanese fleet is repulsed with heavy losses on both sides. Capturing Port Moresby would have given the Japanese a strong platform for the invasion of Australia

MAY 8

German summer offensive against the Soviets begins in the Crimea

1942

GIVE 'EM

BOTH BARRELS

At right, segregation in the U.S. military meant that separate black and white military police were required

A U.S. propaganda poster aimed at boosting morale in industry on the home front. Below, Halloween 1942 and another excuse for a party

1942

MAY 11

In Canada, two freighters are torpedoed in the Gulf of St. Lawrence

MAY 14

In the United States, Congress approves the establishment of the Women's Auxiliary Army Corps

Most people were pretty keen to look smart. What would you think if you were in the British Army, working beside me, getting £1 a day and I was getting £5 a day? Bound to be jealous . . . and if you've got more money, you get more women, take 'em out, and send home to get silk stockings and cigarettes.

Until victory at el Alamein, late in 1942, defeats had demoralized the British Army. And the huge disparity in pay between the British and the North Americans didn't help. Prudence Portman:

The girls went mad. They'd never had such a good time. They'd never been with fellows who had so much money. But a lot of the local lads lost their girls to the Americans and loathed it.

The pub was escape and battleground. Prudence Portman:

The beer would come in in the morning and the Americans, being freer, went down at lunchtime while the farm laborer was working out in the field, expecting to have his drink at night. By the time he got there, the pub was dry.

In 1943, Iris Pilons was a teenager, bombed out of Southampton and living with her parents in the nearby village of Medstead. British, Canadian, American, and Polish soldiers were based at local camps.

They drank the pub dry nearly every night! The punch-ups and the fights there were. One Canadian put his fist through a plate-glass window. He was roaring drunk.

MAY 14

Japanese messages indicating a proposed invasion of the island of Midway are intercepted and decoded by the Americans

MAY 15

Gasoline rationing begins in the eastern United States

African-American troops attend a hymn service at a camp in England. At left, African-American women soldiers arrive in England in October 1942. At right, women ferry pilots in the classroom learn about aircraft engines

MAY 15

170,000 Russians are taken prisoner when the Germans capture Kerch in the Crimea

MAY 24

Basic pay for U.S. Army privates, Marine privates, and Navy seamen is raised to $40 per month

The Americans and the Canadians didn't get on at all well. The Americans and the local people, and the Canadians and the local people—they mixed very well.

The Americans' arrival changed Britain; it also challenged the U.S. armed forces, which, unlike the Canadians and the British, enforced racial segregation. The British government covertly tried to dissuade Washington from sending African-American soldiers to Great Britain. British authorities then very often tacitly backed American segregationist "separate but equal" policies. This outraged black service people from the Empire, American and British antiracists and sections of the British press. There were no "Jim Crow" laws in Britain and the public had not been versed in American segregation. Indeed, with no more than 8,000 black Britons, most of their fellow citizens had never seen a black person. Prudence Portman developed a friendship with a white U.S. Army captain from Philadelphia.

We were cycling to Hungerford. We went into a pub for a drink. And a black man, the first time I've ever seen this, came in and sat down next to me while my friend was up at the bar buying the drinks. My friend came back, and he was very rude to this black man. He told him to clear off—"How dare you sit beside a white woman?" He went. It was like that then, very, very much; no black man to be seen with a white girl. That was absolutely taboo.

England was a shock to Benny Gordon:

I found that the white people in England treated me better than the white people in America. It was a very good experience that I'll treasure as long as I live. In pubs, in a lot of instances, the Englishmen were a little harsh. They would come out and insult the young lady because of the association. I did have an English girlfriend. She was born in England, she wasn't white. Her dad was English and her mother was something

---

MAY 26

Fierce fighting continues in the deserts of North Africa, where the Allies are locked in combat with Rommel's Afrika Korps

MAY 27

Czechoslovakian agents critically injure SS leader Reinhard Heydrich in an assassination attempt in Prague

1942

A female ferry pilot delivers an Avro Anson to an RAF airfield. At right, an American pilot prepares for takeoff in his B-17 Flying Fortress with the image of General "Ike" Eisenhower painted on the side. Below, Paul Kaiser from Philadelphia loads a Bofors antiaircraft gun somewhere in England

else. She was a beautiful person, a teacher, she had been subjected to a lot of the things that we were subjected to. There was a lot of devotion and sincerity. She said: "When you go back to America, you are going to marry an American. But what I want you to do is always remember the times we've had together." It was just so warming.

Time passed. Relationships solidified. Patrick Lewis was redeployed to the south coast.

The landlady of the local pub took to me, I don't mean as a girlfriend. She was a lady in her early sixties. "You are wasting your money," she said. "You shouldn't be drinking so much. I want you to hand over your money to me and I'll dish you out so much a night." In the end I gave in. Also they'd have me in for a meal. They treated me like a son. Her two daughters were married and we would stay at their homes. I was in heaven. The message went out—these people are treating us so well that if you get out of line, you're gonna have to deal with the rest of us.

We were astounded how the English girls were prepared to help and take us home to their families, not having much food to share with us. We appreciated that very much and felt yeah, they're worth fighting for.

MAY 27

Japanese transport ships carrying invasion troops bound for Midway leave Guam and Saipan

MAY 30

"Bomber" Harris orders a major raid on Cologne involving more than 1,000 bombers, using almost every serviceable RAF bomber aircraft, and offloading more than 2,000 tons of bombs; with a total

MAY 31

of only 40 aircraft lost, RAF chiefs claim to have destroyed
more than 200 factories

In Australia, three Japanese midget submarines
raid Sydney harbor

1942

*It was the first time I had ever carried a torpedo on an aircraft, and
was the first time I had ever taken a torpedo off a ship. I had never
even seen it done.*

ENSIGN GEORGE GAY,
TORPEDO SQUADRON 8
U.S.S. HORNET

CHAPTER ELEVEN

FARAWAY PLACES

In January 1942, U-boats decimated Atlantic convoys and U.S. coastal shipping. German and Italian units had pushed back British Commonwealth forces in the Western Desert. The Japanese were engulfing swaths of Asia and the Pacific. Yet, by December 1942, the mention of obscure places and strange cities signaled hope rather than fresh disaster: El Alamein, Guadalcanal, Stalingrad . . . and Midway.

Japanese naval successes had continued after Pearl Harbor. In late February, at the Battle of Java Sea, a makeshift force of 14 American, British, Dutch, and Australian warships, without air cover, was routed. Only four U.S. destroyers survived. On March 8, the Dutch East Indies surrendered.

But then, on April 18, Lieutenant-Colonel James H. "Jimmy" Doolittle led a raid by 16 B-25 bombers, flying 600 miles from the aircraft carrier *Hornet* to Japan. The raid caused little physical damage, but the psychological impact was considerable. It reinforced the aim of Japan's naval Commander-in-Chief, Admiral Yamamoto, to eliminate U.S. carrier forces and thus make some kind of Japanese victory possible.

In early May, three Japanese convoys assembled at Truk, in the Caroline Islands, and Rabaul, in New Guinea. Their initial aim was to secure Port Moresby, New Guinea, on the way to isolating Australia. To guarantee success the Japanese deployed three aircraft carriers, six heavy cruisers, and seven destroyers.

But the Americans and the Australians, thanks to Ultra code-breaking, knew about the Japanese dispositions. Three task forces were gathered, two around the U.S. aircraft carriers *Lexington* and *Yorktown* while a third comprised U.S. and Australian cruisers. The protagonists' ships never sighted each other; the Battle of Coral Sea was the first all-carrier naval encounter. By its conclusion, the Japanese had lost a light carrier and the Americans the *Lexington*, but the other Japanese carriers limped out of the battle and were unable to participate in the next crucial naval confrontation, at Midway.

That tiny island was by then the farthest west of the U.S.'s Pacific bases. Admiral Yamamoto saw its capture as a prelude to an onslaught on Hawaii—and imagined that this might presage a possible U.S. surrender. Yamamoto had mobilized more than 140 ships, including four aircraft carriers.

At left, Lieutenant-Colonel James H. "Jimmy" Doolittle with his crew on the deck of the U.S.S. Hornet prior to the historic raid on Japan. On the previous pages: Dauntless bombers await action aboard a U.S. Navy aircraft carrier. In the background, depth charges are fired from a U.S. Navy destroyer hunting Japanese submarines

At right, U.S. soldiers host a 1942 "Thanksgiving Day" party in England for children who have suffered during the war. Above right, the Grumman Avenger first saw action at Midway

1942

JUNE 1
The RAF mass raid on Cologne is followed by a 1,036-strong bombing attack on Essen

JUNE 3
U.S. ships and carrier-borne aircraft engage Japanese naval forces at the Battle of Midway, resulting in the withdrawal of the Japanese fleet, with heavy losses, four days later

JUNE 4

SS leader Reinhard Heydrich dies
as a result of wounds received
during an assassination attempt

JUNE 10

In reprisal for the killing of Heydrich, German troops execute 172 men and boys from
the Czech village of Lidice, send most of the women and all of the children to
concentration camps and totally destroy the village, deleting it from German maps

Thanks to Ultra, the U.S. Pacific Fleet's Commander-in-Chief, Admiral Chester W. Nimitz, knew his opponent's plans. But the Japanese—partly thanks to U.S. deceptions—did not know that they were facing a substantial U.S. naval force built around three carriers, the *Yorktown*, the *Hornet*, and the *Enterprise*. On June 4, 41 U.S. Navy torpedo bombers caught Vice-Admiral Nagumo's fleet by surprise. They scored no hits and suffered the loss of 35 aircraft. But they succeeded in diverting Japanese fighters—with catastrophic results for Nagumo's carriers.

Ensign George Gay was 24 and would be the sole survivor of the *Hornet's* Torpedo Squadron 8.

> It was the first time I had ever carried a torpedo on an aircraft, and was the first time I had ever taken a torpedo off of a ship. I had never even seen it done. None of the other ensigns in the squadron had either. We had had no previous combat flying. We'd never been against the enemy. Our only scrap with them had been in taking Doolittle to as close to Tokyo as we went. But when we finally got into the air on the morning of June 4, we had our tactics down cold and we knew organization and what we should do.
>
> The Zero fighters jumped on us in full strength that day, just caught us off balance. Torpedo 8 and the other Torpedo squadrons sucked those fighters down so that when the dive-bombers did get there, there weren't nearly as many fighters as there would have been if they hadn't come down to get us. So I think that is one thing that helped save the day as far as the battle was concerned.
>
> I came in with, of course, the rest of the Squadron. We came in to make an attack on this ship on her starboard side. Well, when I got in close enough to think about dropping a torpedo, I saw that she was in this hard turn, and I pulled out to the right and swung back and gave her a lead and it was a perfect setup. I couldn't have missed it if I'd wanted to because all I had to do was to give her about a ship's length lead, and then, instead of the ship turning away from me, by the time the torpedo got to her she was broadside and she just turned right around into it. It was easy. I dropped the torpedo and was fortunate enough to get away from the antiaircraft fire.

Gay had sustained injury.

> I had a left leg that was burned and a left arm that was gone, the plane was still flying, and I felt pretty good. But then the Zeros returned.

JUNE 13

Four German saboteurs equipped with explosives and incendiaries are landed by submarine on a beach near Amagansett, Long Island, New York

JUNE 17

Four more German spies are landed by submarine in Ponte Vedra Beach, near Jacksonville, Florida

The pain of wartime separation—Private D. N. Daniels kisses his wife good-bye at the Greyhound bus terminal in Chicago. At left, Douglas Devastator torpedo planes on the deck of the Enterprise

The Zeros jumped on me and I was trying to get out of the fleet. Before I got away from them, though, the five Zeros dived right down on me in a line and about the second or third one shot my rudder control and ailerons out and I pancaked into the ocean. The hood slammed shut, I couldn't keep the right wing up. It had hit the water first and snapped the plane in, and bent it all up and broke it up and the hood slammed shut and it was in the sprained fuselage. I couldn't hardly get it open. That's when I got scared. I was afraid I was going to drown in the plane.

Gay clung to a seat cushion float and watched the rest of the battle unfold around him. He was later rescued by a Catalina flying boat. Commander John Thach, leader of *Yorktown*'s fighter pilots, was escorting torpedo planes attacking the Japanese carriers:

I was utterly convinced that we weren't any of us coming back because there were still so many Zeros. And then I saw a glint in the sun that looked like a beautiful silver waterfall. It was the dive-bombers coming in. I could see them very well because they came from the same direction as the Zeros. I'd never seen such superb dive-bombing. After the dive-bomber attack was over, I stayed there. I could only see three carriers. And one of them was burning with bright pink flames and sometimes blue flames. Before I left the scene, I saw three carriers burning pretty furiously.

Mitsuo Fuchida observed the battle from the aircraft carrier *Akagi*:

The attackers had gotten in unimpeded because our fighters, which had engaged the torpedo planes only a few moments earlier, had not yet had time to regain altitude. The American dive-bombers' success was made possible by the earlier martyrdom of their torpedo planes.

We had been caught flatfooted in the most vulnerable condition possible—decks loaded with planes armed and fueled.

JUNE 21

Tobruk, in Libya, falls to Rommel's Afrika Korps, with the loss of more than 20,000 Allied prisoners

JUNE 26

Bremen is hit in an RAF bomber raid of more than 1,000 aircraft

1942

Eventually, Pollard went onto the flight deck. The first thing he noticed was what was left of an emplacement.

> A pair of legs attached to the hips sat in the trainer's seat. A stub of spinal column was hanging over backwards—there was nothing else remaining. The steel splinter shield was full of men, or rather portions of men, many of whom were not identifiable. Blood was everywhere. I turned forward and saw great billows of smoke rising from our stack region. We were dead in the water.
>
> Yet fires were brought under control and preparations made to head home. We were really beginning to have some hope that the Japs would not return but, alas and alack, about 16:00, our radar picked up enemy planes at 40 to 60 miles coming in fast.

John Thach took off to defend the *Yorktown* and spotted a torpedo plane:

> I got him on fire. The whole left wing was burning and I could see the ribs showing through the flames. But that devil stayed in the air until he got close enough and dropped his torpedo. That one hit the *Yorktown*. He was a dedicated torpedo plane pilot, for even

Despite the crippling of three of the Japanese carriers, the fourth, the *Hiryu*, counterattacked against the *Yorktown*. Lieutenant Joseph P. Pollard was a young medical officer:

> General quarters sounded, Jap planes were upon us. I dived down the ladder for Battle Dressing Station One. Our antiaircraft guns were in full bloom. I had never before heard such a roar. Then all hell broke loose. I saw a burst of fire, heard a terrific explosion, and in less then ten seconds was overwhelmed by a mass of men descending from the gun mounts and flight deck into the Dressing Station. An instantaneous 500-pound bomb had struck just aft of the starboard side of the middle elevator.
>
> Wounded were everywhere. Some men had one foot or leg off, others had both off; some were dying—some dead. Everywhere there was need for morphine, tourniquets, blankets, and first aid.

JUNE 27

Acting on information obtained from one of the eight saboteurs recently landed in the United States by U-boat, the FBI arrests the last of the German spies

JULY 4

USAAF units based in Britain take part in their first action during a combined attack with the RAF on Dutch airfields used by the Luftwaffe

A Wildcat fighter of the type flown by John Thach has its guns aligned at a U.S. Navy shore base. At left, Charmaine Stadler, aged 7, whose father served with the Free French forces, briefly turns on the illuminations at the Statue of Liberty to celebrate its 56th anniversary in 1942. The monument's lights were turned out due to blackout restrictions. Below, the damaged Yorktown listing badly

though his plane was on fire and he was falling, he went ahead and dropped his torpedo. He fell into the water immediately after. As far as determination was concerned, you could hardly tell any difference between the Japanese carrier-based pilots and the American carrier-based pilots. Nothing would stop them if they had anything to say about it.

Joseph P. Pollard:

There was a sickening thud and rumble throughout the ship and the deck rose under me, trembled and fell away. One torpedo hit had occurred. Just then word came over the speaker, "Prepare to abandon ship."

Pollard, having ensured that all the wounded from his area of the ship had been transferred to life rafts, jumped over the side more than 75 feet into the sea.

As each wave broke over our heads, the oil burned our eyes and noses like liquid fire. It was impossible to keep from swallowing some of it. Someone would swim alongside and say "hold me up a minute, please," and proceed to vomit the oil and then swim on.

Two-and-a-half hours later, he was picked up.

JULY 6

General Auchinleck, Commander-in-Chief Middle East, takes personal command of Eighth Army and drives back Rommel's forces in the First Battle of El Alamein

JULY 12

A township near Joliet, Illinois, is renamed Lidice after the Czech town destroyed by the Germans

1942

The Japanese had suffered a crushing defeat. For the loss of the carrier U.S.S. *Yorktown,* the destroyer U.S.S. *Hammann,* and 147 aircraft, the Americans had sunk three Japanese destroyers, a cruiser, and four aircraft carriers with 280 planes. Another 52 were shot down. Three hundred and seven Americans died in the action, while an estimated 4,800 Japanese lost their lives.

In the spring of 1942, growing pressure was being applied to the British from Washington, Moscow, and Ottawa. The Soviet Union wanted an invasion of western Europe to relieve pressure on the Red Army. The United States, too, hoped for an early invasion. From Canada, whose forces in England were idle and facing morale problems, there were also calls for action.

On August 19 came Operation Jubilee, a raid from southern England on Dieppe. Canada provided 4,963 troops, Britain 1,075, and there were 50 U.S. Rangers. The raid's aim was to test German port defenses, but there was inadequate naval and air bombardment and poor intelligence. A bloody fiasco ensued. American James Goodson, then still flying with the Royal Air Force, was one of the pilots providing air cover.

Battle-weary Canadian soldiers and commandos feature on the cover of topical magazine Picture Post, *below, following the raid on Dieppe. At left, the British lion and a fearsome Canadian beaver fight side by side on a Canadian war poster*

JULY 16

In Paris, French police begin rounding up almost 13,000 Jews who are then handed over to the Gestapo for transportation to concentration camps

JULY 30

The Women Accepted for Voluntary Emergency Services (WAVES) organization is approved by the U.S. Congress

Canadian soldiers bring blindfolded German prisoners ashore in England on their return from the Dieppe raid

We were flying right down among the weeds, we could see the whole thing happening. The Germans had all the defense in the world, and to see these troops going in and getting mowed down—it was like wheat being cut by a reaper. It was just terrible.

Toronto-born war correspondent Ross Munro described life and death on a beached landing craft:

One lad crouched six feet from me. He had made several attempts to rush down the ramp, but each time a hail of fire had driven him back. He had been wounded in the arm but was determined to try again. He lunged forward and a streak of tracer slashed through his stomach. I'll never forget his anguished cry as he collapsed on the bloody deck. "Christ we gotta beat 'em. We gotta beat 'em." He was dead in minutes.

Twenty-nine-year-old French-Canadian Lieutenant Colonel Dollard Ménard was commanding a unit of Les Fusiliers Mont-Royal. Having been hit twice while on the beach heading for a pillbox, he watched a major and close friend being shot down in front of him.

He was holding his stomach, a bad place to be hit because nothing outside a hospital operating room could help him. His face was gray and he was sucking hard for breath. I began fumbling for my first aid kit. My friend was watching me but didn't say anything. I got out some morphine tablets, put one on his tongue and he swallowed it. There was nothing else I could do. He knew it and I knew it.

I went on toward the pillbox. Up to that point I'd been more or less brave because of discipline and training. I hadn't felt any particular anger because of my own wounds. But now, with my friend lying there, I was so blind angry that it seemed to push everything else out of my head. All I wanted was to kill, get even. I had to direct my unit, so I had to control this rage. But it seemed to clear my head, to make me think harder and faster. It also seemed to act as a sort of

AUGUST 7

American troops storm ashore on the Pacific island of Guadalcanal

AUGUST 8

Six of eight German saboteurs arrested by the FBI in the United States are executed. One of the remaining two is sentenced to life imprisonment, the other to 30 years

1942

A Canadian Spitfire pilot embarks on a mission in North Africa. At left, Allied armor closes in on Hitler for the good of British propaganda

general anesthetic. Trying to get over the parapet, I was hit again—this time by a bullet. It knocked me backwards onto a steel picket, seriously injuring my spine. The bullet went clean through my right arm above the wrist and smashed two bones. I barely felt it.

Ménard made it back but in less than half a day, 3,367 Canadians had been captured or wounded, 689 of whom would die. There were 825 British casualties and the United States suffered its first World War II fatality in France.

James Goodson:

The excuses made were, well, it gave us experience for the later invasion. But it didn't. The people who were supposed to get the experience were dead.

British Commonwealth successes in the deserts of Libya had been reversed in 1941 with the redeployment of key units to the failed defense of Greece and the arrival

in Tripoli, in February 1941, of formidable German General Erwin Rommel. By June 1942, he had captured Tobruk—which had earlier resisted a series of sieges—was made a field marshal, and won again at Mersuh Matruh. British Commonweath forces fell back to Egypt. However, from an obscure railway outpost, El Alamein, between July 1 and 4, General Sir Claude Auchinleck checked the German-Italian advance. Then, in early August the British Eighth Army welcomed a new commander, General Bernard Montgomery.

Derek Mayne was working with a film unit attached to the New Zealand Division, and soon after he was appointed, Montgomery was inspecting units:

1942

AUGUST 17
Churchill visits Moscow for talks with Stalin

AUGUST 19
Almost 6,000 Allied troops, mostly Canadians, are involved in a disastrous attempt to raid Dieppe. The landing is completed, but only a fraction of the targeted installations

General Bernard Montgomery, shown at left, commanded the British Eighth Army "Desert Rats" in North Africa. Above, Montgomery's German counterpart, General Erwin Rommel, the "Desert Fox"

He stopped when he saw a platoon of men digging some rear defenses quite a long way behind what was called the Alamein Line and said very loudly, "Good morning, what are you doing here?" The officers said, "We are digging a reserve position, Sir." Montgomery said, "You can stop all this, this will never be required, the army will never retire, the army will go forward."

At the end of August Rommel made another attempt to break through in what became the Battle of Alam Halfa. Derek Mayne:

Alam Halfa was the great forerunner of Alamein. The order of the day, which Montogomery issued before the battle, was that there would be no retreat and no surrender.

Mayne and his crew had been ahead of the main force, but then came back into the Alam Halfa defenses:

There was a most extraordinary scene. Down below us, because this ridge was fairly pronounced, I think it was the Eighth Armored had come up and they were laid out there almost in a parade formation it looked, and slogging against them was part of 15th or 21st Panzer, two very large armored formations doing that. About 5,000 yards off in the dust and the haze were Rommel's supply vehicles. He thought he was going to come through. Our gunnery and our air force were bombing this thing like mad, and it really was absolute hell.

What followed on October 23 was Montgomery's delivery of firepower, air power, and superior numbers against the Axis forces. Peter Salmon was serving with the Ninth Australian division on the northern perimeter of what became the Battle of El Alamein. It began with an 882-gun barrage, the biggest by British Commonwealth forces since the First World War 24 years earlier.

AUGUST 25

are attacked. About 4,000 men are killed in action, wounded or captured, and over 100 aircraft are lost, along with a destroyer, 30 tanks, and 36 landing craft

The Duke of Kent, youngest brother of King George VI and a serving RAF officer, is killed in an air crash

1942

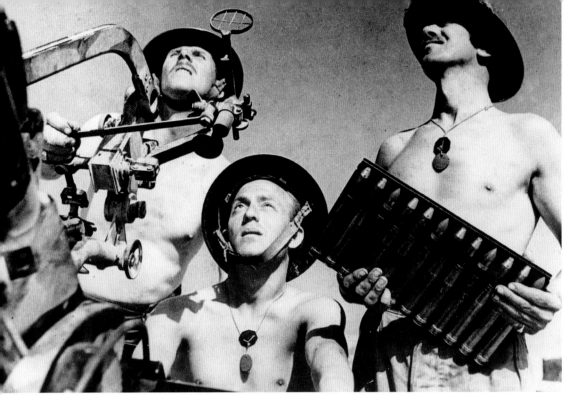

Three British Desert Rats man a captured German gun at Tobruk. At right, German prisoners awaiting transport after the Battle of El Alamein

Below, an American-built Curtis P-40 of the RAF. The man on the wing is guiding the pilot, who has only limited forward vision while on the ground. Below right, one of the workers who helped produce the 1939-43 Star of Africa campaign medal ribbon

Obviously it was going to be a really big battle. We were just told we were going to move forward. One of my most unpleasant experiences was having to jump into a slit trench and landing fair and square right onto a corpse, which had been there for a very long time. So I had a very long time putting up with a very unpleasant odor—coming from me. Little things like that stick in your mind.

It was quite a while before we actually came into contact with machine-gun fire and mortar fire. The machine guns were set up to give a cross fire, the Germans were particularly good at that. The cross fire was pretty horrific and, of course, they had the 88mm, which were nasty.

That battle was a turning point in the West. By November 4, Rommel had begun a skillful retreat. But four days later, Operation Torch, Anglo-American landings in French Algeria and Morocco led by General Dwight D. Eisenhower, began. In the Pacific, conflict on the Solomon island of Guadalcanal was intensifying,

1942

SEPTEMBER 8
The German Sixth Army confronts an entire Soviet army in Stalingrad, thus beginning the siege

SEPTEMBER 16
The Women's Air Force Service Pilots (WASPS) is established and will go on to supply more than 1,000 auxiliary pilots to the U.S. armed forces

and on the Eastern Front the immense battle for Stalingrad was moving to a climax. For Winston Churchill, this was not the end—"It is not even the beginning of the end. But it is, perhaps, the end of the beginning."

Peter Salmon:

It was the first time Churchill had given out the orders to ring the bells of London. It was quite an emotional time, it really was. We thought we had done our bit. At the back of most of our minds there was a bit of worry of home, I think. A lot of Japanese propaganda came through the Germans and the Italians, and made all sorts of false claims that the Japs had invaded Australia. They used to talk about the Americans taking all our girls . . .

SEPTEMBER 25

RAF Mosquitos conduct a low-level bombing raid on Oslo, targeting the Gestapo office with great success, and destroying the HQ along with its records of Norwegian resistance fighters

OCTOBER 23

The Battle of El Alamein begins when General Montgomery orders a 1,000-gun bombardment of the German positions and minefields, followed by a nighttime attack

1942

THE NAVAJO CODE TALKERS

SHUSH DZEH WOL-LA-CHEE BA-GOSHI LIN AH-JAH
DIBEH BE-LA-SANA AH-LOSZ AH-NAH CHUO A-KHA
DAH-NEW-TSA A-KEH-DI-GLINI TSE-NILL MOASH
WOL-LA-CHEE THAN-ZIE TKIN TLO-CHIN TSAH

Most of the thousands of U.S. Marines battling their way from one shell-blasted beach to the next around the Pacific, closing ever nearer to Japan, would have loved the above message ... but only around 400 of them would have understood it. All those who could were Native-American Navajos.

Navajos had one of the highest proportional representations of any ethnic community in the U.S. armed forces during World War II. In 1942, there were approximately 50,000 Navajo tribe members. It is estimated that more than 3,600 of them served loyally in the armed forces alongside men whose ancestors had been bitter enemies of their own forefathers. Some 540 volunteered for the U.S. Marine Corps. Of those, 400 were chosen for an elite signals unit. Men from this unit took part in every assault launched by the U.S. Marines from 1942 to 1945, fighting in all six divisions, raider battalions, and parachute units. Their skill was specific, unique, and indispensable. They were code talkers, guardians of a vital cipher that the Japanese, renowned for their expertise as cryptographic analysts, found impossible to break.

Navajo is an unwritten language of great complexity spoken only on Navajo lands in the southwestern United States. In order to understand it, one must have had extensive exposure to its use; had intensive training in the intricacies of its pronunciation; or known that it has neither alphabet nor symbols. In other words, one has to be a Navajo. Only 30 known non-Navajos in the entire world could understand the language at the beginning of World War II. One was Philip Johnston, son of a missionary to the Navajos. Johnston was a veteran of World War I and knew the importance of code. He also knew that Native-American languages, such as Choctaw, had been used by the U.S. military to create codes in the past. He believed the Navajo language could form the basis of an unbreakable code.

When Johnston presented his idea to the Marines, he was asked to prepare a demonstration. Tests were carried out under simulated combat conditions. Johnston's Navajo volunteers proved they could successfully encode, transmit, and decode a three-line English message in fewer than 30 seconds. Encoding machines at that time would have needed 30 minutes to carry out the same task. The Marines were convinced.

The code talkers started out as a unit of 29 Navajo recruits. All could speak perfect English and all had attended high school. In May 1942, they were put through basic training and assigned to Camp Pendleton, in California, where their task was to create a Navajo code. Many English words, especially military terms, had no Navajo equivalent. This group of 29 gave Navajo names to things such as the submarine (besh-lo, "iron fish") or fighter plane (dah-he-tih-hi, "hummingbird") and defined a way in which Navajo words could be used to represent letters of the English words being encoded. The encoded messages were constructed in such a way that the Navajo code talker being sent a message would receive a whole list of apparently random Navajo words. He had to translate each word or phrase into its English equivalent and then use only the first letter to spell out the message.

For example, while the word "tank" had been given a Navajo equivalent as chay-da-gahi (tortoise), it could also be spelled out in code as than-zie (turkey), tse-nill (axe), tsah (needle), klizzie-yazzie (kid). Each letter of the alphabet could be represented by several alternative Navajo words, meaning that the same word or phrase need never be transmitted in the same way twice. That way, it was impossible for the eavesdropping enemy to attribute specific meanings to frequently used phrases or terms and thereby devise a key to unlock the code.

The complete Navajo code dictionary, including 450 English words given Navajo equivalents, had to be memorized by each new code talker recruit as part of his training. On completion of training, he was assigned to a Marine unit deployed in the Pacific where, beyond performing general duties, he would relay battlefield

A two-man Navajo Code Talker team relaying messages on a field radio somewhere in the Pacific

communications by talking on the telephone or radio. Major Howard Connor, Fifth Marine Division signals officer, had six code talkers operating throughout the first two days of the battle for Iwo Jima. In that time they sent and received, flawlessly, over 800 messages. Connor later announced, "Were it not for the Navajos, the Marines would never have taken Iwo Jima." While that may sound exaggerated, the fact is while the Japanese did crack codes used by the U.S. Army and the Army Air Force, they never managed to work out the Marines' Navajo code. Even when they forced a Navajo prisoner of war, a soldier captured at Bataan while serving with the army, to listen to the code talkers' transmissions, he could not understand what was being said.

The Navajo code was seen to have great value to the military long after the end of World War II and was consequently kept secret. But the secret was not be kept forever. In 1981, code talkers were awarded a Certificate of Appreciation by the President of the United States, and on July 2, 2001, the original 29 volunteers were awarded the Gold Congressional Medal of Honor at a ceremony in Washington, D.C. Only five were still alive and only four were able to attend. In November 2001, the remainder of the Navajo code talkers were given the Silver Congressional Medal of Honor.

The message at the top of the page? It could represent one possible encoded version of "beaches are for vacation."

We loved escort work because we were so upset at seeing these daylight bombers getting slaughtered without escort that we were determined to give these boys some protection. And we did.

USAAF Mustang Pilot
James Goodson

CHAPTER TWELVE

ROADS TO HELL

Several paths led to Hiroshima and Nagasaki and the atom bombs of August 1945. One opened in September 1915, when an Imperial German Zeppelin bombed London. Over 560 people died in airship raids on England during World War I. In June 1917, 14 German Gotha bombers raided the British capital, killing 835 people. Amid the ensuing public outcry, South Africa's General Jan Smuts, a member of the British war cabinet, recommended formation of the Royal Air Force, the first such independent force in the world. Its main job was strategic bombing. The whirlwind would be reaped a quarter of a century later . . .

By May 1941 the German Blitz on Great Britain was over. Raids continued but on a smaller scale. The Luftwaffe had turned eastward. But post-Battle of Britain, the RAF was sending its fighters on sweeps over France. In 1942, the U.S. 8th Air Force began to join in. Texan William Ash was still flying with the RCAF out of southern England.

These sweeps were usually escorting six bombers over Lille or some place like that. The idea was to force the German fighters to come up. We also used to do strikes, a pair, or four, flying over France or over Holland.

In March 1942, Ash's flying war ended.

There were slight swings in superiority between the aircraft being flown. I was flying a Spitfire V when I was shot down. The Focke-Wulf 190 was coming into action and was probably a bit better, well certainly in speed, than the Spit V. A 190 attacked me, pulled away to the left, and I could see it below me and managed to get on its tail. And I got that one.

I could see another one of my section under attack from another Focke-Wulf and went into attack, when I got hit myself. My hydraulic system was out, my guns wouldn't fire and the engine was faltering. I was much too far from the coast to think of being able to get back even as far as the Channel. So there wasn't anything to do except bail out or crash-land in France. And I decided that I would have a better chance of escaping if I picked out a fairly isolated-looking place and crash-landed, because to float down by parachute gave them a much better chance to spot you. So I found a place, got away from my aircraft, and ran into the nearby village.

It was a time when the only British war on mainland Europe was the air war focused on Bomber Command's attack on Germany. In the 1930s, the expected shape of things to come was summed up in a sentence: "The bomber will always get through." It didn't. Expectations were wrong.

In September 1939, just after Great Britain declared war, 29 RAF bombers set off for Wilhelmshaven on a daylight raid. Thirteen got lost and went home. One bombed what was then neutral Denmark. Fifteen reached the target—and caused little damage. Seven

Canada's contribution to the Allied war effort extended to hats at The Hamilton Cap Company, Hamilton, Ontario, at left. On the previous pages, Lieutenant W. Groscoe of South Dakota with his Mustang and ground crew. In the background, replacement B-17 Flying Fortress bombers ready to be delivered to 8th Air Force squadrons in England

Above right, twin brothers Staff Sergeants John and Don Echols at the waist gun port of a B-17. At right, a stalwart of America's daylight bombing offensive, the B-17 first entered service with the USAAF in 1937

1942

NOVEMBER 4
Following Montgomery's successful breakthrough of the Afrika Korps' front line at El Alamein on November 3, Rommel is reported to be in full retreat

NOVEMBER 8
Main Allied task force landings of 400,000 troops begin in North Africa at Oran, Algiers, and Casablanca. Troops come under fire from Vichy French forces in many areas

planes were shot down. When, in 1940, the RAF began its long-planned bomber offensive against Germany, it was at night. But in 1941 it was found that, of 100 raids on 28 Bomber Command targets, only 22 percent of RAF sorties dropped their bombs within five miles of their targets. The effective choice for the British was to abandon bombing of Germany or improve navigational and bomb-aiming aids.

For the U.S. 8th Air Force such decisions came later. When the Boeing B-17 "Flying Fortress" entered service in 1937, it was the world's first four-engined metal monoplane bomber. Five years later it provided the backbone for the 8th's European offensive. The Americans, confident of the B17's defensive firepower, resolved to focus on daylight raids. One man who flew in B-17s was coalminer's son James Kirk, who swapped work in a steel mill to become a bombardier in the USAAF on January 1, 1942.

> We had three months of training that was mostly learning about the use of the equipment and dropping the bombs. B-17s were made for teenagers. I found out many years later I couldn't fit into one anymore.

NOVEMBER 13

American shipyard workers set a record by building a 10,500-ton merchant "Liberty ship" in less than five days.

NOVEMBER 24

A desperate airlift of supplies to surrounded German troops at Stalingrad begins

1942

At right, ground crew prepare the payload of a Lancaster bomber

U.S. airmen, at left, admire the twin .50-caliber machine guns in the tail of a B-17. Below left, a Canadian navigator checks his equipment in the nose of a Handley Page Hampden medium bomber

They were cold and cramped, but fairly efficient as far as the aircraft itself went. We learnt how to shoot a machine gun, and how to take it apart. I never fired at a moving target in my training. Nobody told us that there were German and Japanese aircraft that might be shooting at us while we were doing all this accurate bombing. Nobody told us much about the antiaircraft fire and we were still being told about aircraft that were obsolete. German aircraft we all thought were things like Stukas and would never get up to our altitude, so we didn't have to worry.

They hadn't planned many of the defensive arrangements. The principle was that we would fly so high, and so fast, that no fighters could reach us. They weren't keeping up with what the Germans were doing, because they had no trouble at all reaching us. It was a great shock when we discovered Focke-Wulf 190s and Messerschmitt 109Gs, and 20-mm cannons. Some of our equipment was very poor, oxygen masks used to freeze up and you couldn't breathe. You were going to sleep and finding out "Oh, I am frozen up again." They finally developed armored vests and flak suits, big waistcoats and helmets that you could wear. With his country now in the war, James Goodson made the switch from the RAF to the USAAF.

I wasn't quite sure that the Americans would have the same determination, bravery if you like, courage that I had seen with the RAF. And I was very proud, rather surprised, to find that they did. Some of the Americans are a little more—perhaps—down to earth. They might have said: "To hell with this." But, no, there was just the same instances of bravery in the American daylight bombers as in the British bombers.

In August 1942, James Kirk arrived in Bovingdon, England, with what was becoming the 92nd Bomber Group.

The war was not the only difficulty. We were cold all the time. They used to say they had central heating, one stove in the middle of the barracks, and one bucket of coal per day, to heat this quarters. You had maybe 20 people sleeping in there. I think it was body warmth that kept us warm most of the time.

The biggest problem seemed to be sinuses. Everybody seemed to have the worst cold in their life trying to get people used to this climate. It was aggravated as soon as you got up to altitude. Any pressure would send you screaming with pain. People were grounded completely, they couldn't fly any more because of the sinus problems.

After an initial sortie to Cherbourg that October, James Kirk took part in another raid on France.

It was the most ambitious operation they had so far. Most of those people were very poorly trained. We got across the French coast all right, we had an escort of Spitfires, but they only went just over across the Channel.

We were approaching the target area of Lille's steel mills and we were starting to get anxious. People were jockeying for position to get in a nice tight formation. And somebody at the rear of us pulled up over the top of our three-ship formation and chopped the throttles back too suddenly and dropped back, and just managed to hit our tail with his two propellers and a ball turret probably. I was flying in the tail and saw a shadow or a feeling of something coming, and I managed to duck as far down as I could, which wasn't very far in the cramped little space at the rear of the plane. There was this terrible impact, and I found us going straight down towards the coast of France. I started to reach for my parachute and found that my parachute pack had gone out through the hole in the plane. It's hard to move when the plane is going down at about 4 to 500 miles an hour. It gradually leveled out over the Channel.

I crawled up into the main part of the plane on my

DECEMBER 2
The world's first sustained nuclear chain reaction is achieved at the University of Chicago

DECEMBER 4
The U.S. 9th Air Force attacks Naples in the first U.S. raid on Italy

1942

The Lancaster bomber, shown above, entered service with the RAF in 1942. Opposite above, a factory worker making "window," also know as "chaff," which was dropped from bombers to confuse German radar. Opposite below, two young sergeant pilots study their routes prior to embarking on a mission

Wing Commander Guy Gibson with part of his "Dambuster" crew—Pilot Officer Spafford (RAAF), Flight Lieutenant Trevor-Roper, Flight Sergeant Deering (RCAF) and Pilot Officer Taerum (RCAF)

DECEMBER 7

The U.S. Navy launches the U.S.S. *New Jersey*, one of a dozen U.S. warships launched on the first anniversary of Pearl Harbor

DECEMBER 21

Butter is added to the list of rationed foods in Canada

hands and knees, and my oxygen was gone, too. By the time I got up there, I was flat out on my face. Somebody put his oxygen mask on my face and brought me round. And then I was searching around to see if we had a spare parachute. I found one, but it was for someone about half my size. By that time we were coming back over the airfield at Bovingdon and I didn't need the parachute.

In February 1942, Sir Arthur Harris took over as commander of RAF Bomber Command. The following month the first in a new wave of navigational aids for bombers, GEE, was introduced. GEE stood for "Grid" and used radio waves to help bombers fix their position as a map grid reference. GEE was used when, on May 30, 1942, Bomber Command launched its first 1,000-plane raid on Cologne. Two more such raids followed in June on Essen and Bremen.

In 1940, Reginald Lewis was bombed out in East London. He went to Canada to train as aircrew. By 1942, he was over Essen with Bomber Command.

The Ruhr, of all targets, was, I always thought, the most awe-inspiring. If you happened to be bombing somewhere like Essen, which was in the center of the Ruhr area, a very heavily defended area, one had something like 10 minutes, a quarter of an hour, maybe 20 minutes of flying through a fairly rough area, inasmuch as flak was bursting all over the place. There were certainly hundreds of searchlights in the sky. One could see other aircraft, coned in the searchlights, being shot at. One could see aircraft going down in flames. It was, all in all, I would almost say, a frightening experience. Certainly exciting as a first entry into battle. And one was very grateful to get home.

Another navigational aid, Oboe (a radar transmission beamed out from England which the aircraft could follow to the target) was made available to Bomber Command in December 1942 and H2S inflight radar in 1943. These were used by Pathfinder squadrons which flew fast Mosquito bombers ahead of the main bomber force and identified the area to be bombed by "lighting it up" with flares and target marker bombs.

Bomber Command's crew was an international

DECEMBER 24

At Peenemünde in Germany, 30-year-old Werner von Braun successfully test-launches the world's first surface-to-surface missile

DECEMBER 30

Hysterical teenage girls faint and swoon at the packed Paramount Theater in New York City where Frank Sinatra stages a concert

1942

A B-17 comes in to land, having fired flares to warn the ground crew that there are wounded aboard. Below left, war correspondent and photographer Peggy Diggins lines up a shot on the wing of a P-47 Thunderbolt

Below right, Sergeant George Baltimore (drop tank), Corporal Jack Kazanjac (engine), Sergeant Howard Buckner (cockpit) and Private Albert Asplint (guns) working on a P-47 in England, 1943

brigade drawn from Great Britain, Canada, New Zealand, the West Indies, South Africa, Poland, the United States, Rhodesia (Zimbabwe), and elsewhere. In May 1943, it pulled off its most famous raid when 617 Squadron's British, Canadian, Australian, and New Zealand aircrew proved nighttime precision bombing was possible.

Nineteen Lancaster bombers hit the Ruhr's principal dams. Had the RAF returned the following night,

observed Nazi industrial supremo Albert Speer, the results would have been catastrophic for the German war effort. As it was, while civilian life was dislocated and many Ukrainian prisoners of war were drowned, Ruhr industry recovered rapidly. Eight Lancasters never made it back to England, 53 men died, 13 of them Canadians. According to Canadian Flight Sergeant Kenneth Brown, British scientist Barnes Wallis, who invented the unique bomb used in the raids, wept on hearing of the RAF's losses: "All those boys. All those boys . . ."

In January 1943, the 8th Air Force had begun flying daylight raids into Germany. Meanwhile, from July 24 to August 2, 1943, RAF Bomber Command, having jammed German radar, carried out Operation Gomorrah on Hamburg. The 8th launched daylight raids on the city on July 25 and 26. On July 28, the fires the RAF started coalesced into a 150-mph firestorm, sucking in oxygen, raising temperatures to more than 1,400 degrees and killing that night more than 45,000 people. Half the great seaport was destroyed, and most of the surviving civilian population was evacuated. Hamburg never recovered.

Myrtle Solomon was a 22-year-old Londoner.

When I realized the quantities of material we were dropping on Germany—and we were told it was very much more than what they'd dropped on us—I thought how terrifying it must be be.

JANUARY 8

General Paulus, commanding the surrounded German Sixth Army at Stalingrad, is invited by the Soviets to surrender. He refuses

JANUARY 14

Churchill and Roosevelt meet in Casablanca to discuss war strategy

Later in the war, Canon John Collins, chaplain to Bomber Command, was to ask, "Are we talking about the ethics of bombing? Or the bombing of ethics?"

The 8th, meanwhile, was faced with the same problem on daylight raids that had befallen the British—and the Germans: no fighter cover. No Allied plane had enough range to escort the bombers to the target. The theory was to employ daylight precision bombing. The reality at Schweinfurt—home of German ball-bearing production—in August and October 1943, was disaster. James Goodson was one of the American fighter pilots.

> We were so grateful to get the P-47 Thunderbolt, with which we could at least escort daylight bombers as far as Germany. We extended our range somewhat with droppable tanks, but we had a terrible experience of Schweinfurt. We escorted the American bombers as far as we could. When we had to turn back, we saw hundreds of 109s and 190s. They had been just waiting for us fighters to turn back. They came in on the bombers and just slaughtered them. There were tremendous casualties on those raids, until the American bombers realized they could not afford to hit any target in Germany that was so far away that they could not have fighter escort.

In August, the 8th sent out 376 bombers to Schweinfurt and lost 147. In October, it lost 60 at Schweinfurt from a force of 291. Raids into Germany by the USAAF were suspended.

Meanwhile, post-Hamburg, the Luftwaffe devised

JANUARY 17
London is subjected to a nighttime raid by 118 German bombers, the first bombing since May 1941

JANUARY 22
Canadian, Australian, New Zealand, and U.S. troops capture the southern part of New Guinea, protecting Australia from invasion by the Japanese

1943

The USAAF was ever improving its bombers. James Kirk recalls:

The B-17 E-model that we brought over had a couple of .50-caliber machine guns, point 5s, in the nose, and was operated by the navigator on one side and the bombardier on the other. And in the middle was a little .30-caliber machine gun, mounted in the center of a piece of Perspex in a swivel mount. The first time I tried to fire that at a German fighter, the Perspex gave way, came back in my face and knocked one of my front teeth loose— I eventually lost it about 20 years later. They changed that in a hurry and put a power-operated gun turret in the nose of the plane, which was a big help.

They came along with the F-model, which had a better oxygen system, different masks which didn't freeze up, the engines were more powerful, a lot of the electronics were better, they improved a few of the gun positions, until the G-model came out, and it was the one they finished the war with, with extra power turrets which would deter some of the fighter planes—not many, but they helped a lot.

new tactics against Bomber Command, albeit at the expense of resources diverted from the war against the Soviet Union. In the winter of 1943-44, the RAF launched a string of attacks on Berlin. The Luftwaffe's radar-based night fighter and antiaircraft system accounted for nearly 500 British bombers in attacks on the German capital. It became clear that the RAF's visitation of terror and devastation upon Germany had come with unacceptable losses.

In 1944, Petrea Winterbotham was a 24-year-old plotter at Fighter Command's operations room at Bentley Priory in Stanmore. Her brother was a 20-year-old Bomber Command pilot.

He did, I think, over one and a half tours and he was going out on the big raids: Emden, Kiel, Cologne, those terrible ones. That was pretty ghastly because I obviously kept an eye on the place he flew from—he was at Medmenham—for a time, so when you saw a lot of flight of bombers going out, you were a little inclined to wait until they all got back.

JANUARY 27

USAAF planes fly their first mission against Germany with over 60 B-17 and B-24 bombers attacking Wilhelmshaven

JANUARY 30

Hitler promotes General Paulus, stranded at Stalingrad, to field marshal in the hope that he will commit suicide rather than surrender. No German field marshal had ever surrendered

At left, a ground crew collects spent .50 caliber shell casings from the floor of a B-17 after its return from a raid. Ammunition of this caliber had to be fed carefully into the wings of planes to avoid jamming, as shown below left

A German bombed-out family wheel the remains of their possessions past the ruins of the Propaganda Ministry in Berlin

But the real answer to the 8th Air Force's vulnerability was provided by an American aircraft with a strange pedigree. Ordered by the RAF from the United States at the beginning of the war, the P-51 Mustang had proved to be a passable, but not outstanding, warplane. Then the British suggested it be fitted with a Rolls-Royce Merlin engine. The result was a fighter equipped with huge fuel capacity and an American-built Packard Merlin engine. It was called the "Cadillac of the skies" and established air superiority over Germany. James Goodson:

> The Mustang had as much range as the bombers. We could escort the bombers wherever the bombers could go. We even did a shuttle raid to Russia and to Italy. We loved escort work because we were so upset at seeing these daylight bombers getting slaughtered without escort that we were determined to give these boys some protection. And we did. I used to get cases of Scotch sent to me by bombers that I had protected. You'd shoot 109s and 190s off a bomber and very often you'd come past the bomber. This one straggler, who had been attacked by about ten 109s, and I took my squadron down and chased the 109s away. Instead of chasing the Germans on down to the deck to build up your score, I always led my squadron back to protect the bombers. On this occasion, I went past this straggler bomber and we'd taken about five 109s off his tail, and he was badly hit. They had these doors in the side where the side-gunners were standing with their half-inch machine guns, and they both got down on their knees and "salaamed" to me. That sort of spirit made you feel good.
>
> I was once trying to get these German fighters off this one B-17, but finally he was going down. The little tailgunner on the B-17 that was spiraling down, I could see those tracer bullets coming out. He kept firing until his plane went right into the deck.

Germany's industrial strength would not be the only thing to suffer as the Anglo-American strategic air offensive in Europe accelerated. The cost in lives, combatants and civilians, was vast.

JANUARY 30

While the German Air Ministry in Berlin commemorates the tenth anniversary of Hitler's regime, British Mosquito fighter-bombers launch a daylight raid on the German capital, hitting the radio broadcasting building with two aerial mines

JANUARY 31

Paulus surrenders to the Soviets but in the north of Stalingrad, General Stecker continues to fight

1943

DAWN OF THE JET AGE

The first thing that Generalleutnant Adolf Galland noticed was the silence. Then came the novelty of unobstructed, all-around vision and, finally, the sheer exhilaration of incredible speed. Galland had first flown the Me 262 prototype in 1943 when it was still undergoing flight tests. Prior to settling himself in beneath the bubble canopy of the 262, he had been used to sitting behind the roaring V12 engine and spinning propeller of the Messerschmitt 109 in a cockpit constantly assaulted by noise and turbulence. Perched back on its tail wheel, the old 109 pointed its nose skyward when on the ground, limiting the pilot's forward vision. Even in the air one could look straight ahead only through the spinning prop. Sitting proudly on its tricycle undercarriage with its tail in the air, the 262 gave Galland a clear view ahead. As for the noise—well, comparatively speaking, there wasn't any. The two Junkers Jumo Turbojet engines were slung under the wings. From Galland's point of view, all the engine noise was left behind.

But it was the smooth acceleration and shatteringly fast top speed of this new fighter that Galland truly relished. It could achieve 540 mph—over 110 mph faster than the best American or British fighter planes—allowing it to outstrip Mustangs or Thunderbolts escorting the lumbering Flying Fortress bomber formations and create havoc among the American "Terror Flyers."

It was for this very purpose that Hitler had given Adolf Galland a free hand to recruit the cream of Germany's fighter pilots to form his "Squadron of Experts" in February 1945. Tactics that had evolved since the Me 262 first saw operational service in the spring of 1944 were to sweep down through fighter escort formations and attack bombers from the rear, first with the 262's new wing-mounted rockets and then to close in and bring the nose-mounted cannons to bear. At last Galland and his aces had a machine that gave them an edge over the Allied pilots. Unfortunately for the Germans, the turbulent history of the plane they called "The Turbo" meant that it was a case of "too little too late."

In 1937, the first jet engine designed to power an aircraft was demonstrated by Englishman Frank Whittle.

Unimpressed, the British authorities did not give Whittle's new engine the highest of priorities. In Germany, meanwhile, a similar engine was being tested with the backing of aircraft manufacturer Ernst Heinkel. Heinkel's involvement ensured that the first jet-powered flight, in the experimental Heinkel He 178, took place in Germany on August 27, 1939. Thus began the race to develop the new technology.

The race, however, developed into something of an all-German event. In fact, the British hardly seemed to realize that they were in a race at all. Development of the Whittle engine progressed slowly and on the outbreak of war in 1939, the British government plowed its resources into conventional aircraft production. The same government attitude prevailed in Germany, although there, in the absence of Whittle, the race was being run between Heinkel and Messerschmitt. Each had a new jet fighter plane in development and each knew that only one would be chosen for production by the air ministry. The Heinkel He 280 first flew in April 1941, the Messerschmitt not until July 1942. But the Messerschmitt would prove the better performer.

In Britain, meanwhile, the Gloster E.28/39 enjoyed an uneventful maiden flight lasting just 17 minutes in May 1941, powered by the British jet engine. Government interest was now more acute, and the development of Britain's first jet fighter, the Gloster Meteor, was underway. The first airworthy prototype was flown in early March 1943, and the Meteor eventually entered service with the RAF in July 1944.

The first Meteor "kill" came on August 4, 1944, when Flying Officer "Dixie" Dean attacked a German V1 flying bomb bound for London. With all four of his nose-mounted cannons jammed, Dean slipped one of his wing tips under that of the V1 and flipped it over, causing it to crash.

While the RAF slowly took delivery of new jets and trained pilots to fly them, by 1944 the Luftwaffe was reduced to sending aloft whatever aircraft it had left, flown by whoever was available. The Me 262's production had suffered catastrophic delays. Hitler had decreed that the new aircraft should be produced as a bomber in order to strike at invading Allied forces, and by the time he was persuaded it was needed as a fighter to tackle the bombers devastating Germany's cities, it was too late. Manufacturing materials were in short supply, spare parts likewise, experienced pilots were scarce, and while the engines ran on reasonably plentiful diesel fuel, the lifespan of temperamental power

plants was just 12 hours. Many of the German jets were destroyed by Allied bombing raids at the factories where they were produced, others were attacked on the ground at their airfields. Allied pilots soon discovered that the Me 262 was most vulnerable on takeoff or landing, and the bases from which they flew were regularly targeted. Only about 1,400 of the world's first operational jet fighter were ever produced, and of these a mere 300 saw limited combat. Arguably, however, had the Me 262 been introduced sooner, it could have ended Allied daylight bombing over Germany.

The only allied jet to see action in World War II, the Meteor was flown on operational sorties over Germany from bases in Belgium, but never came into contact with the Me 262. About 3,900 Meteors of various types were produced before 1954 and served with the air forces of over a dozen countries around the world.

As for Generalleutnant Adolf Galland, his aces

accounted for 56 Allied planes before the end of the war. When hounded from one base to the next by the rapidly advancing U.S. 7th Army, and without Galland (who had been wounded in action), the jet squadron destroyed its remaining two dozen "Turbos" before their latest airfield at Salzburg-Maxglan was overrun in May 1945.

Above: Sir Frank Whittle, who invented the first working jet engine, sits in his study with models of the E.28/39 Gloster "Whittle" and the twin-engined Gloster Meteor on his desk

Left: The Messerschmitt 262, the world's first operational jet fighter aircraft

We were all exhausted. We had no clothes. All I had was my shoes, no socks, no underclothes, a pair of torn dungarees, and a khaki shirt. I had gone to Guadalcanal weighing about 150; I left weighing about 110.

LOUIS ORTEGA
PHARMACIST'S MATE FIRST CLASS
7TH MARINE REGIMENT

CHAPTER THIRTEEN

AGAINST THE EMPIRE

Reverberations from the Battle of Midway in June 1942 washed over other fronts where the Japanese advance had seemed inexorable. A string of Allied defeats had been checked. It was a vast eastern front, reaching from Manchuria to Sydney, from Assam to Hawaii, but also a hand-to-hand struggle of small bloody conflicts on tiny islands, in jungle pockets—and over mountains on the roof of the world.

After the battle for the Philippines, the land battle with the Japanese Empire resumed on the island of Guadalcanal in the southern Solomons. On August 7, 1942, 19,000 Marines went ashore, catching the enemy by surprise. But two days later a Japanese cruiser squadron sank one Australian and three American cruisers at the Battle of Savo Island. Nonetheless, Guadalcanal, it seemed, would be a quick Allied victory.

Louis Ortega was a Pharmacist's Mate First Class with the 7th Marine Regiment. On September 15, 1942, he and his comrades landed on Lunga Beach. They were shelled by a submarine. Moving inland, they were bombed from the air. A string of sea battles accompanied the land battle at Guadacanal—where taking the airstrip, Henderson Field, was a key Japanese aim. Ortega and his comrades pulled back for a rest at Henderson Field.

We were laying down in our pillbox. A whistling noise and then boom! "What the hell was that?" And then another one. For the next four hours we were bombarded by four battleships and two cruisers. You can get a dozen air raids a day, but they come and they're gone. A battleship can sit there for hour after hour and throw 14-inch shells. I will never forget those four hours. The next morning, when they stopped shelling, there was a haze over the whole area. Five miles of coconut groves were gone! Where the day before you had miles and miles of coconut trees, now five square miles were wiped clean. Every tree was gone.

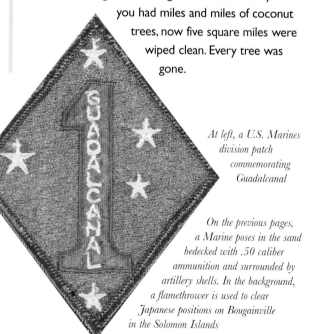

At left, a U.S. Marines division patch commemorating Guadalcanal

On the previous pages, a Marine poses in the sand bedecked with .50 caliber ammunition and surrounded by artillery shells. In the background, a flamethrower is used to clear Japanese positions on Bougainville in the Solomon Islands

Crucially, American fliers maintained air superiority. But for Ortega the landing on Guadalcanal had also been accompanied by the sinking of the regiments' supply ships:

All they got ashore was Spam and pancake flour and peaches. Fortunately for us, we had a guy who had worked at the Waldorf Astoria. He made pancakes with peaches, he made pigs-in-blankets with peaches and Spam. And we were having it twice a day, then it was down to once a day. We'd get a hunk of peach on top of Spam or you would roll it up, or he'd bake it, but it was always Spam, and that's all we had: Spam, Spam, Spam, and peaches and hotcakes, for five months.

FEBRUARY 2

The remaining German forces in Stalingrad surrender. Over 90,000 Germans are taken prisoner, but only 9,000 will survive to return home ten years later

FEBRUARY 6

A jury clears actor Errol Flynn of rape charges in a Los Angeles court

One mutual enemy did not discriminate between the combatants:

> When you got malaria, you might have it five times. Everybody was getting it over and over again. If they evacuated people who had it five times, there would have been no one left in the field. If you had it ten times, they would finally evacuate you. By the first of December, we had more casualties—four or five thousand casualties—from malaria and dengue fever than we did from battle.

But disease and hunger hit Ortega's enemies harder:

> Our planes would come and bomb their food supply and sink their ships. But they could go 16 miles a day with a little ball of rice. Their diet caused them to explode when they died. Within a couple of hours they were bloated. And the next day, boom, they exploded. The maggots were all over them. An American boy would take two days before he'd turn purple and start bloating.

At left, with wings still folded, aircraft on the new carrier Yorktown *warm up their engines prior to flying against the Marshall and Gilbert Islands*

Lieutenant John Clark, at right, guides aircraft onto the deck of the Lexington *after a raid on the Marshall Islands. Above right, wounded U.S. Marines arrive at Vella Lavella after being evacuated from Bougainville*

FEBRUARY 7

Shoe rationing begins in the United States

MARCH 3

178 people are suffocated or crushed to death as a crowd rushes to a London Underground shelter during a daylight air-raid alert in Bethnal Green

1943

At right, war workers take a break from the factories on holiday in Cornwall, England, September 1943. Below right, Prime Minister Mackenzie King of Canada, President Roosevelt, Prime Minister Winston Churchill and the Earl of Athlone, Governor-General of Canada, on the terrace of the Citadel in Quebec during the first Quebec Conference, August 1943

Manning an antiaircraft gun on the Missouri, Charles Hansen displays tattoos that commemorate shipmates lost in action in the Pacific. Below, Private Wesley Smith from Brooklyn, based in the Aleutian Islands in the North Pacific, writes home to New York

On January 9, 1943, Ortega and his Marine comrades were relieved by the U.S. Army.

> We were all exhausted. We had no clothes. All I had was my shoes, no socks, no underclothes, a pair of torn dungarees, and a khaki shirt. I had gone to Guadalcanal weighing about 150; I left weighing about 110.

At the end of January 1943, the Japanese were defeated on Guadalcanal. In June the Allies renewed their attacks in the Solomon Islands and on New Guinea, where a particularly horrific war was raging. The Allies were launching a two-pronged attack on the Japanese garrison at Lae. Peter Salmon, back from the campaign in the Western Desert, and his 2/28th Battalion, Australian Army, were part of the amphibious assault.

> There was swamp on one side and the sea on the other. You were in this narrow stretch and you were very vulnerable. That made it easy for the Japanese to shell us and shoot mortars in. We were quite close to the mouth of the river; we had to get across, and we had to take haversacks, Bren guns, rifles, mortars, everything had to be held above your head. That made

MARCH 13

A bomb smuggled aboard Hitler's plane by senior German Army officers in an assassination attempt fails to explode

MARCH 29

Meat rationing is introduced in the United States

it very hard for some fellows who weren't good swimmers and got swept out to sea—the river came up to your neck. Some tried to help those, which was an impossible task. The Japs were on the other side, firing.

We managed to get to the other side. We clambered up and consolidated ourselves just on the bank. I was with my company. They were soaking wet. We spent a terrible night. We didn't have anything to eat. The next day I had to take a small party and rescue some of our fellows who went out on a scouting job and got pinned down. Anywhere where you are fighting in the jungle you got snipers and an immense number of cases in which people can lose their lives without being able to do much about it. Forward scouts were to prevent ambushing, snipers were sometimes pretty well hidden in the tree, and it took a while to find out where the shots were coming from. The only cover was to get out of sight. Sniper fire killed quite a lot. I had a Bren gun on my hip, which I was firing—it was rifle fire, Bren guns, and grenades.

APRIL 1

With meat, fat, cheese, canned goods, gasoline, rubber, and many other items now rationed in the United States, the government introduces a freeze on salaries and prices

APRIL 19

Jews in the Warsaw Ghetto, armed with smuggled weapons, rebel against their Nazi captors, and fierce fighting erupts

1943

By mid-September 1943, Lae had fallen and the Japanese melted into the jungle. Peter Salmon:

> You get a lot of rain in the mountains in New Guinea; it rains every day. It was a very enervating heat. We were always wet, and after you had worn clothes for a few days, they rotted on you. Being wet didn't demoralize us at all. We just pressed on. We were just determined to get the job done. We would crack jokes—there was always someone who was funny.

For U.S. Marine Louis Ortega, after Guadalcanal, the next target, on Christmas Day 1943, was Cape Gloucester, New Britain.

> Aerial reconnaissance had showed luscious green, a nice road. We figured we'd get our jeeps in there. When we landed, we found a muddy road and about 10 yards after that was swamps and petrified forest. And then it started raining. It rained for almost 60 days without stopping. We were in the water, the sick bay was in the water. Our camp was in the water. We went out on patrols. It took about a week to take the airfield, and then when we got there, we were up on high ground. But all around that area was mud, mud, mud.

On New Britain, jungle warfare pitting Americans, Australians, and local units against the Japanese continued until August 1945. Americans, Australians, and New Zealanders island-hopped against fierce opposition across the Solomon Islands. In November 1943, the Japanese garrison on Bougainville, just to the east of New Britain, became the target. George Green was a 21-year-old with the 2nd Battalion 3rd Marines Division.

> By the time we got into fighting, we pretty well had the confidence that we were better trained, had better equipment, we had better food, and we had better air support. Japanese equipment, some of it, was fairly good, but it was inferior to ours. We were pretty well convinced that nobody was going to stop us.
>
> The idea was for us to grab a piece of the island and build airfields so we could attack Rabaul. We landed at Cape Torokina, got on the beach, dug in foxholes—slit trenches—which were only a foot deep because of the high water level. Then the bombers were coming in. We were no more than 15 feet away from where this bomb hit—right in the middle of the mess tent. The

APRIL 29

Major-General H.L.N. Salmon, commander of the Canadian 1st Division, is killed, along with several senior officers when his plane crashes taking off from an airfield in Britain

MAY 1

Meat joins the list of staple foods already rationed in Canada, although Canada's rations are more generous than elsewhere, and Canada continues to export food to a beleaguered Britain

Prisoners of war, especially those who were ill, were sometimes exchanged via the International Red Cross. At right, the Chaplain of the Canadian Red Cross holds communion for returned Canadian POWs in the Chapel on Viscount Astor's Cliveden Estate in England, 1943. At left, the Children's Hour *Christmas and New Year broadcast from the BBC, December 1943*

Below, Marines take time out during the fighting on Bougainville for laundry day

next one went into an area where some infantry were bivouacked. The next night the same bombers came over and they hit right next to one of our gun positions. As we moved inland, they moved from other areas towards the beach.

By August 1945, battered by American and Australian troops, the Japanese were confined to a corner of the island. Allied forces, meanwhile, fought their way across the central Pacific. Success in the Marianas, the outer citadel of the defenses of Japan itself, would open up the Japanese mainland to air raids. Thus began battles for Saipan, Tinian and Guam.

By July 1944, the war had taken George Green to Beach Red Two on Guam.

We had about 200 yards of water and coral to cross before we could get to the beach. We had to land all our gear from the LCPV, ammunition and everything, on the coral reef, in the water under mortar fire. I tried to get the Navy crew to help us unload, but they wouldn't do it. They pulled up the ramp and they didn't back up more than 20 feet when a mortar hit right in

MAY 13

The North African campaign draws to a close with the surrender of 250,000 German and Italian troops

MAY 16

The Warsaw ghetto uprising is crushed when the Germans blow up the synagogue; 56,000 Jews are captured, 7,000 are shot, and the rest sent to extermination or concentration camps

1943

In a propaganda exercise, the British female munitions workers, shown at left, try out the mortar bombs they manufacture on a beach in England, above. Above right, General Joseph Stilwell leads a column through the jungle in Burma

1943

MAY 16

The RAF's 617 Squadron deploys inventor Barnes Wallis's famous "bouncing bomb," which skips across the surface of the water to explode against dams on the Mohne and Eder rivers in Germany

MAY 29

Vigorous fighting on Attu, in the North Pacific Aleutian Islands, leaves U.S. troops in possession of territory occupied by the Japanese for over a year

the middle of the boat and the boat sank. They came swimming in to the shore—none of them were wounded very badly.

We carried all our gear up the beach under mortar fire, set up our guns, and started firing. I don't think I slept for the first night. The second night I had the duty until about midnight, and Lieutenant Coles said, "I'll take over." I hadn't had time to dig a foxhole. He said, "Crawl in mine." I crawled in his and I went sound asleep.

I woke up after dawn to a racket going on. I put my head out of the foxhole and I see our shells bursting in front of the cliffs right in front of us—when before we were firing over the cliffs. The gunners were facing a Banzai charge when the Japanese, outnumbered and facing defeat, launched attacks regardless of the odds.

The Japanese attitude was, "We'll beat 'em on the beach." They would get to a certain point, then make this attack, mostly at night. They could break through, but if the Marines were well dug in, you could really destroy them. And then you could move fairly fast because they would be so totally disorganized.

I was told we were to cut our crews down to three men, put everybody out as infantry, and start mopping up. On several gun positions there were people who didn't want to go. I said, "You just gotta go." The whole day was spent mopping up. We didn't do too much

firing because the lines were all intermingled. It seemed like those people who were worried about being killed or wounded would be the ones who were killed or wounded. I never thought I would be killed. It never entered my mind, being young.

Once we were into the Marianas, we were in the inner defense lines of the Japanese. It was a pretty tough fight because when you are fighting in the jungle, you can't see much of the enemy or anything, so your imagination runs wild. The Japanese had brought up some artillery and were firing at night, and you could lay there and visualize them putting the shells in, and imagine all sorts of fear because you can't see. You knew they were there. Where you could see somebody, your fear was less.

When you had to go five feet and there would be nothing but jungle and you don't know what would be on the other side of the jungle and you gotta go—then it's a little bit different. It was a tough battle, but after the Banzai attack, it went much faster. They broke the back of the main resistance, and you would be running into groups. But the Japs just didn't surrender. They would be in caves. There were a lot of caves on Guam.

Being with the artillery, they never got close enough to us that we had to do any hand fighting except when they would infiltrate at night. This one night I kept

JUNE 11
SS Chief Himmler orders all Jewish ghettos in Poland to be liquidated, with the occupants transported to execution or concentration camps

JUNE 22
Violent race riots in Detroit leave 34 people dead

1943

hearing hand grenades going off. I had to go around and say, "You guys are trigger-happy. Just take it easy because you are liable to kill some of your own people."

The next morning they replaced the camouflage and they were dumping it in a hole. Lo and behold, there was a Japanese officer in the hole. He had been wounded because someone had thrown a grenade. They didn't even give him a chance. They just shot him. He had a Japanese saber and Seiko gold watch. The fellow that found him took the watch, and some officer from the battalion came and said they had to take that stuff. I went to the battery commander and said, "He deserves something." He's still got that watch.

Another night we ended up with a pig. They killed the pig, we had some farmers with us and they boiled

that pig, cleaned it and we had pork. You never knew what you would run across as far as the jungle goes.

Far to the north, from 1942 to 1945, an extraordinary mix of nationalities fought to wrest Burma from the Japanese. The key British commander was General Sir William Slim of the 14th Army. The key U.S. commander was General Joseph Stilwell, commander of Chinese and American forces in the China-Burma-India theater. Richard Leacock, a naturalized American, was an NCO cameraman posted to a film unit with the British 36th Division in northern Burma.

It was a mixture of Chinese artillery, British fighting troops, Gurkha fighting troops, Indian army sappers and engineers, an American surgical team, an American film unit, and a wonderful little unit of American engineers who built airstrips as we went down through Burma with a bulldozer.

It was a strange hodge podge. At one point General Stillwell was visiting us. He singled me out. "Soldier," he said, "what the hell army are you in?" I snapped to attention. "United States Army, sir!"

He said, "You sure as hell don't look like it." We looked like a mixture of Australians, Indians, Chinese, God knows what. No one liked steel helmets. We all wore the Australian bush hat. Never with the side turned up, always down as a certain kind of chic snobbery; you didn't want to look pukkah. I had just become an American and was happily accepted by the British troops who called me "Yank," which delighted me.

In 1944, at Imphal, the Japanese Army suffered its greatest single military defeat. For two years before that the fact of a Japanese-occupied Burma meant that the only land route to China and Chiang Kai-shek's nationalist forces had been cut. In July 1942, the "Hump" opened. The war's most dangerous air transport route was operated by the U.S. Air Transport Command and ran from eastern Assam, in India, over mountains 15,000 feet high, to Kunming, in China—and a different world.

Evelyn White was a nurse who had worked in the East End during the London Blitz. Impressed by the pacifists of the Quaker Friends Ambulance Unit, she joined them. In June 1943, the 21-year-old flew over the Hump into China. Soon after, while based in Baoshan, a Chinese troop train was derailed nearby.

JULY 4

Leader of the Free Polish forces, General Sikorski, is killed in an air crash near Gibraltar

JULY 4

At Kursk, the biggest tank battle the world has ever seen starts to unfold, involving up to 2 million men and 6,000 tanks

It was a revelation to me, in spite of being in the Blitz in London. That was comparatively civilized, because we all had the facilities, the hospital wards, the blood plasma, the Civil Defense, the Fire Brigade. We had a backup of wonderful people, air-raid wardens, and all the facilities, buses, and ambulances to transport.

Here, in the wilderness, where there were no ambulances, no backup, no blood plasma, very few medicines that we needed, or splints, it was improvisation. They were lucky to survive. I don't know what would have happened if we hadn't been there.

Air gunner Roger Sandstedt from Omaha was 21. He found himself flying bombs and gasoline to Chengtu.

India, it was real warm and China, it was real cold, and I got a sore throat. We were up there, we had cabbage soup and I thought the bread was so wonderful. I don't know what the butter was made out of, yak milk or something, and it was real good. Then I saw the Chinaman cleaning the mess hall—and the butter had soot on it. He was blowing the soot off. I never ate any more butter.

In 1944, 22-year-old Jon Pensyl from South Carolina flew into ChichChiang. He was to fly with 17th Fighter Squadron, Chinese Air Force.

I looked down and there was a P-40 on the runway burning and I thought, "That's my introduction. Bejesus!" This is war. The strip sat up on a plateau. One end had a 150-foot drop, sloped straight down, leveled off slightly,

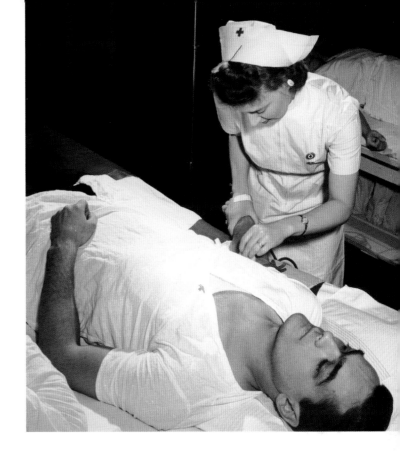

and went into the river. At the other end it sloped up into the hills. They brought in 50,000 coolies who made trips down into the river to bring big rocks up in baskets slung over their shoulders. They would walk, I think, five miles down to the river and 20 miles—two round trips—a day. They had great big concrete rollers, about 9 foot around and ropes which they would pull. The strip was about 2,500 feet long. In three months— 90 days—they added 700 feet to our runway. By hand.

At left, Britain's Gurkha soldiers from Nepal fought not only in the Far East but also in North Africa and Europe, gaining a fearsome reputation for unflinching bravery and the use of their "kukri" bush knives

Moving supplies by tractor, the squad at right flounders in the Bougainville mud. Above right, a New York firefighter donates blood that will be used to help treat men wounded in the Pacific

JULY 9
An Allied force of almost 500,000 men under Generals Eisenhower and Alexander begins the invasion of Sicily

JULY 10
Canadian troops land unopposed at Pacino Beach on Sicily

1943

BATTLE GEAR

THE CANADIAN SOLDIER

There were very few career soldiers in Canada when hostilities between Germany and Canada began in September 1939. Canadians who joined the army came from farms, factories, and offices. Some came straight from the unemployment lines, lured by the army's daily pay of $1.30.

The Canadian soldier's battledress did not change between the end of World War I and the year 1939. Yet just a few months before World War II commenced, the Canadian National Defence Dress Clothing Committee approved a new uniform, based on a new British version. November 15, 1939, was the date on which the army expected delivery of blouses and trousers for the 1st Canadian Division. Alarms were raised when, on November 6, a mere 3,700 blouses and 6,700 trousers had been completed. Hard work and extra hours ensured the entire 1st Canadian Division was wearing the new battle dress when it left for England in December 1939.

The greatest difference between the new British and the new Canadian uniforms was hue. The Canadian uniform was a darker, greenish bronze khaki. Made of wool, the Canadian battle dress was considered to be of better quality than the British. As a result, the Canadian uniform was highly prized by British soldiers.

The Canadian soldier sported a World War I vintage Mk I helmet in September 1939. By the end of the war, more than 1,130,000 helmets were produced—most of them Canadian-made Mk IIs. A net, olive green, khaki, or greenish-brown, was usually worn over the helmet. Between the net and the helmet was stuffed khaki cloth to increase camouflage.

In 1942, the Canadian Army considered switching to the then new American Mk I helmet because it offered better protection. Canada ordered 250,000 of the helmets, but decided to adopt the new British Mk III a year later.

Having bought the American helmets, the Canadian Army issued them to soldiers in British Columbia, as they were likely to serve alongside their American allies in the struggle against Japan. The 13th Infantry Brigade was wearing American Mk I helmets when their troops helped U.S. forces liberate Kiska Island, Alaska, on August 15, 1943.

Completing the uniform were laced boots made of black pebbled leather, leather soles, steel toes, and steel heel plates. The Canadian soldier was issued with at least 50 rounds for his own Lee Enfield rifle, but was also expected to carry a minimum of two magazines for his squad's light machine gun, the Bren gun, and at least one hand grenade.

In battle order, he carried his gas mask and a gas cape, an entrenching tool, a two-pint water bottle, and a small backpack. In it was his mess tin, rations, washing kit, spare socks, and an assortment of other clothing and equipment. He also carried any of his most treasured personal possessions—perhaps a picture of his wife or children, or a letter from his sweetheart. Infantrymen left their large backpacks and/or kit bags at a drop-off point before going into combat. They never knew when, or if, they would ever see them again.

THE AMERICAN G.I.

bag for his gas mask, and in the pack on his back he would carry his canteen, rations, shelter half (two men together could make a "tent"), wash kit, spare clothes, and other items of gear.

Although they entered World War II with their old British-style World War I helmet, G.I.s were soon issued with the new "pot" seen here.

The U.S. uniform was generally of high quality and was much admired, as was the U.S. infantryman's weekly pay, which was around four times the paltry 14 shillings that his British equivalent was paid. Canadian soldiers'

A s with the British Army, Americans adopted khaki around the beginning of the 20th century, and their infantry combat uniform at the outbreak of World War II was based on gear introduced 15 years earlier. This was supplemented, however, in 1941 by a versatile and practical field jacket with zipper and button fastenings. The troops shown in the landing craft at right, about to set off for the beaches of Normandy, wear different versions of the field jacket over wool trousers.

The sergeant in the picture above is wearing olive-drab cotton battledress. The British, too, had a lighter uniform with battledress–pattern denim fatigues often pressed into service for warm-weather combat. The sergeant is carrying an M1 Garand semiautomatic rifle with fitted bayonet, and on his belt he has a pistol holster and binoculars (lower ranks would not carry these items), ammunition pouches, first-aid pack, and water bottle. Slung under his left arm is a kidney-shaped

pay was more in line with the Americans.

Nearly 3.5 million servicemen from North America passed through the U.K. during the war, and elements of the U.S. soldiers' kit were manufactured in the U.K. for easy resupply. Some British battledress was also manufactured in the United States from around 1943 under the War Aid scheme. It was issued to troops in Italy and the Mediterranean, was slightly greener than the U.K.-made versions, and of notably better quality.

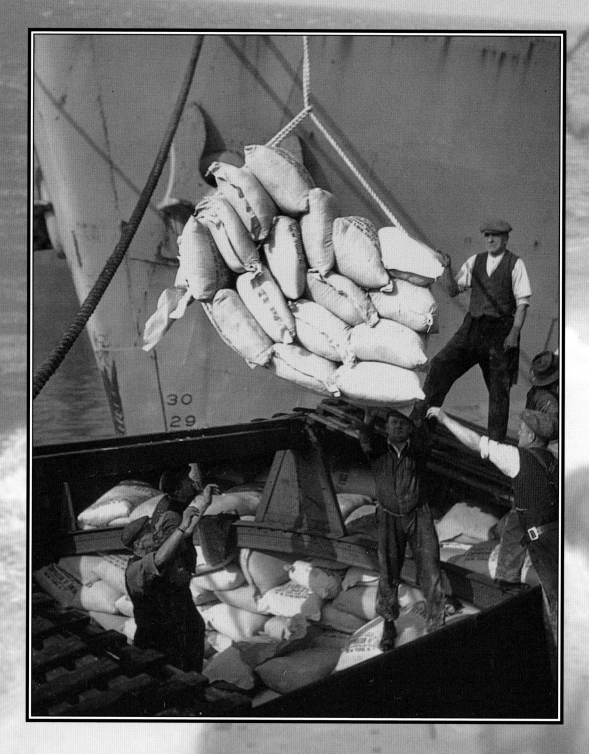

*If anything was going to win that war it was those U-boats. If they'd cut that
lifeline from America and Canada—we couldn't have done anything.*

23-YEAR-OLD HOWARD INSTANCE
H.M.S. WITHERINGTON

CHAPTER FOURTEEN

AGAINST THE SEA

It was a battle that lasted as long as the war and in which merchant seamen died by tens of thousands. The location was an ocean bordering Hudson's Bay and Murmansk, Sierra Leone and Miami Beach, the River Plate and the River Mersey. The Battle of the Atlantic pitted sailors and fliers from Canada, the United States, Great Britain, the Soviet Union, France, Holland, Norway, Belgium, Poland, and elsewhere against submarines, surface raiders, and aircraft of Nazi Germany. At stake was the survival of arteries through which North American industrial and military power was pumped into Great Britain—and the Soviet Union.

Admiral Doenitz, commander of the U-boat fleet, addresses the crews of one of his "Wolf Packs" on their return from an Atlantic foray. On the previous pages, a cargo of precious flour from North America is unloaded at a British port. In the background, the view from the bridge as a British submarine surfaces

At right, British sailors in the North Atlantic man an outdated deck gun. Below right, A U-boat on the surface. The U-1 was launched in 1935 and was sunk, probably by a mine, with the loss of all 24 crew in the North Sea in 1940

In 1939, commander of U-boats Admiral Karl Doenitz began implementing his strategy of winning the war: sinking Allied merchant shipping through submarine warfare. The British responded with convoy operations as protection against both surface ships and submarine attack. But the Royal Navy's position was weakened with the fall of France in summer 1940, which opened up Brittany as a U-boat base. Doenitz strung a line of U-boats across convoy routes. They were in coded radio contact with Berlin, ready to cluster for attack—often on the surface at night—as a "wolf pack" once convoys were discovered. Doenitz's U-boat force in 1940 was small; that summer he had little more than a dozen vessels in the Atlantic. But in the winter of 1940–41, it seemed possible that not only Great Britain's merchant fleet, but the country itself, would go under.

In 1940, 23-year-old Howard Instance was serving on the V&W class destroyer H.M.S. *Witherington*.

In the early part of the war, if you set out with a convoy of 50 ships, you'd be lucky if you got home with 12. Four or five a night once they found you, the wolf packs would come in—and in those days we were short of escorts. Four escorts, one up ahead, one on either side, one astern. Fifty ships in four rows or five rows of ten. You had very little chance at all and you just saw them go up night after night. And when you got to Liverpool, you'd go "one, two, three, four—oh, we got eight home."

Germany's surface fleet was small in comparison with the Royal Navy—but modern. The commander in chief of the German Navy, Admiral Erich Raeder, launched attacks on shipping, intensifying pressure on the Royal Navy, which found itself short of armed escorts for its convoys. One response was "armed merchant cruisers," converted from cargo and passenger ships like the *Jervis Bay* which, in November 1940, was

JULY 19

Rome is raided by a force of 270 USAAF B-17 and B-24 bombers

JULY 24

A four-day-and-night bombing offensive against Hamburg by RAF and USAAF planes begins, causing a firestorm in the city and 40,000 people die

JULY 25

Having been ousted from power in a political coup the previous day, Italian dictator Mussolini is arrested by Italian authorities

JULY 29

With all eligible men committed to the war, the British government announces that all women under the age of 50 must register for war work

1943

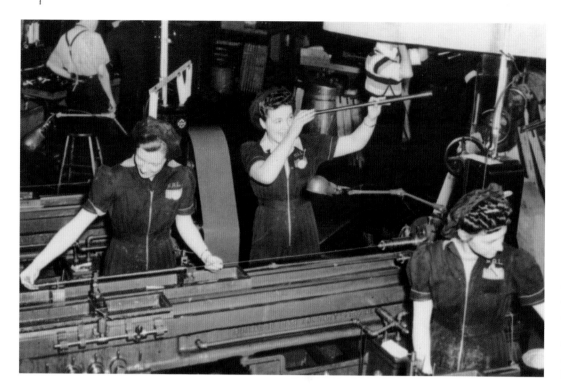

Workers in a Canadian munitions factory producing barrels for machine guns

Below, a G.I. on guard duty in Iceland poses with a local girl in Icelandic national costume. At right, the crew of a U-boat crowds the bridge to watch its latest victim, an American merchant ship, go down

escorting convoy HX-84 toward North America when the German pocket battleship *Scheer* attacked. J. Arthur served on the *Arawa*, the *Jervis Bay*'s sister ship.

> The *Jervis Bay* was just used as target practice. The convoy scattered. The *Jervis Bay* engaged the *Scheer*. The battleship just stood off and pounded her and sank her. The guns we had were 1899 six-inch breech loading. They'd fire seven miles if you rolled in the right direction as you pulled the cord for firing it. They were absolutely useless. The most modern gun we had were two three-inch 1914 ack-ack guns. But they played their part. They did what they were supposed to do. They appeared to be protecting the convoys, but when it came to the crunch, they were completely useless.

Canada began the war with 2,000 sailors and 10 ships—so in 1940, they began a major corvette-building program. By late spring 1941, British and Canadian forces arrived in Iceland—and by summer U.S. Marines had relieved the base. So pre-Pearl Harbor Americans were involved in the Battle of the Atlantic. Meanwhile, the Newfoundland Escort Force ran protection to Iceland.

The Royal Canadian Navy's Rear Admiral L. W. Murray was the force's commander:

1943

AUGUST 1

Flying from Benghazi, in Libya, over 160 U.S. 9th Air Force B-24 Liberator bombers attack the Ploesti oilfields in Romania. More than 50 aircraft are shot down

AUGUST 1

Future U.S. President John F. Kennedy begins a week of escape and evasion in the Solomon Islands after his motor torpedo boat, PT-109, is sunk by a Japanese destroyer

A 35-day cycle to and from Iceland, leaving overnight, picking up an eastbound convoy the first day out, escorting it to a point off Iceland and turning it over to another escort. In Hvalfjord there were no fresh provisions and very little rest. Bridge and engine room were manned day and night against the possibility of the anchors dragging, as the winds roared in the fjord. About four days of that, until a westbound convoy came past. Then the long beat back, covering slow ships, probably insufficiently ballasted, and against the prevailing wind, with about seven days in St. John's again before repeating the dose.

At midday on May 9, 1941, Sub-Lieutenant David Balme was on watch on the destroyer H.M.S. *Bulldog*, part of the escort for convoy OB-318, when two of its ships were torpedoed by a U-boat, which was depth-charged by H.M.S. *Aubretia*. U-110, out of Lorient, Brittany, surfaced under heavy fire and the U-boat crew had to abandon ship. David Balme:

Normally you'd expect the submarine to come up, the crew come out and set the detonating charges, and then down forever, there she goes. But she didn't. She stayed on the surface. And that is when my captain said, "Right, we'll board her." And the captain turned to me and said, "Sub, you take this seaboat."

Balme and eight sailors rowed the 300 yards to U-110 and the sub-lieutenant descended into the submarine.

I went just up to each end through the watertight doors, which were swinging, and there wasn't anybody there. That was a great relief, that was the worst moment of my life, going down there.

The British took every code, cipher, and map. Meanwhile, a telegrapher went to the wireless room. David Balme:

He said, "Look, Sir," and pointed to this typewriter. We both said this looks an interesting bit of equipment. So there it was, the famous Enigma, as we now know it. We never heard or knew about Enigmas or coding machines in those days.

The machine had that day's German naval code settings. It was a priceless haul. Back at the Royal Navy base at Scapa Flow, David Balme was greeted by an expert from Bletchley Park, center of code-breaking operations.

He said we had never had any of these things, it was absolutely untold heaven. These were the ciphers and the machines and the settings, list of settings, and so on. The captain said, "Now, you must never breathe a word to any of your family or anybody about what we have done."

The capture of that Enigma machine provided a key to unlock U-boat strategy, and it was submarine warfare, far more than surface ships, that was doing the damage to merchant shipping. Indeed, the Luftwaffe accounted for more Allied shipping than surface ships. In July 1941, Irishman Michael Moran was supply officer on H.M.S. *Malvernian*, a converted merchant ship, 600 miles off Finisterre.

A German freighter had been reported having left New York—this was before America was in the war—and it was felt that she might cross our patrol area and, if possible, a Catalina flying boat might be sent out to assist us in our search. I got up at the usual time, had breakfast, filled my pipe, went out on deck, and suddenly spotted an aircraft low on the horizon. So I rushed back to my cabin to get a camera. By the time I got out on deck, "action stations" went. Instead of one aircraft, there were four.

The planes were Focke-Wulf FW200 Condors, four-engined long-range aircraft that worked with U-boats and dominated the Atlantic skies:

They hit us with three bombs. One of them went straight down into the engine room and destroyed everything there, killed all the engine-room staff who were on duty. Another went through the signals office and through the sick bay, killed everyone there. We had ten communications cadets with us on that particular patrol. These were youngsters, 18, 19, sent to sea on a patrol for sea experience. They were all killed. The *Malvernian* had no power, no communications. The dead were collected. We shoved these chaps over the side as best we could and said whatever prayers we could remember. By that time the ship was burning furiously and listing over. The next thing was to get some lifeboats in the water.

AUGUST 8

Having enlisted the help of local natives in finding a U.S. "Coastwatcher," Kennedy and his surviving crew are rescued

AUGUST 15

The Devil's Brigade, a U.S./Canadian special forces unit, leads 35,000 troops ashore to capture Kiska in the Aleutian Islands and finds that Japanese forces have been evacuated

At left, a British sailor stands by his antiaircraft gun, scanning the skies over the Atlantic; and the radio room of an American destroyer— communications were vital to the protection of the convoys

American sailors take a break from the engine room in the middle of the Atlantic. Above, fresh baked bread in the galley of a Royal Navy vessel, ready to feed the crew

AUGUST 17

Allied military leaders meeting in Quebec are joined by Roosevelt, Churchill, and Canadian Prime Minister Mackenzie King to review plans for the invasion of France

AUGUST 17

Allied forces take Messina to complete the conquest of Sicily. Over 100,000 Italian troops have been taken prisoner

1943

The lifeboats' launch mechanism was crippled. Survivors boarded the boats that had been placed in the water by old-fashioned human strength. One boat, with the seriously wounded, departed. But the blazing ship, full of ballast, was still afloat, and the remaining survivors decided to stay by the ship. But six days passed and they were far from the sea lanes.

> Things were really getting a bit dreary because you could smell the burning bodies, or at least you felt you could smell them. It was purely a question of sitting there and hoping that something would come along. And morale was getting low.

Michael Moran volunteered to head off on a 27-foot lifeboat with a rigged-up sail and 30 other sailors. A week later, they glimpsed land and thought they had reached Innistrahull in Scotland . . . .

> There was a naval hospital at Innistrahull and we started pulling for Innistrahull and looking forward to survivors' leave, to pretty little nurses stroking our brows and telling us what wonderful chaps we were. Something to drink, eat, plenty to eat.

But Innistrahull disappeared into the distance. In reality, they were 1,000 miles away from Scotland, in the Bay of Biscay. Two sailors had died. Rations then were two tablespoons of water a day.

> One of the chaps had a bottle of Galloway's Cough Syrup. We put our finger to the top of the bottle, turn it over so that you got a dab of syrup, and put it on your tongue. That was an absolutely immense relief. Two of the chaps had been drinking bilge water in the bottom of the boat and wouldn't pay any attention whatsoever. One of them had pushed over the side. He'd just said, "I'm off." He was grabbed and pulled aboard. They both died. But I suppose we were all round the bloody bend.

An encounter with a French trawler brought supplies, but if they accepted rescue, German detention would follow. Then, after 21 days adrift, the survivors spotted an aircraft.

> I can see us now standing up in the boat. I can see myself hanging onto the mast and waving. And the aircraft circled round and pushed off. And then the

AUGUST 17

376 bombers from the U.S. 8th Air Force attack Schweinfurt and Regensburg, with massive losses of 60 aircraft and a further 60 damaged

AUGUST 17

RAF Lancaster bombers attack the Peenemünde Island rocket research base in the Baltic Sea

Aboard a British submarine in action. At left, British Wrens are put through their paces aboard the submarine depot ship H.M.S. Forth

next day we spotted some smoke on the horizon. We were absolutely mad with excitement. The ship got nearer; it was a peculiar sort of battleship gray, and we were arguing about which of our fleets it belonged to: the Atlantic Fleet, or the West Indies Fleet, or the Mediterranean Fleet, or the Home Fleet. "Which one is it?"

There was a bloody great swastika flying from the stern. It settled all those arguments.

It had been a German aircraft which alerted the German destroyer. Moran and his comrades were splendidly treated by its crew—and became prisoners of war.

After Pearl Harbor, merchant ship losses continued to mount into 1942, but by then the United States was a full combatant. Howard Instance:

I remember going out on H.M.S. *Witherington* to pick up the first American troops coming over in two liners. When we got within about 15 miles of them, we saw two enormous shell splashes. An American cruiser was firing its 8-inch at us, not quite understanding what we were. It was rather strange to find three old V&W destroyers going to escort two liners full of American troops. We were taking over from one battleship, three cruisers, and about six destroyers.

American reluctance to adopt a convoy system initially decimated U.S. shipping on the eastern seaboard. In 1942, more U-boats were loose in the Atlantic than ever before and their numbers were rising. Howard Instance:

AUGUST 19

Secret negotiations begin in Lisbon between Italians and Allies to secure an Italian surrender

AUGUST 23

The Soviet government, having left Moscow almost two years previously, returns to the capital

1943

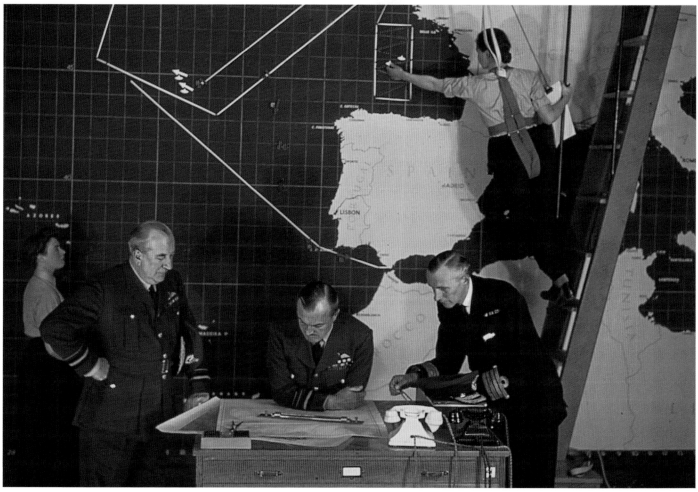

AUGUST 25

American forces take New Georgia,
in the Solomon Islands

SEPTEMBER 2

H.M.S. *Valiant* and H.M.S. *Warspite* bombard
Reggio, on the Italian coast

At left, a Hawker Hurricane fighter is carried aboard ship on convoy duty. The Hurricane could be launched using the catapult on which it sat, but could not be recovered— the pilot had to ditch in the sea near the ships he was protecting. At bottom left, the Operations Room of RAF Coastal Command in 1943. In addition to antisubmarine and antishipping patrols, Coastal Command flew air-sea rescue missions and helped protect convoys

The crew of a B-17 Flying Fortress of RAF Coastal Command study charts prior to takeoff

You are in very, very heavy weather. You are rolling all over the place and shipping the water in. And your whole attitude was, "Well, we shouldn't get attacked in weather like this." But you blooming well did.

There's a chap out there in a little submarine, about 600 tons, cramped conditions, wet, cold. He still carried his attack out. If anything was going to win that war, it was those U-boats. If they'd cut that lifeline from America and Canada, we couldn't have done anything.

There were other lifelines to be maintained. In summer 1942, a land war dwarfing any in history raged between Nazi Germany and the Soviet Union. American supplies were crucial for the Russians. The most dangerous, the most horrific, sea route linked British and Icelandic ports with northern Russia. There were threats of U-boats, warplanes flying out of occupied Norway, and big ships of the German Navy, notably the *Tirpitz*, sister of the *Bismarck*, waiting in the fjords. The film star and naval officer, Douglas Fairbanks, Jr., sailed north:

The convoys were terrible because of the weather. Mountainous seas and terrible climatic and oceanic problems that would be met during the winter months. The worst part of the winter was just a physical discomfort, bashing back and forth and no sleep, day or night. Tossing and turning and twisting, and shipping water and terrible storms, as opposed to the summer months, always calm, equally terrible, because that was when the enemy was able to attack, 24 hours a day, with the everlasting sun.

In June 1942, the 37-strong convoy, PQ-17, set sail, escorted by British and American warships. Fairbanks was aboard an American cruiser:

We thought we had the thing pretty well under control and we could make Murmansk. The Russians were supposed to come over and join us and help us to get in and overlap with us. And when the trouble started, they didn't come.

The "trouble" had originated with information reaching the British Admiralty that a force led by the

SEPTEMBER 3

Italy surrenders in secret when General Castellano signs the deed in Sicily, but fears over the German reaction mean the surrender is kept under wraps

SEPTEMBER 3

The 1st Canadian Division leads the Allied invasion of mainland Europe when they go ashore in Italy, taking Reggio di Calabria with minimal opposition

1943

Tirpitz was preparing to attack PQ-17. Admiral Sir Dudley Pound ordered the escorting warships to sail west and the convoy to scatter. Douglas Fairbanks:

> The Germans were able to pick off the ships one at a time, both from wolf packs of submarines and also from continuous air bombing, night and day, because we were way up north, the Arctic Circle, in July, 1942, so we had the midnight sun. We were just left up there with everybody scattering, and the poor convoy was just picked off. You weren't allowed to pick up survivors because it would endanger your own ship. We could have gone and picked them up had we been allowed to. But it would have put in danger an enormous cruiser with what, 1,500 others on board, to pick up maybe two or three survivors. The only ones who could survive were those who made lifeboats of rafts. It went on day and night for several days. And so that was pretty awful.

Only 11 ships made it to the Soviet Union. In the wake of the disaster, recriminations ensued.

> Quite a lot of ill will developed. Even the top-ranking officers of both navies blamed the Admiralty and possibly also the U.S. Navy Department, to a lesser degree, for this decision to scatter. It was terrible, absolutely awful, everybody blaming everybody else. The ultimate blame rested with the Admiralty in London, who made a false assessment on the basis of information or intelligence, which was in error. Nobody did it deliberately, but it was a decision that was made hurriedly without checking with the boat on the spot.

It was more than two months before another convoy sailed; it included an escort aircraft carrier. Allied losses were still mounting, but the United States could outbuild the sinkings, Great Britain was being supplied, and the battle was turning. In March 1943, U-boats were decimating shipping, yet by the end of May, aided by Ultra intelligence, long-range aircraft, support carriers, and better radar, it was the wolf packs that were being decimated. Howard Instance:

> Two things changed the tide of the U-boat war. One was the long-range bomber armed with depth charges. The submarines didn't like aircraft. They could be spotted so far away. And the other was the Americans making the pocket carriers. We had this 600-mile gap that our aircraft couldn't reach. But once the pocket carriers were being built, with every big convoy of 100 ships you'd have a pocket carrier. Any sort of sighting or echoes, and off they would go in twos. One would be a Grumman Hellcat with four or six .5 machine guns and the other would have either depth charges or a homing torpedo.

After surviving the sinking of the battleship *Prince of Wales* off Malaya, Colin McMullen became commander of six escort ships. Once, 300 miles southwest of Cape St. Vincent, he found his convoy being shadowed by a Focke-Wulf Condor.

SEPTEMBER 6

German battleship *Tirpitz,* accompanied by the *Scharnhorst* and a flotilla of destroyers, sets sail from Altafjord to attack Allied bases on Spitsbergen in the Arctic Ocean

SEPTEMBER 8

Montgomery's Eighth Army establishes another toehold in Italy, at Pizzo

There appeared on the scene an American Liberator. We managed to vector this anti-submarine aircraft on to the Focke-Wulf. There then occurred a battle over the convoy. It was a Jules Verne scene with these two enormous aircraft weaving about, shooting at one another. Finally, the Focke-Wulf lost height and ditched about five miles ahead of us. Then, to our horror, we saw the Liberator losing height. She got rid of her depth charges and ditched just about a quarter of a mile ahead. So we dashed off and picked up the American crew—who were extremely angry at being shot down. We rescued them all except one chap.

Then I saw this smoke going up in the distance, so we found where the Focke-Wulf had gone into the sea. There were three Germans swimming for Portugal, which was rather a long way away. We picked up the crew who, as they came on the upper deck, up the ladder, came face to face with the American crew. It was only by great tact that we managed to prevent them continuing the engagement on our upper deck.

Above, a Hellcat on the deck of a U.S. Navy aircraft carrier. At right, the vital lifeline of supplies from America arrive at a British dockside

At left, volunteer worker Mrs. Evans sews Allied insignia on a special curtain at the American Red Cross Washington Club in London in November 1943

SEPTEMBER 8

Eisenhower and Italian Prime Minister Marshal Pietro Badoglio, appointed when Mussolini was deposed, announce the Italian surrender

SEPTEMBER 9

Further Allied landings take place at Taranto, where the British 1st Airborne Division takes the port with ease, and Salerno, where the U.S. 5th Army meets fierce German resistance

1943

He said, "We'll train you. It will take you three weeks and you'll be able to run a crane yourself." I was running one in three days. It just came to me. I loved it.

ROSE KAMINSKI
CRANE OPERATOR
MILWAUKEE

CHAPTER FIFTEEN

CLOSE TO HOME

Millions of young North American men and women headed overseas. So did big bands, movie stars, filmmakers, crooners, comedians, and athletes. American popular culture became a global brand. But the world also turned upside-down for those who stayed behind. In 1940 U.S. unemployment was almost 15 percent. By 1944 it was just over 1 percent. War had blown the percentages away. Twenty million Americans, following the job trail, moved home. Old ways were shaken— and often it was African-Americans and women doing the shaking.

On January 9, 1942, at Madison Square Garden, New York, Alabama-born Joe Louis, the first African-American world heavyweight champion since Jack Johnson, knocked out Buddy Baer after two minutes and fifty-six seconds. Baer thus became a member of the Brown Bomber's "Bum of the Month Club."

Together with African-American athlete Jesse Owens, whose triumph at the 1936 Olympics had infuriated Hitler, Joe Louis's media battle with Germany had begun long before the war. In June 1936, Germany's Max Schmeling beat Louis in the 12th round. Two years later, as world champion, Louis defeated Schmeling in two minutes and four seconds, a triumph that sent the country wild and became a symbol of American triumph over Hitler. Louis, in an era of segregated sport, had crossed the racial divide.

Soon after Pearl Harbor, President Roosevelt met Louis at the White House, checked out his biceps and said, "We need muscles like yours to beat Hitler." Louis at Madison Square Garden, Louis at the White House, symbolized an America that could seemingly wage war while sustaining a vast civil economy.

In March 1942, London RAF recruit Brian Atkins arrived for pilot training in New York:

> I was a 19-year-old who had never been out of England except for the odd day visit to the Channel ports. The skyline of New York is a scene I'll never forget. We suddenly were in a land of plenty: steaks, no blackouts, a completely different world. We were in Brooklyn for maybe a week or ten days, entertained by the local community. We went to see Joe Louis fight Abe Simon—I think it lasted a matter of a few minutes.

U.S. World Champion heavyweight boxer Joe Louis training for his fight with Abe Simon at the Fort Dix U.S. Army camp, left. On the previous pages, a worker at a smelting furnace in a chemical plant near Muscle Shoals, Alabama, in 1942. In the foreground, a female technician working on blackout lamps used by the U.S. Air Force

In order to appeal to those left behind at home, war bonds advertising, as in this U.S. poster at right and the Canadian one above, was unashamedly sentimental. Ordinary people in America, Canada, and Britain were encouraged to buy government bonds with their savings or as investments to help swell the Allied fighting fund

In the 16th second of the sixth round at Madison Square Garden on March 27, 1942, Louis KO'd Simon. Three months later the heavyweight champion of the world joined the U.S. Army. Back at the Garden for a sold-out armed-forces benefit, Louis told the audience:

> We're going to do our part ... and we'll win because we're on God's side.

Burton Stein was still at school when he took a job:

> I started working in 1943 on a swing shift at the Wisconsin Steel Works in South Chicago as a laborer. The steel mills were working three shifts. There was about a dozen of us who would just go out to the steel mill every day after school. It was mostly laboring. There was a great deal of money around. The people who were working there were people who had been in the workforce in the late 1930s—for whom jobs were risky. And here were secure jobs with quite good pay. So I don't know that they had to think too much of the advantages of there being a war on—it was a great relief to have a good steady income. People did wonder why it was necessary to feel some security in their employment only because there was a war on. That was a part of my political education. It was good money. It was good fun for a young person, drinking beer with the grownups after work.
> And it was all war work. It brought women into the

SEPTEMBER 12
Having been imprisoned at a ski lodge in the Abruzzi Mountains, Mussolini is rescued and spirited away by a German special forces team

SEPTEMBER 13
Chiang Kai-shek becomes president of China

1943

work force. At the steel mills, less so, because steel workers, open-hearth men and crane operators, were exempted. But at the gear factory the women ran a great many of the machines. For women it was terrific to be able to work—the enormous liberation from being at home, for not just young women, but middle-aged women who found this an extraordinarily exciting time, a time when they were really sort of important and independent, and loving it.

Rose Kaminski was in her mid-20s and her husband was in the U.S. Navy. In 1943, she was working in a Milwaukee machine shop—and becoming a "little robot." She went for another job:

We went into the factory and this gentleman came up and said, "Well, we're going to be hiring inspectors and we're also going to be needing several crane operators."

My ears perked up right away because my stepfather was a crane operator. I said to him, "Oh, I'd like to see what a crane looks like and what I'd have to do. I'd be really interested because my dad was a crane operator."

So he took several of us and walked into the factory. And here was this great big ordnance plant with machines all lined up in rows. They were making great big howitzer barrels. Overhead were the cranes,

SEPTEMBER 13

Italian troops battle with German units on Cephalonia, in Greece, but are forced to surrender after suffering 1,500 casualties. Many prisoners are killed by the Germans and others sent to concentration camps

SEPTEMBER 14

Yugoslavian partisans under their commander, Tito, advance along the Dalmatian coast

The workers at right in a U.S. East Coast factory in 1942 are sewing harness tabs on gas masks. Labor shortages led to a recruitment drive for war workers in the United States. The recruitment truck, at left, is parked in New York's Fifth Avenue on a snowy winter's day, 1943

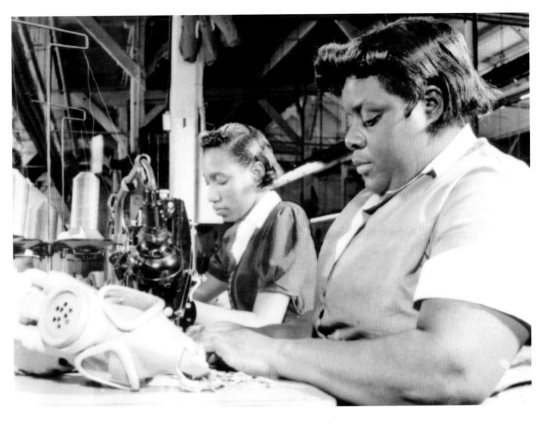

The fashion industry's idea of war work, as seen in magazine photos like the one below, was a far cry from reality

and he showed us what we'd have to do. I thought, "Oh, is this what my father used to do?" I said, "I'd like to try and see if I can do it."

He said, "Well you just have to learn how to work the crane, and all you'd have to do is pick up these great big"—they're like grinders that would go in and thread the barrels of these big howitzers—"and you'd have to set them in, and then you'd just have to sit and wait until all of this goes through a procedure before you would take up and lift this part and move the gun barrel on to a flatcar."

I thought, "Well, gee, that sounded pretty nice."

He said, "We'll train you. It will take you three weeks and you'll be able to run a crane yourself."

I was running one in three days. It just came to me. I loved it. And here I thought, "You can see the gun barrels. You know that it's part of the war."

Her daughter was two, so she had a childcare problem. A neighbor solved it.

She was about sixty-five—an old grandmother—a little German woman who was just wonderful. She had about three children. Would you call it a day care

SEPTEMBER 15
Safely in Germany, Mussolini declares he is the real leader of Italy, and Hitler awards the Knight's Cross to his rescuer, Otto Skorzeny

SEPTEMBER 16
Australian troops capture Lae, New Guinea, after almost two weeks of fighting

1943

center now? She had a fenced-in yard and she took care of those children and she was wonderful. She taught them their ABCs and their numbers and she taught them little song. And the kids would dress up in clothes and take a flag and parade round the neighborhood. This is where my daughter stayed. I don't think I would have gone into any work had I not been able to leave her with somebody as fine as this woman was. She devoted her time just to the children and in her old German brogue she always used to say, "I know that I am needed."

Not everybody doing war work supported the war. Spencer Coxe came from a middle-class Quaker background in Pennsylvania, and was a pacifist.

I always saw an important difference between Hitler and the Allies, and I realized there was an enormous difference there. I was not neutral in that sense.

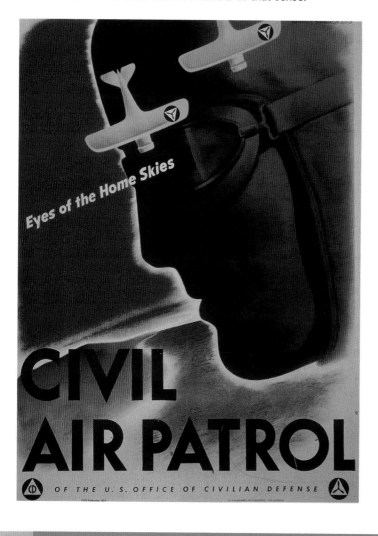

In World War II the United States recognized conscientious objectors on the grounds of "religious training and belief." There were around 100,000 of them. Spencer Coxe was sent to do forestry work in Massachusetts.

It was a very heterogeneous group of guys, some Jehovah's Witnesses, Episcopalians, some Jews who'd had a very hard time getting classified as non-Quakers. And a lot of the people came from really poor families. To me the camp was like going camping—a lark. Here I was out in the woods doing things I'd never done before and eating very plain food and being cold a lot of the time and sleeping in a barracks. It was fun for a while for me. But for these poor people having come from a hard background, it was a real hardship.

Civilian Public Service was set up by the government. Large numbers of COs were assigned to mental hospitals; a number volunteered for medical experiments. The man who later became my brother-in-law was in an experiment testing DDT, which was a

1943

SEPTEMBER 16
The Women's Air Force Service Pilots (WASPs) is founded in the United States. It will go on to supply over 1,000 auxiliary pilots during the war

SEPTEMBER 19
Italian troops seize control of Sardinia as Germans evacuate the island

brand-new discovery, on killing lice. They were inseminated with lice and then DDT sprayed on them.

A good friend of mine was in the seawater experiment: COs immersed for hours, days, and weeks in a tank of seawater to see what effect of long-term immersion was. Others were testing the effects of long-term starvation.

In 1942, Charlie Johnson was trapping in the Yukon woods.

I looked up and saw big trees toppling and thought I'd gone crazy. When I saw a bulldozer and some Yank soldiers told me they were building a road to Alaska, I realized they were crazy. Hadn't I heard of the road? I hadn't even heard of the war.

The Alaska Highway—the Alcan Military Highway—was completed in 1943 and stretched for more than 1,500 miles from Dawson's Creek, British Columbia, to Fairbanks, Alaska. It was worked on by 16,000 Canadian and 11,000 American soldiers. It symbolized a new Canadian-American relationship. War gobbled up distances. Spruce logged on Alaskan islands found its way alongside Canadian ash into warplanes flying out of England. New factories, ports, and airfields sprang up across Canada, and as in the United States, living standards rose and strangers turned up with strange ways. Patrick Lewis observed the arrival of the U.S. Army and the effect the American soldiers had on the population.

A cold and dirty winter job, women railroad workers clean the fast freight train at left in Edmonton, Canada, in January 1943. Below left, The Civil Air Patrol was formed on December 1, 1941, an organization of civilian pilots and their aircraft tasked with patroling the U.S. East Coast on search and rescue and submarine-spotting missions

Wartime leave was over all too soon—a long goodbye at Chicago's Union Station, February 1943

SEPTEMBER 20

Canadian destroyer H.M.C.S. *St. Croix* is torpedoed off Iceland. H.M.S. *Itchen* picks up five officers and 76 men, but all but one are lost when *Itchen* herself is sunk two days later

SEPTEMBER 22

British midget submarines evade detection in Altafjord to place explosives on the hull of the *Tirpitz*, causing damage that will take six months to repair

> All the girls ran after them because they were jitterbugging. We Newfoundlanders didn't know too much about jitterbugging, so we were sidetracked by the Americans, who could throw the girls all around the room.

Lindy hops and jitterbugs cut a rug across North America and the world. So did the music. Bandleader Artie Shaw was in the South Pacific; Bing Crosby made it to England where St. Louis's Flip Pallozola organized sound for him on USAAF bases.

> A very nice person, very laid-back. He said it was the best sound that he had had since he'd been overseas, which made me feel very good. I wrote back to my mother and told her about that. I traveled around to a few bases with the Glenn Miller Army Air Force Band. I really enjoyed this music. Dinah Shore was with him. Johnny Diamond was with him and Ray McKinley—the singer who did "Chattanooga Choo Choo."

Swing music was peaking. Warships, bombers, and platoons were models of collective endeavor. So was the streamlined, coordinated big band, masterminded by the likes of Duke Ellington and Benny Goodman, Harry James and Tommy Dorsey, Count Basie and Louis Prima.

In action at home—the crew manning the coastal gun pictured above on America's eastern seaboard had to be constantly vigilant as U-boats patrolled off shore and had been known to land saboteurs. At left, rationing was a reality in North America by 1943; this American housewife watches as the required amount of point stamps are torn from her ration book by the cashier

At right, the fear of drastic food shortages prompted a massive U.S. propaganda campaign with the president suggesting "Meatless Days" each week and the First Lady broadcasting recipes for healthy and frugal meals. Above right, hoarders are warned of the consequences at a grocery store in New York City

SEPTEMBER 22

Plans for PAYE—Pay As You Earn—income tax deductions direct from workers' wages are announced by the British government

SEPTEMBER 22

Around 650 RAF bombers attack Hanover, Germany

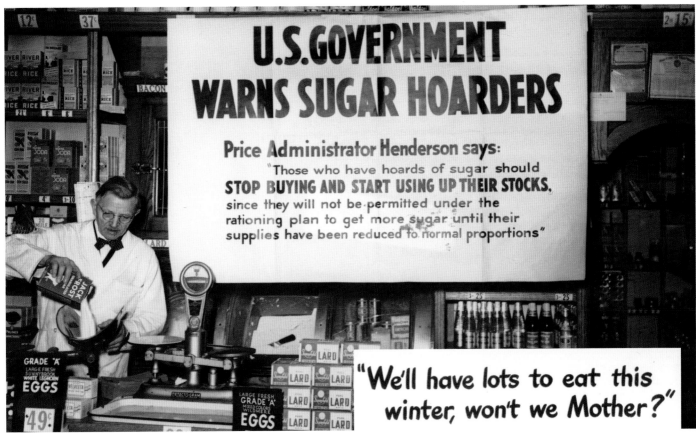

U.S. GOVERNMENT WARNS SUGAR HOARDERS

Price Administrator Henderson says:

"Those who have hoards of sugar should **STOP BUYING AND START USING UP THEIR STOCKS**, since they will not be permitted under the rationing plan to get more sugar until their supplies have been reduced to normal proportions"

"We'll have lots to eat this winter, won't we Mother?"

Grow your own Can your own

But there were other, more anarchic, more individual sounds—and looks. Fats Waller, for one; and a skinny 28-year-old Hoboken tough guy, Frank Sinatra, who left Tommy Dorsey in 1943 for a solo career.

On the streets dress was the austerity look, army style, and the Zoot suit, big and baggy. It was a style popular among California's young Mexican-Americans, and in 1943 became the catalyst for violence in Los Angeles and elsewhere when servicemen attacked the Zoot suiters. Similar riots hit Montreal in 1944. Once in a U.S. Army barracks, Burton Stein was subjected to patriotic propaganda movies:

> The films were, say, on subversives in the society and the kinds of people that were supposed to be depicting the villain. They're so hard to do in the United States because of the variety of racial types. There's no such thing as a spivvy-looking person because a lot of us look spivvy. So they had to do it by dress, and the spivvy people became guys with very wide fedoras, wide-shouldered suits and peg

SEPTEMBER 22

U.S. destroyers and landing craft disembark Australian troops at Finschhafen in New Guinea

SEPTEMBER 23

Mussolini declares the Italian Social Republic, putting Germany in control of large areas of northern Italy

1943

pants. For many of the kids who came from places like Detroit or Chicago, that didn't look spivvy. To them, it looked rather classy, the way high-classy tony people in the neighborhoods they knew dressed.

We were always so tired when we were taken to see these films, we really were run flat-out most of the time. That was when they put us in a warm building to watch a film; we all went to sleep. It was the job of the non-commissioned officers to come round and bop you. You heard a stick coming down on people's heads. It was all done in a slightly joking way.

I don't think there were many people in my training group that were malingering or bolshy. It was a gung-ho, enthusiastic young crowd, very much of an age, 18 or 19 years old, rather happy to be involved in all this physical stuff. Motivation was not a big problem.

Hollywood was big on motivation. Audiences wanted movies about anything but the war, but there were movies for all purposes: to sell the alliance with the Soviet Union (*Mission to Moscow*), the Pacific war (*Bataan*), French resistance (*Casablanca*), and an ever-present British theme. The 1940 best movie Oscar went to *Rebecca*, set in the west of England. In 1941, it was *How Green Was My Valley*, set in a Welsh mining village. In 1942, it was *Mrs. Miniver*, with Greer Garson as a heroic British housewife. For New Yorker Stephen Weiss the plot was familiar. . . .

SEPTEMBER 24

With Germans in heavy retreat, Russian forces approach the outskirts of Kiev

SEPTEMBER 26

An Australian special forces unit operating from a fishing boat places mines in the harbor at Singapore, sinking 37,000 tons of Japanese shipping

The effect of Hollywood and the quality of motion pictures that were produced in the 1930s and early 40s in combination—and I think the combination is crucial—the people who had the leading roles in these films were English.

There was a level of comradeship and morality that was essentially the message: *Dawn Patrol, They Died With Their Boots On, The Charge of the Light Brigade, The Lost Patrol, The Four Feathers, Gunga Din.* Most of the ones I mentioned were played by English actors and actresses and the stories either took place in British India, England, or World War I in France.

Consider *The Dawn Patrol.* The simple thesis of the story is that one man gives up his life for another, goes out on a suicide mission for the good of the group, the country. And it really was for King and country, and even though we were Americans, this was the basis of a kind of morality, a kind of attitude that yes, this is what one does.

In 1940, as arms orders from Europe revitalized the U.S. economy, A. Phillip Randolph, who had built the Brotherhood of Sleeping Car Porters into the first successful black labor union, began a new campaign. It was to stop industry from denying African-Americans and other minorities decent wages and jobs.

On January 1, 1941, Randolph announced that on July 1, he would lead a march on Washington. By June President Roosevelt signed Executive Order 8802. All defense contracts were to have a clause outlawing discrimination. It wasn't the promised land, but it was progress. Randolph called off the march. Northern and western cities witnessed the arrival of a new wave of African-American workers. There were hints of a new time, a new era beginning.

Rubie Bond, born in Mississippi in 1906, moved to Beloit, Wisconsin, in 1916. There she settled and married. Then came the war.

I remember going to this meeting for the Girl Scouts and telling this girl that I'd just come from the bank to buy a bond to support the war, so she could sit behind her mahogany polished desk and tell me that black girls couldn't be in the Girl Scout troops in the schools.

A Boeing factory employee working on the nose cone of a B-17 bomber

Taking time out to pose for the propaganda camera, these Canadian engineering students are taught about aircraft construction

SEPTEMBER 26

Despite heavy German opposition, advancing Allied units approach Naples

SEPTEMBER 27

The capture of airfields at Foggia, in Italy, puts U.S. bombers within striking distance of industrial targets in southern Germany

1943

Sergeant Franklin Williams shares a soda with girlfriend Ellen Hardin while on leave in Baltimore in 1942. At right, food supplies from the United States and Canada kept Britain alive— here wheat is harvested in Walla Walla County, Washington

The students below are learning about camouflage techniques in 1943 at New York University, prior to military service

SEPTEMBER 27

Despite another raid on Hanover, the targeted industrial sites remain in operation

SEPTEMBER 27

German troops fight pitched battles with Italian soldiers on Corfu, in Greece, before taking control of the island

Military camps helped revitalize the South's economy. But they also brought northern African-Americans face to face with southern racism. Benny Gordon:

> I was drafted at school. During the medical procedure we were all in line together, black and white. But after we had been accepted, then they would segregate the black soldiers to one area of the facility and the white soldiers were in another. In most instances the white soldiers had the best.
>
> Officers were all white, and most of them were from the South, and they didn't like having Negro troops. I found that most of them were outcasts. They couldn't lead the white troops, so they'd put them over with the Negro troops. It's demeaning to have an ignorant meany person to lead you. We had officers who didn't even finish high school. We referred to them as 90-day wonders because they didn't know anything about what they were doing, or how, and in a lot of instances it was the black soldiers that made the white officers, because the non-commissioned officers, like I was, we knew how and what, so we ran the thing. The officer got the credit.

The byways of discrimination were odd. In 1944, 20-year-old Dorothy Keating from Laona, Wisconsin, a full-blooded Oneida Native American joined the Women's Volunteer Service, the WAVES.

> You were either black or white, and on many of my documents and things like that that I have, and on my discharge papers, I'm considered white. There was no "other" or there was no check for American Indian. There wasn't even red. You were either black or white, and if you were American Indian, you were considered white.

Amid problems there was the wonder. City boys who had never seen forests, Midwest girls who had never seen an ocean had their eyes opened—and many resolved one day to return. Burton Stein was posted around the country en route to the war against Japan. He ended up in the Pacific northwest.

> We sat around waiting for a boat. There was no training there. It was a lovely, very beautiful camp near Portland, Oregon. Great pine trees, and for kids from Chicago it was an amazing natural experience. Texas was raw and harsh and all. But the northwest coast of the United States was a gloriously beautiful place and we were all overwhelmed with the beauty, the great smell of pines.

THE ROLE
OF THE
MOVIES

Humphrey Bogart and Ingrid Bergman in Casablanca

At the beginning of the 21st century, worldwide communications are so advanced that if the President of the United States catches a cold, people in Australia, Europe, even China will know about it before the second Presidential Sneeze. Satellite communications, fax machines, the global telephone network, the World Wide Web and, of course, broadband and digital radio and television can flash information around the world instantly. It is almost unthinkable nowadays that you should have to make a time-consuming trip to the cinema to catch up with the news, but at the outbreak of World War II in 1939, the cinema was a major source of news and current affairs information.

Newspapers, of course, played an indispensable part in keeping the general public up to date with events around the world and radio was the instrument of mass media, yet to be usurped by the infant upstart, television. But the only place where you could see moving pictures of events at home and abroad was at the movie theater. In darkened picture houses, "newsreel" documentary films covered the kind of current affairs and, naturally, the progress of the war effort, in much the same way—albeit with a different style and emphasis—as television news does today. The newsreels, however, played second fiddle to the main feature presentations. Movies, like radio, had yet to suffer the incursion of television and as the western world entered the 1940s, regular visits to the cinema to see the latest offerings from Hollywood's superstars were both a treat and a highlight of the week.

It comes as some surprise, then, that one of the first things the British government did at the beginning of the war was to order the closing of its theaters in most major cities. The propaganda value of cinema newsreels was not yet seen as so great an asset that it could outweigh the danger of thousands of venues packed with thousands of people falling prey to Nazi bombs. The movie

Clark Gable did his duty as a waist gunner in a Flying Fortress

Leslie Howard, who died while working for British intelligence

ban in Britain was, however, soon lifted and audiences flocked to see sensational new films like the 1939 Academy Award winner for Best Picture, *Gone With the Wind* or *The Wizard of Oz*, the film that introduced the number that won that year's best song, "Over the Rainbow." The following year, *Pinocchio* produced the best song, "When You Wish Upon a Star." It went on to become Disney's theme tune. Disney's other productions in the early war years were the remarkable *Fantasia* (1940) and remarkably sentimental *Dumbo* (1941). Adult audiences could enjoy the wonderful *Citizen Kane* (1941) or the wisecracking private eye Sam Spade, portrayed by Humphrey Bogart in *The Maltese Falcon* (1941) before both the British film industry and Hollywood shunned pure escapism to put their full weight behind the war effort.

Some established movie stars felt that they had to do their patriotic duty by serving in the armed forces— Major David Niven, Colonel James Stewart and Captain Clark Gable, for example—but others concentrated on their role as entertainers. Between the start of World War II in 1939 and the end of hostilities, John Wayne made over two dozen movies. Bob Hope and Bing Crosby made their first four "road" movies starting with *The Road to Singapore*, and Crosby starred in *Holiday Inn*, the movie that took the best song Academy Award in 1942, for the unforgettable "White Christmas."

The power of the cinema to boost wartime morale, and as a pure propaganda tool, came into its own almost from the outset with a plethora of patriotic adventure films, many of which endure as classics. Noel Coward's *In Which We Serve*, 1942 Academy Award winner

Mrs. Miniver and Humphrey Bogart in *Casablanca* still rate as some of the best movies of all time. Other morale-boosters like James Cagney playing a maverick Canadian pilot in *Captains of the Clouds* or Leslie Howard in *Pimpernel Smith* or fur-trapping Laurence Olivier in *Forty-Ninth Parallel* remain very much of their time.

The unashamedly patriotic propaganda movies of the 1940s will remain as a unique reflection of the united front presented against the enemy during a war that touched the lives of ordinary people everywhere. It is almost inconceivable in that modern politics, the nature of war, freedom of expression, and public opinion will allow such movies ever to be made again.

Bing Crosby was one of many American stars who toured abroad to entertain Allied troops

The firepower of the Allied forces was enormous. I can't understand why they didn't achieve more in that particular time. They were far superior to the German forces.

Wehrmacht paratrooper
Herbert Holewa
Defending Force, Anzio, 1943

CHAPTER SIXTEEN

TORCH TO ROME

On November 8, 1942, the Anglo-American Torch landings took place in Algeria and Morocco. Commanded by Lieutenant General Dwight D. Eisenhower, the largely U.S. invasion forces signaled that the soldiers of the New World were very much back in action on the Old World's side of the Atlantic. It was the beginning of a campaign that would involve forces drawn widely from New Zealand and Nepal to Brazil and Canada. They would drive Axis armies from North Africa, only to become enmeshed in a grim war through Italy that would continue well into 1945.

From the time of the initial landings, Torch's diplomats would spend a whole year trying to win the full backing of the Vichy authorities in France's North African territories. In Algiers, 41-year-old Colonel Charles Dunphie was commanding the British 26th Armoured Brigade.

> We were welcomed. We landed at Algiers, moved forward to Medjez el Bab where there was a hope that one might be able to rush Tunis before Christmas.

The Germans occupied Tunis's airfields, and Berlin diverted forces from the eastern front to the French colony. Charles Dunphie:

> The opposition stiffened up very quickly. They had complete air superiority and our airfields were way back in Algeria. The weather, too, turned completely sour. It rained and rained. Tunisian mud is equal to any, anywhere.

On February 18–19, 1943, at Tunisia's Kasserine Pass, the Afrika Korps mauled parts of the U.S. Second Corps. General George S. Patton took over as commander of the Corps, restored its morale and began a legend. Charles Dunphie was appointed an assistant chief of staff.

> General Patton told me on arrival he didn't like the British, that he'd only met one British officer he really liked. "He's partly Jewish, not a typical British officer but," he said, "you are completely executive. I'm sure we shall get on and if you want to tell anyone he's the goddam son of a bitch, you have my permission to do so."
>
> He got that corps into working order in no time.
>
> We became great friends and I had a great admiration for him. A lot of the pistol packing was rather an act put on for the press. He had this "blood-and-guts" reputation but he was also extremely kind-hearted and sentimental. To show his blood-and-guts thing, he issued an order that the corps were to look like soldiers and everyone must wear a steel helmet and none of these knitted caps any longer. I was driving with him in a jeep when we passed an officer by the side of the road in a knitted cap.
>
> Patton shouted "Stop!"
>
> He got out, took him by the neck and shook him like a rabbit, took his cap off, threw it on the ground, fined him $10 for the Red Cross and then stomped off and got into the jeep again.
>
> And I said, "Steady, General, wasn't that a bit rough?"
>
> He said, "It'll be all around the corps by tonight and you'll never see one of them goddam caps again."
>
> We never did.

Amid the fog of battle, the 43-year-old British war artist Edward Ardizzone, advancing with the Allied forces, continued his work.

> We had gone ahead, I and my driver, and we had bedded down for the night among the spring flowers. I'll never forget the scent of them, wild mignonette, all out of a sterile desert. Every type of spring flower you can imagine with this wonderful scent. And waking up, it was a fine dawn; there was no rain, thank God. And, far away, hearing the bugles of a highland regiment. It was gorgeous. It really was.

The Nazis and 250,000 soldiers surrendered on May 15. Classical dancer Marika Phillips's mother was Russian

1943

SEPTEMBER 27

The Continental tire works at Hanover is targeted in another huge attack by RAF bombers, but this factory and other war-related industrial sites are barely hit in the attack

OCTOBER 1

Allied troops liberate Naples, Italy

On the previous pages: Two wounded Highlanders in Sicily arrive at a church being used as a field hospital. In the background, American troops go ashore at Salerno, near Naples. At right, King George VI inspects the Second Medium Regiment, Royal Canadian Artillery, in Italy, July 1944

A clothesline at the front line. Two U.S. Army nurses below take a break on laundry day, somewhere in Italy. Below left, a U.S. engineer clears mines on the beach at Viareggio, Italy

OCTOBER 2

Orders are issued for the expulsion of Danish Jews. Danish resistance workers smuggle 7,000 to Sweden, but 415 are captured by the Nazis

OCTOBER 10

Chiang Kai-shek is sworn in as president of China

1943

During a pause in the action in Italy, Lieutenant H. Aldridge, at left, enjoys reading a letter he received from his home in Surrey

Private C. Kolano from Buffalo, New York, kneels by the grave of his former lieutenant, below. At right, Marlene Dietrich sings for wounded soldiers at an evacuation hospital in Italy, 1944

and her father was the artist Diego Rivera. She was living in North Africa.

> I took the electric train to Tunis to celebrate liberation accompanied by a couple of singers and a very elegant transvestite. We had to stop, there were hundreds of German youngsters. This silly priest, he came out of the train and wanted to talk and say something about God. They urinated on him.
>
> They asked for some water. There was no water. No sanitation. Nothing. It was this vision of all this blond, blond hair. It was like they were floating in the middle of space.

In Tunis she performed for Allied soldiers, including the French soldiers who, commanded by Lieutenant General Philippe Leclerc, had marched from Chad, across Africa to join Commonwealth forces in Libya.

> I started with a prelude of Chopin. When I finished I took off my black coat and I remained all in white, with one side the British flag, and one side the French. I can't tell you what it was like. You can't replace these things. Those young men gave their lives, their everything.

In March 1943, a wave of workers' strikes had rocked Milan and Turin. Allied bombers were now wrecking Italian industrial output. On July 10, 1943, General Patton's Seventh U.S. Army and General Montgomery's Eighth Army began the invasion of Sicily, the second largest European landing—after Normandy—of World War II. George Henderson, from Springfield, Massachusetts, was on a landing craft.

One big ammunition ship was hit off our beach and it burned for three days and three nights and it was a perfect beacon for German bombers to come in. That's where our first bomb of the war was directly aimed at us. As gunnery officer, I'm up there on the bridge with the telephones on to give orders to the guns, and all I remember about that plane is weeaow! We just barely saw, or at least I did, to my right 100 feet up on the

OCTOBER 22

The Fiesler aircraft factory at Kassel is raided by 486 RAF bombers following the discovery by British intelligence that it was working on Peenemünde's VI rocket program

NOVEMBER 18

Berlin is attacked again by more than 400 RAF bombers dropping 1,600 tons of bombs

1943

beach, this silver thing glinting in the sunlight, a bomb, and it came down from the right over the starboard side, over the mast and hit in our port quarter. A few men were on the stern anchor watching, and several of those fellows were injured by the shrapnel.

It would have been our last bomb of the war if it had hit us directly. We had a British barrage balloon and it saved us. It went up maybe 75 feet. And luckily that German pilot coming over the ridge didn't spot it until he was almost on top of us, and then he pulled out at an angle. That pullout is what caused him to miss us.

Nineteen-year-old Theron Dosch, from Auburn, Indiana, was a quartermaster striker on another landing craft.

Sicily was my first action. It was just glorious adventure that I'd read about in papers; all these sparklers going off and everything. I didn't realize until later that these sparklers could come down and hurt.

Twenty-six-year-old Martin Hastings was a senior officer with Malta Independent Brigade. Having struggled ashore, he headed for a battery of British field guns.

We were struggling up a plowed field which had vines in it and I met two Americans—paratroopers—sitting under a vine and I said, "What on earth are you doing here?"

"I don't know," they said. "We dropped."

And I said, "I see you have but I think you must be something like 50 miles out of your proper place."

It gives some idea of the chaos that the paratroopers had, of being dropped in various different places. The same sort of chaos happened to our own paratroopers.

A few days later, Edward Ardizzone came across a line of tanks in a shady road.

We had only just passed them when one was hit by a shell. And we got on to the big road and there we picked up with this chap with his hand blown off. The next thing we saw our troops running away—it's the first time I'd ever seen it happen—all haring out of the woods. They were off. They said their officers had all been killed, the Germans were coming back with anti-tanks. We picked the chap up with the blown-off

Above right, wounded evacuated from Italy are cared for aboard a British hospital ship in 1944. Below right, a German soldier taken prisoner in Italy is interrogated by his British captor

Regimental Sergeant Major Prévost leads a Canadian Army ski patrol on the outskirts of Colledimezzo, Italy, in 1944

1943

NOVEMBER 22

Roosevelt and Churchill meet with Chiang Kai-shek to discuss the future of the Far East and the new Pacific Charter once the Japanese have been defeated

NOVEMBER 24

An entry in Goebbels's diary reveals his unhappy surprise at the way the British have been able to inflict so much bomb damage on Berlin in a single raid

hand and took him back. We hadn't gone more than another mile or two down, when we met old Monty [General Montgomery] turning up to see what was happening.

On July 25, Italy's dictator, Benito Mussolini, was ousted. Yet Italy was still part of the Axis. The campaign in Sicily, accompanied by wrangles between the Allies, continued. Montgomery's forces were making slow progress. Martin Hastings was injured and sent to a field hospital.

A young Italian lieutenant there had been very badly wounded by tommy gun bullets by the Canadians. We said to him, "Well what happened to you during the landing?"

He said, "Well, I commanded a platoon and I was overlooking the beaches and the telephone, it rang and I said, 'Allo, Allo.'"

Somebody said, "There's ships off the coast."

And we said, "Well, what did you do?"

He said, "I went on playing cards and drinking vino with my soldiers. A bit while later the telephone rang

NOVEMBER 26

A number of diversionary raids lures away some of Berlin's fighter cover, enabling the city to be bombed once again

NOVEMBER 28

Churchill, Roosevelt, and Stalin meet in Tehran to discuss the invasion of France

1943

NOVEMBER 28

Photo-reconnaissance film from a flight over Peenemünde shows constructions similar to others in northern France, confirming to British intelligence that Britain will be targeted by new rocket weapons

DECEMBER 5

Acting on the information obtained from the photo-reconnaissance flight, raids on the V1 sites in northern France are mounted by Allied aircraft

German POWs are issued rations in Italy in the spring of 1944. At left, a British soldier tastes grapes offered by a local Sicilian girl as they sit on the hood of a jeep

again and I said, 'Allo, Allo.' And the same voice said, 'They're landing on the beach.'"

So we asked, "What did you do then?"

He said, "Oh, I went on playing cards with my soldiers and drinking vino."

And the next thing I think he knew he was being assaulted by the Canadians and had these bullet wounds. So it all seemed to me a pretty lackadaisical way of going to war, and obviously he didn't want to go to war. He was a happy-go-lucky sort of fellow. Didn't bear the Canadians any grudge at all, either.

The first Allied soldiers ashore on mainland Italy were three Canadian brigades and other units of the Eighth Army that crossed the Straits of Messina from Sicily on September 3, 1943, landing in Calabria. John Bowie of the Royal Scots Fusiliers was among them.

The landing was done under cover of a tremendous artillery barrage overnight: heavy, medium, and field guns firing across the straits. We didn't land on the right beach. I was landed with my company about a mile behind enemy lines. Fortunately, it was an Italian battalion guarding that particular stretch of coast and as soon as we landed they all came out of their pillboxes with their hands up and said, "Good morning, nice to see you, welcome ashore."

This brief complacency was boosted by Italy's armistice on September 8. Francesco Cavalera, a pilot with Italy's air force, had been fighting the Allies.

DECEMBER 6
Roosevelt and Churchill are back in Cairo for further meetings with Allied leaders

DECEMBER 10
The House Foreign Affairs Committee in Washington announces that 600,000 people fleeing Nazi persecution have been granted admission to the United States since 1933

1943

With the city secure, two British soldiers embark on a sightseeing tour of Rome at left, followed by the propaganda cameras

At right, G.I.s take an unconventional tour of Venice in amphibious trucks

On September 8, 1943, I didn't know anything about the armistice. I was then in a corner of Ciampino Airport with two or three aircraft, while being bombed by USAAF Liberators. I was sent to fight against them but we were three aircraft against, I suppose, 40 or 50 Liberators. We tried to fire at the last part of the formation without any success—the fire of a formation of Liberators was really a great fire.

On September 9, we were surrounded by Germans. We had no arms. We realized we were occupied. A German officer told me, "You are not to fly."

I told him, "I receive the orders of my superiors."

They put sentries with arms by the aircraft. Little by little, I suggested to my people to go away. During the night I realized we were completely occupied by the Germans.

1943

DECEMBER 19
Three Germans are found guilty of atrocities and hanged at Kharkov following the first war crimes trial

DECEMBER 20
Some 1,000 Allied aircraft drop 2,000 tons of bombs on Frankfurt, Mannheim, and other industrial cities in southern Germany

Cavalera eventually reached Italy's provisional government. He ended the war with the Balkan Air Force, dive-bombing a Spitfire against German positions in Yugoslavia.

That same September 9, 1943, Edward Bedford, a private with Third battalion, 142nd U.S. Infantry Regiment, was en route to Paestum as part of the Salerno landings. He had heard of Italy's surrender.

> That made us very happy. We thought we might not have much fighting to do. We didn't expect to get what we did. When we got on the beach, that was when we kinda got bogged down, and some colonel came along. He was chewing his mouth and trying to get everybody to move because artillery and tanks were pretty strong along that beach, all along. That first day we moved pretty slow because the rifle companies had run into a bunch of tanks. That first day was a nightmare.

Theron Dosch:

> At Salerno, the glorious adventure changed into fear. We were ordered to go into Salerno and unload soon after we got there. All I can remember was the ships were steaming in a line formation; then we were ordered to turn 180 degrees, which made a U-turn, and the Germans were landing 88 shells right down the middle of our group. I didn't think they hit any of us but it was so scary I was just devastated then.

First Lieutenant Bert Carlton was with the U.S. 143rd Infantry Regiment. Off the beaches, the 143rd had been detailed to Mount Soprano, where Bert was with his comrade, Harry Stokes.

> The Germans would come in directly over the fleet and fly right over the beaches straight towards Soprano, zoom up at the last minute and by that time all the flak was catching up with them. The airplane was gone and we were catching the flak. Harry wanted to know if I would help him find a German machine gun. He had the mount. I did find one and gave it to Harry. When the planes flew over, he opened up. Well, the plane was gone, the firing ceased, we were just standing there laughing—and we drew every piece of small arms fire in the area on us. He looked at me and I looked at him, and we took the gun and threw it over a cliff. That was the end of messing around with German weapons.

The Allies had hoped for a speedy victory. Twenty-five-year-old Herbert Holewa was a Wehrmacht paratrooper, a veteran of Crete, the Soviet Union, and North Africa. He was posted near Anzio.

> It was very sharp fighting in Italy. The fighter bombers—the Jabos, we called them—you couldn't walk on the road. If you were on a cycle, they would come down and shoot at you. The firepower of the Allied forces was enormous. I can't understand why they didn't achieve more in that particular time. They were far superior to the German forces. You couldn't get anything during the day, and at night they bombed and strafed the roads with heavy guns. The paratroopers were still a very, very good fighting force. There were so many old—and the young ones looked up to the old ones.

DECEMBER 22

In Britain it is announced that a turkey shortage means that nine out of ten families will have to go without at Christmas

DECEMBER 29

Berlin is targeted by Allied bombers for the last time this year, as RAF and USAAF forces drop 2,300 tons of bombs on the capital

1943

In January 1944, an Allied bridgehead established by sea at Anzio remained just that, hemmed in by German forces until the spring. Meanwhile, in the first five months of 1944, four great battles were fought over Monte Cassino, as French, American, British, Indian, and New Zealand soldiers fought to take it from the Germans. Eventually it was taken by Polish troops, while a 1,400-year-old Benedictine abbey was destroyed in Allied air raids.

On June 4, U.S. troops arrived in the Italian capital. Pope Pius XII was to receive many visitors in those times. Among them, before the arrival of the U.S. Army, was Holewa and his fellow paratroopers.

> We took 250 in civilian clothes to see the Holy Father at St. Peter's Square. He came and received us, he gave us his blessing, and he gave us a coin which, apparently, was the rosary of a soldier. There were little notches in it.

A later visitor was Martin Hastings.

> It must have been about the 12th June. We went to the Vatican and parked our jeep. And there were a whole lot of Allies, Americans, French, British, Scots, you name it, we were all going in. We went past all the Swiss Guard in their rather unusual uniform and took our seats. The hall filled up and eventually the Pope came in. And we didn't know whether we were to stand up, kneel down or what we were supposed to do, so we sat still. Some people stood up and other people knelt down forward to try and kiss his ring. The Pope then gave us a little talk. First of all in English and then in French, and then indicated that the photographs and the rosaries that we had each been given were blessed, and that the audience was at an end.
>
> And suddenly from the back of the audience chamber came a real English voice which said, "Three cheers for his holiness the Pope, Hip, Hip!" Then there were three sort of ragged cheers. I gradually sank lower and lower in my chair.

Benito Mussolini, after his overthrow and imprisonment, had been rescued by an SS commando group. In September 1943, he had set up his "Italian Social Republic," entirely dependent on the Nazis for its survival. By 1944, the German artillery officer Karl Günther von Hase, fresh from the eastern front, had been posted to the little town of Predappio, southwest of Rimini.

> This was the birth place of Mussolini. It was obvious that we, under the pressure of the British and the Poles, would have to withdraw. Mussolini came to see, once more, the graveyard of his parents and his old birthplace. We had a rather small dinner—my general and our chief of staff, the ADC of the general and myself, and Mussolini and his private doctor, one or two Italian officers, and also one or two officers wearing SS uniform.
>
> He was a broken man. He didn't look that, but when he talked and how he treated everybody else, the old fire was extinguished. He spoke a little bit of German. We tried to explain a little bit of the campaign in Russia, and what had happened in the winter of 1943–44 when we had suffered heavy losses. He was not properly informed about the situation. He didn't know what had really been going on there. He didn't have a realistic view. His optimism was gone.

JANUARY 1

The first feature-length foreign movie to be screened on American TV, *African Journey*, is seen by viewers in New York

JANUARY 3

A helicopter is used on a mercy mission for the first time when blood plasma is flown to New York to treat victims of an accidental explosion on board the U.S.S. *Turner*

Allied soldiers chat near a fountain in St. Peter's Square, Rome, 1944. At left, Lieutenant Paul E. Vincent, along with other Canadian servicemen, meets Pope Pius XII in Rome, just before Christmas 1944

JANUARY 4

Soviet troops cross the pre-war Polish border

JANUARY 4

Hitler orders the mobilization of all children over the age of ten

1944

Morale-boosting Music

The most pervading influence on the lives of everyday people in the late 1930s came when they visited the cinema. Hollywood's grip on popular culture was, perhaps, most apparent when it came to fashion. Movie stars could make a particular look or hairstyle the absolute height of fashion overnight. Fans, mainly female but males to a lesser degree, clamored to ape their idols. But the movies were also a showcase for another highly volatile barometer of youth culture—music.

Swing music and the Big Band sound had grown to dominate the concert halls and night clubs of America, with leaders like Benny Goodman, Count Basie, Duke Ellington, and Glenn Miller playing up-tempo, jazz-based dance music. It was music like this that the outside world first heard via Hollywood, rare imported recordings and the more daring radio shows—and they wanted more. The popularity of the Big Band orchestras had almost peaked by the time World War II came along, with singers such as Bing Crosby, Frank Sinatra, Ella Fitzgerald, and Doris Day, once employed by band leaders to give them an edge over their rivals, starting to turn the tables and hire the bands to back them. The need for escapist entertainment, however, breathed new life into the Big Band.

While it's not entirely true to say that U.S. troops were responsible for introducing the new music and the shocking new "jitterbug" wherever they went (the first "All-England Jitterbug Championship" actually took place in London in 1940—before America entered the war), having U.S. servicemen around to show local girls the new dance moves made it irresistible. Music, dancing, and having fun helped to keep the war at bay for an evening and the "feel-good factor" worked wonders for morale.

Along with the upbeat band music came upbeat songs.

The Andrews Sisters were the original "girls next door" for the American forces

The jitterbug was the sensational dance craze of World War II

Although the jitterbug craze took something of a back seat following the war, the legacy of the new high-energy music lingered on, with the general public eager to keep an upbeat, optimistic outlook for the future—and marking time for the emergence of rock 'n' roll.

Gracie Fields, already a major international star by 1939, and Vera Lynn, who would become the British "Forces Sweetheart," tugged at the heartstrings with numbers like "White Cliffs of Dover" or "We'll Meet Again." But America's Andrews Sisters set feet tapping with "Boogie Woogie Bugle Boy" and "Don't Sit Under The Apple Tree."

It all went to show that patriotism could be packaged in different wrappings—both the emotional ballads and the more light-hearted dance tunes played an important role in boosting morale among the troops as well as on the home front.

Gracie Fields, an honorary captain in the Canadian Women's Volunteer Reserve Corps of Montreal

Vera Lynn, the British "Forces Sweetheart"

He showed me the mechanics of the rifle, handed it to me and said,
"This was your basic training, you are now a partisan fighter."

AUSTRIAN-JEWISH REFUGEE

HARRY BURGER

Italian Alps, 1943

CHAPTER SEVENTEEN

SECRETS AND NIGHTMARES

In 1940, Great Britain was driven out of continental Europe. Winston Churchill spoke of setting Europe ablaze with the Special Operations Executive (SOE) operating in occupied territory. Two years later, Franklin Roosevelt set up the Office of Strategic Services (OSS). In the summer of 1944, as the Allies closed in on the Nazi regime, Hitler reached for his surprise secret weapons—the jet and the rocket. But civilian resistance to the Axis powers was growing, and thanks to the resistance movements, there was no surprise at all . . .

When William Ash was shot down over France in 1942, he was initially aided by a 10-year-old child and her mother, who provided him with a change of clothing before he headed off—down a sewage canal. Three days later, he heard people singing World War I songs in a village café.

> I decided to take a chance, knocked on the door, and told them who I was. They were delighted to see me, they gave me a meal of eggs, which was about all they had, but it tasted delicious. I'd had hardly anything to eat.

He moved to the capital.

> I stayed in Paris for two months, hiding in this flat with a very nice couple near the Bois de Vincennes. He had been in the French Air Force, a pilot. But it was just too long for me to be left there. Somebody in that same apartment block obviously informed the Gestapo that they'd seen this strange character. And so one morning about four o'clock, the Gestapo carted us off.
>
> I never saw the two young people again. And after the war, I was never able to get in touch with them. It's something I'll never forget, the help given me by people in France.

William Ash became a prisoner of war.

As the war progressed, the French Resistance diversified greatly. It had its own underground newspapers and magazines, it embraced—not always easily—Communists, Royalists and Gaullists, Catholics and Jews, refugees and locals, blacks and whites. Communications weren't always perfect. One night in 1943, Robert Maloubier, a 20-year-old French SOE operative, set ablaze a subpower station that was supplying Rouen's industry.

> We left by bicycle about 11 o'clock and as I passed by, just behind Rouen Cathedral there was a huge explosion—the local terrorists had just bombed the German mess on the square. Just a few minutes after, the whole damn place was surrounded by Germans checking up on every passerby. If I had been three minutes later, I wouldn't be here. Because in my bag I had my Sten gun, some explosives left, and detonators.

At its peak, nearly a quarter of the SOE's agents were women. One of them was Yvonne Cormeau. Born in China, she was fluent in English and French, and spoke Spanish and German as well.

JANUARY 7

The U.S. Air Force announces production of its first jet fighter, the Bell P-59

JANUARY 15

5,000 die in an earthquake in Argentina

On the previous pages: A partisan fighter, one of thousands who harassed the Nazis throughout the occupied countries. In the background, a coastal gun emplacement in France, part of Hitler's Atlantic Wall defenses. At right, German Grenadiers scrub the winter white camouflage off their half-track

Violette Szabo, below, a British French Resistance fighter who became a secret agent to avenge the death of her husband at El Alamein. She was posthumously awarded the George Cross, having been tortured and shot by the Gestapo after resisting all attempts to force her to divulge secrets. Below left, A group of French Resistance fighters. The poster proclaims "French We Are, French We Will Remain"

They gave us some ideas about living and operating in France, but they said, "You've got to judge. When you're on the spot, things might change. All we can tell you is there may be certain days of the week when you can't have certain drinks or foods in certain cafés, so don't ask. Just try and look out and see what is on the menu and advertised for those days. Please don't do too much dyeing of your hair or have very noticeable makeup or things like that, because you'll fall foul at some time or other. Try and dress as they do locally as much as possible. If you're going to live in the country, don't have a manicure."

In 1943, came the Sunday afternoon when she set off for France as an agent and wireless operator.

We took off in a beautiful sunset in England. At one moment I was given a nice hot drink by the dispatcher and then he opened a hole in the floor of the fuselage. I knew when the green light came on and the dispatcher gave me a sign, I had to fly through the hole. Slowly but surely, my parachute opened out on

JANUARY 16

General Eisenhower takes command of the Allied Invasion Force in London

JANUARY 21

Air raids are launched against London and southern England; 270 German aircraft attack but only 96 reach their targets. In contrast, almost 700 RAF bombers raid Berlin, Kiel, and Magdeburg

1944

LES BEAUX YEUX ONT DES OREILLES

SOIS DISCRET

"Beautiful eyes have ears. Be discreet." This Canadian propaganda poster warns servicemen of the dangers of loose talk. Bragging to a pretty girl could unwittingly pass information to the enemy

Although women were not used in combat roles by the Allies in regular military units, the female partisans shown at right were fighting alongside Allied units near Castelluccio, in Italy. Below, King George VI, U.S. Lieutenant General Mark Clark, and British General Sir Harold Alexander embark on an inspection of the Fifth Army in Italy early in 1944

its own and I didn't even feel the jerk on my shoulder.

I only had a handbag with money, strapped behind my back, filling the lower vertebrae of the spine so that the shock wouldn't damage anything. I was dressed in what I thought was normal for France, a black coat and skirt and silk blouse—and that went very well indeed—and black shoes. My ankles were bandaged because I was in shoes and not jump boots.

Yvonne was parachuted into southern France. But the Germans picked up her radio transmissions. And Gestapo money bought an unexpected informer.

By 1944 the Gestapo had found someone willing to talk, one of the communist Spaniards who had left Spain, running away from Franco. And he said, "Yes. At the village of Castelnau there is an Englishwoman."

There were, in that one *département,* eight Castelnaus. The Germans never happened to come to the one where I did go. There was no electricity, no running water, just one well. And in their methodic way, they'd decided no Englishwoman would live in such conditions.

Yvonne Cormeau was never captured.

JANUARY 22

Allied troops land at Anzio, in Italy

JANUARY 27

Berlin is raided by nearly 500 RAF bombers in bad weather; there are a number of collisions because of heavy clouds

Manchester-born Harry Ree was a conscientious objector in 1939. By 1943, the 29-year-old SOE operative was parachuted into France. One of his schemes—echoed elsewhere in France—was a deal with a Peugeot factory whereby, provided the plant was regularly sabotaged, the RAF would call off its bombers. He kept in contact with London, and even, via the BBC, heard of his daughter's birth. But one day, knocking on the door of Jean, a Resistance comrade, he ran into a stranger with a pistol.

I said, "Don't be an idiot, it's very dangerous to play with firearms like that."

He said, "Put your hands up," and pulled out his card which was a Gestapo card or a Sicherheitsdienst, field security.

I said, "Oooph! I beg your pardon," and put my hands up.

He said "Come on inside."

I said, "What's happened?"

He said, "Jean's been arrested and we discovered some arms here. What have you come for?"

"Oh," I said, "I've come to borrow a book, he's a friend of mine, a teacher."

He said, "Oh, well, never mind, come and sit down here and we'll wait until I'm relieved, and then we'll just go along to the Gestapo to clear you and we'll be all right."

I knew that if I ever got inside the Gestapo, I'd never come out free. So I said, "What about a drink?"

I got a couple of glasses and a bottle, and when I was walking behind him with the bottle, I hit him on the head with it. He was wearing a hat, it was stupid of me, I didn't hit him anything like hard enough. And he stood up, turned round and fired and as he fired I remember thinking, "Good heavens, how extraordinary!" I was by this time hitting him. He tried hitting me on the head with the back of the pistol and then he dropped it, and pushed me downstairs into a cellar. I managed to push back up again, and then he got my head into one of

JANUARY 31
It is decided that Operation Overlord, the invasion of France originally scheduled for May, will be postponed until June

JANUARY 31
In the Pacific, U.S. forces begin the invasion of Kwajalein Atoll in the Marshall Islands

1944

This map of the United States was drawn and painted by London schoolboys while in their air-raid shelter

Above, a British soldier searches for souvenirs among some wrecked German equipment north of Rome, 1944. At right, Italian civilians clamber over the ruins of the Ponte alle Grazie, destroyed by the Germans as they evacuated Florence

1944

FEBRUARY 15

The monastery at the summit of the strategic stronghold, Monte Cassino, is bombed prior to an assault by Allied troops

FEBRUARY 16

Following an 800-bomber raid on Berlin, Goebbels overemphasizes the amount of damage sustained in an effort to convince the Allies that the capital is no longer a crucial target

those bloody grips, a sort of half-nelson. I remember it going through my mind, "If you're ever going to see your daughter, you've got to get out of this one."

I put my hands right back and pushed them up into his stomach and he let go. He fell back against the wall and said, "Sortie! Sortie!"

I didn't ask twice. By that time he had got my identity card, but I didn't think of getting it back off him.

The SOE and OSS operated across the Mediterranean and Balkans. In 1942, in Prague, two SOE-trained Czechoslovaks assassinated Reinhard Heydrich, architect of the genocide of Europe's Jews. In Norway, the heavy-water plant crucial to the Nazi atomic program was wrecked by Norwegian SOE agents.

As Allied battlefield successes grew, so too did the scope of operations undertaken by undercover agents and resistance groups, their confidence and morale boosted immeasurably by the certain knowledge that liberation from the Nazis was no longer just a forlorn fantasy.

At the time of the 1943 Italian armistice, Harry Burger was a 19-year-old Austrian-Jewish refugee in Italian Fascist-occupied southern France. The SS were approaching, so for two days a large party of refugees followed Italian soldiers as they scaled the 10,000-foot-high mountains into Italy. There they were helped by local army units and partisans. While many of the refugees were to be trapped by the SS, Harry and his mother pressed on and were cared for by peasant farmers.

This was the turning point in my life. A few days after that, some maybe two or three dozen Italian officers came by armed to the teeth, ex-Fascists. I asked them where they were going. They said: "We are going into the mountains."

I said to myself, "You know, Harry, you're 19. How long are you going to run?" And I asked the man, "Could I possibly join you?"

One of the officers, he had a rifle in his hand and he says, "Have you ever shot one of those?"

FEBRUARY 16

The 577-mile-long CANOL pipeline, linking the oil field at Norman Wells, Northwest Territories, with the refinery at Whitehorse, in the Yukon, is opened, having cost $134 million

FEBRUARY 18

London is targeted by the Luftwaffe in an air raid involving 187 aircraft dropping incendiary bombs

1944

And I said, "I don't even know what the heck it is."

And he said, "Well, here's how it works."

He showed me the mechanics of the rifle, handed it to me and said, "This was your basic training, you are now a partisan fighter."

And I said, "Wow, I learned the basic training in two minutes. This is incredible!"

His mother stayed with the peasants. Harry went on.

That first group of people I came across became the military police of the First Alpine Division. This became a very important fighting force that had three major battles with the Nazis. The first was in January 1944. Then we had one right after D-Day, when they tried to join their friends in France and were not allowed to go through, and there was one in November. They always had to retreat again.

It was a question of fighting, retreating, blowing up a little bridge, making it a little more difficult, waiting for them again, and attacking. The Nazis burned down villages if they found out they helped partisans. The partisans were adored and revered in that area. A lot were natives, peasants, a lot of others were deserters who couldn't stand the Nazi doctrine.

We had to sleep wherever we could. Sometimes we were outside. In winter, when the snow fell in the Alps, it was totally brutal. I landed a mule called Gina, a big animal. She was my helper. She helped me out of snowstorms when I didn't know where I was. I would definitely have died without that animal.

We were never left by the people to go away hungry. If they had something to give us, even a couple of boiled potatoes, they would do it. At times we had

FEBRUARY 19

RAF Bomber Command loses 78 aircraft from a total of 730 when night fighters and antiaircraft fire decimate a raid on Leipzig

MARCH 15

Allied attempts to storm Monte Cassino continue to be thwarted and a barrage of 1,400 tons of bombs, combined with 190,000 shells, is directed against the stronghold

Below left, PFC Mary Jane Ford becomes the first WAAC to receive the Soldier's Medal, awarded for trying to save a drowning soldier. At right, a British soldier tours the ancient ruins of the Acropolis in Athens, Greece

nothing. We found a cow that had died, probably from a snake bite. It was all blown up, we cut out pieces of meat, not caring if it was poison or not, and just ate it raw. There was a lot of hunger at times and there was a lot of good times.

After the Italian landings, George Henderson of the U.S. Navy arrived in England—and tuned in to German radio.

We had been hearing from "Berlin Sal." One thing she kept harping on about—and it was in the papers in England, too—was that the Germans had secret weapons.

The one I thought most of was gas.

Henderson was wrong. In August 1942, on the Baltic island of Bornholm, a Danish naval officer had stumbled on a crashed, unmanned aircraft. The Danish resistance sent a photograph and drawing to London. Vital information and parts were to come from the Polish resistance.

At rocket engineer Wernher von Braun's Peenemünde research establishment on the Baltic, the Nazis' Vergeltungswaffen reprisal weapons, the V1 and V2, were taking shape.

In 1943, the RAF launched a 600-bomber raid on Peenemünde. Three USAAF raids followed in 1944. More information on launch sites from other resistance groups led to more bombings. But soon after 4:00 a.m. on June 13, 1944, the first V1 "doodlebug" landed south of London. The RAF's Roland Beaumont was then commanding a wing of high-performance Hawker Tempest V fighters in southern England.

On June 16, we were alerted by noises like a motorbike going through the night sky—which were the first of these V1s—to stand by with a whole wing, and from dawn on that day, we were totally engaged in defense against V1s.

We were able to shoot down a great number of the things in the first few weeks, to such an extent that 11 Group asked me to provide a recommendation for certain ways of improving this defensive action, which

I did. As a result, an area along the south coast from Eastbourne to Dover was restricted for our purposes to Tempests and a squadron of the fastest Spitfires, which were Spitfire XIVs, and a wing of Mustang P-51s.

In the period from June 16 to the end of July, the Newchurch Tempest wing shot down over 600 V1s. The British shifted their forward defenses closer to the coast as a V1 "bomb alley" opened up. A new wave of London evacuations swept over a gray and cloudy summer city.

By early September, when the British 2nd Army overran V1 launch sites in the Pas-de-Calais, nearly 7,000 V1s had crossed the English coast. Some of them passed by Flip Pallozola of the U.S. Army 9th Air Force.

You could hear 'em 15 miles away. As long as we heard 'em, it really didn't bother us. When they were going and their engine suddenly stopped, we all took cover.

MARCH 24

335 Italians, most of them civilians, are executed by German troops in the Fosse Ardeantine caves outside Rome in retaliation for the killing of 35 German soldiers

MARCH 30

During an unsuccessful raid on Nuremberg, the RAF suffers the largest number of aircraft and crew lost in a single raid—96 of the 795 aircraft are shot down by night fighters

1944

Even after the V1's launching areas were overrun, the attacks—more than 10,000 in total—continued, with around 1,600 launches from aircraft. These hit provincial English towns and cities. More were fired at Belgium, and Paris was also hit.

On September 8, 1944, Chiswick, in west London, and Epping, on the eastern fringe of the capital, were rocked by huge explosions. In the months leading up to the end of the war in Europe, more than 1,300 V2 rockets, reaching speeds of more than 3,300 mph, were fired at London and a further 44 at Norwich and Ipswich. Less than half hit their targets, but they cost 2,724 lives.

Flip Pallozola, on leave, was staying in a USO hotel near Marble Arch in central London.

> This one time that I was there, one of the V2s hit right near Marble Arch and knocked me out of bed. The V2s you never heard. They were going so fast they didn't do horizontal damage, they did vertical damage. They would dig in so far, and there would be a big crater.

Victory was approaching, yet exhaustion swept over a capital and a land of bomb sites, wrecked houses, and rationing. Myrtle Solomon was a young civil servant.

> The doodlebugs were pretty frightening, but the V2s were terrifying. And I don't know whether we were tired by then or what it was, but a lot of people would admit to that—that we were much more scared then than when the bombs were raining down on us during the Blitz.

Alongside the rockets was another threat. Rosemary Horstmann was based at the British monitoring center at Bletchley, Hut Three, monitoring the Germans' deployment of another weapon.

> They were tremendously excited at the possibilities that jet aircraft would offer and there was one group, I think it was KG65, which was re-equipped with Me 262s, the first German jet aircraft. We used to spend a lot of time being absolutely sure where that group was.

The British and the Germans both introduced jets in summer 1944. The RAF's slower Meteors were initially confined to attacks on V1s, but the Luftwaffe began to use Me 262s and the rocket-powered Me 163 aircraft against USAAF bombers.

James Goodson was flying his Mustang fighter over Germany.

APRIL 30

General Douglas MacArthur announces in Washington that he has no intention of seeking the Republican presidential nomination

MAY 3

Except for certain select cuts, meat rationing ends in the United States

We were very worried about the Me 262 and the Me 163, particularly the rocket plane, because it was very small, and we thought they could probably produce 500 of these things a month. Up in the air we couldn't touch those things. So every time those fellows went up in those jets and rocket planes, they shot down at least one American bomber.

I said: "The only way we can get at these new planes, which are streaks ahead of ours, is to hit them on the ground."

Our generals in the U.S. Army Air Force were very reasonable and brilliant commanders. And they agreed. So when we had escorted the bombers and were relieved, instead of flying straight home at 30,000 feet, we'd go down, spread out and look for the airfields where the German fighters were. And that's where we got the jets and the rocket planes.

At left, two Canadian soldiers sit astride a V1 bomb that crashed in a field in southern England

At right, Lance Bombardier Jack Grundy of the Royal Artillery joins his family in Cheshire, England, while on seven days' leave in the spring of 1944

MAY 9

The Soviets capture Sevastopol and retake the Crimea. Although the Germans manage to evacuate 150,000 troops, they have lost 78,000 killed or captured during the campaign

MAY 18

The Polish contingent of the Allied force attacking Monte Cassino captures the convent building, marking the end of a battle that lasted more than six months

1944

SECRET WEAPONS

One of the most spectacular German secret weapons of World War II was the Me 163 Komet. A small, single-seat, lightly armed fighter plane, the Komet was the only aircraft in service during World War II that was powered solely by a rocket engine.

The little rocket plane (it was less than 20 feet long with a wingspan of just over 30 feet) had phenomenal performance. It could climb four times faster than the Me 262 jet fighter and, with a top speed of almost 600 mph, was the fastest aircraft of the war.

Intended to intercept Allied bombers, the Komet proved far from effective. Fuel consumption gave it a powered flight time of less than 8 minutes and a range of only 50 miles. Once the fuel was used up, the Komet landed as a glider.

The rocket-powered Komet was able to reach a top speed of nearly 600 mph

Only 300 Komets were built and less than 100 saw operational service, downing only 16 Allied aircraft. Fuel shortages limited their effectiveness, although even when the highly volatile rocket fuel was available, it was prone to explosion and killed several pilots. It could also burst into flames if it came into contact with organic material such as cotton, or even human skin. Pilots wore special nylon flying suits in case of accidental fuel spillages.

A month before the first operational flight of the Komet, Germany unleashed another of its secret weapons. Designated FZG, or Flakzielgerat (antiaircraft targeting device) 76, the weapon was also known as Vergeltungswaffe Eins (reprisal weapon 1), or the V1, to try to fool Allied spies. Mounted on the fuselage of the unmanned cigar-shaped flying bomb was a "pulse jet" engine, the distinctive sound of which gave the V1 its nickname—buzz bomb.

The Allies knew of the "secret" V1's existence from an early stage through information supplied by resistance groups and secret agents. At $500, the V1 was far cheaper than a conventional aircraft, and it could deliver its payload of 1,900 pounds of high explosives a distance of 150 miles (later extended to 250 miles). In the nose of the bomb spun an anemometer (a small propeller). Once the anemometer had completed a specific number of revolutions, equating to the distance traveled, the engine cut out and the bomb tipped forward. People living in the south of England soon came to realize that when the buzz bomb's buzzing stopped, they had better take cover.

The V1 was neither reliable nor accurate—the anemometer, for example, could easily be affected by head or tail winds. 10,000 V1s were launched against Britain at a rate of over 100 per day from their 150-foot "ski-jump" ramps in the Pas-de-Calais area of France, but only 7,000 crossed the English coast. There they then ran into newly developed radar-guided antiaircraft guns and the fastest Allied fighter planes available. Specially prepared aircraft, including Spitfires, Tempests, Meteors, and Mustangs were needed to intercept the 400 mph V1s. There was another method: Pilots sometimes avoided the risky business of firing on almost a ton of high explosives by flying alongside and flipping the V1 over with their own wingtips to send it crashing to the ground.

A great many V1s, however, evaded the defenses. The last of the V1s were air-launched from Heinkel bombers, the final one impacting in Kent on March 29, 1945. In total the buzz bombs claimed over 6,000 lives in England and caused 18,000 serious injuries.

Just as the Allies overran the V1 launch sites in September 1944, a new secret weapon was pressed into service by the Germans—the V2. Developed by a team of scientists led by Werner von Braun, who would later play a major part in America's space program, the V2 rocket was another "secret" about which the Allies already knew. While it was still in development, Polish resistance fighters had recovered a V2 following a test firing at Bliza and were able to pass on vital information.

Unlike the V1, however, the V2 was not vulnerable to

air attack as its launch sites were entirely mobile. Although the launch operation involved scores of personnel and around 30 vehicles, the V2 could be launched under cover of a forest location and the site vacated within half an hour, making air strikes almost impossible. From the first launch in September 1944 to the last in March 1945, the Allies never mounted a successful air strike against a V2 launch site.

At the extent of its 200-mile operational range, the V2 was only accurate to within 5 or 10 miles. Its targets, therefore, had to be large cities. It was, however, completely unstoppable. The V2 reached an altitude of 60 miles before plunging to earth at three times the speed of sound. There was no warning. It couldn't be seen. It couldn't be tracked by radar. It couldn't be shot down by gunners or fighter pilots. It couldn't be heard coming.

The massive explosions caused by the V2s' 2,000-pound payloads were a complete mystery to the general public in Britain. At first, gas leaks were blamed. Finally the government admitted to the existence of a new German weapon against which there

The Allies had no defense against the V2 missile

was no defense and, having endured the Blitz and the buzz bombs, Britain's city dwellers faced up to a new terror.

Approximately 1,300 V2 rockets were launched against London, with Norwich and Ipswich also being targeted. Half of the launches hit their targets, causing over 2,700 deaths and over 6,500 injuries. A further 1,600 V2s were launched against European targets as the Allies advanced toward Germany. Paris, Mons, Lille, Antwerp, and Maastricht were among the cities hit.

General Eisenhower noted after the war that, had the Germans managed to perfect the accuracy of the V1 and V2 and targeted English south coast ports, the invasion of Europe might have been impossible.

An American-built V1 buzz bomb, created to help the Allies learn more about the weapon, on display in New York at a war Bonds rally

*I thought I was going to be killed. I got my picture taken with all my
battle stars, how I would have looked if I'd lived through D-Day.*

U.S. NAVY QUARTERMASTER

THERON DOSCH

June 1944

CHAPTER EIGHTEEN

RETURN TO FRANCE

When they come, Field Marshal Erwin Rommel concluded, the western Allies have to be immediately driven back into the sea, or defeat will follow. Defeat would follow for the Germans, as events transpired, but only after 10 months of bloody warfare. It began when the Americans, Canadians, and British launched the greatest amphibious operation in the history of the world on the Normandy beaches. It was almost over when U.S. and Soviet troops met on April 25, 1945, at Torgau on the River Elbe . . . .

In June 1944, guiled by Allied disinformation, the Nazi high command expected an Allied landing in the Pas-de-Calais. A date had, in fact, been set for the Allied invasion to take place much farther west along the French coast at Normandy: June 5. Quartermaster striker Theron Dosch of the U.S. Navy and his landing craft were assigned to England:

> It was the fourth of June 1944. I had the signal watch and we were scheduled to leave for D-Day, but we had had some stormy weather. I got a message down the line of command. And it said "Fabius Foetus."
>
> I couldn't believe what I saw, so I had it repeated and took this down to the captain. I said, "Sir, I have verified this. This is actually what I have got."

He says "That's all right Dosch, we know what it means. It's a valid command."

> Fabius was the whole amphibious landing force and Foetus meant the baby wasn't born yet. The weather was too bad for the attack to go in.

Newfoundlander Private Patrick Lewis was detailed onto a tank landing craft off Plymouth:

> We stayed for two days. And then we were taken ashore and taken to a movie house, all with our guns all strapped on. Came out of there, back onto the boats again, back out to the Isle of Wight and the next morning back ashore, taken to a village, into the lanes, outside Southampton. We were pretty confused by then. I went to Gosport and got loaded onto a tank landing craft. Then back into the lanes again.

And then came the day . . .

> I was in the tank. We used to have to do radio watch and I heard "H-hour now!" We knew H-hour was going to be the invasion. I listened to it for a while and then got out of the tank shouting "H-hour has arrived!"

Just after midnight on June 6, 23,400 American and British airborne troops landed on the eastern and western periphery of what were to be the landing beaches. Prudence Portman was living in an English village that had become a temporary home to an American airborne regiment.

> They were billeted in a lovely old mansion and became friendly with villagers. When the invasion took place, that was a sight to be seen. Each plane had a glider behind it, and we all sat up in bed, the whole village, watching these planes go out.

At 6:30 in the morning, the seaborne forces arrived. By the end of the day, 75,215 British and Canadian soldiers and 57,500 Americans had landed. There were five beaches: Sword, Juno, and Gold for the Anglo-Canadians, Omaha and Utah for the Americans. Above them were the Allied air forces. John W. Howland from Carthage, Texas, was flying a B-17 with the USAAF's 324th Squadron.

> The weather looked bad, and we were given strict orders to make certain our bombs didn't fall short. We headed south and west across the English Channel. The radarscope was full of reflections from hundreds of boats in the Channel. Until that, I didn't believe it

JUNE 4

Rome is liberated by the Allies

JUNE 6

D-Day landings—Allied troops storm the beaches of Normandy, France, against fierce opposition, especially at the U.S.-targeted Omaha landing area where 1,000 men die on the beach

On the previous pages, Private C. Gikas of Boston, Massachusetts, poses with Florence Le Noray outside the Palace of Versailles near Paris, 1944. In the background, British paratroops prepare for D-Day. Above, men of the Highland Light Infantry of Canada en route to France on D-Day with bicycles to help them move inland quickly once they are off the beaches

General Eisenhower visits U.S. troops on exercise in England during the D-Day preparations. At left, Lieutenant Ben Clemints leads his platoon through a farmyard somewhere in southern England training for D-Day

JUNE 7

With more than 150,000 troops ashore, Allied forces fight their way inland to link up and consolidate the coastline

JUNE 10

Over 600 people are murdered by German troops in the French village of Oradour-sur-Glane. The men are shot; the women and children locked in a church, which is then set on fire

1944

U.S. Rangers wait in their landing craft in Weymouth Harbour, England, prior to heading off for France on D-Day

was the real thing. At our 15,000-foot bombing altitude, we had a solid undercast.

At "Bombs Away" I came up for air and to look out my window. But all I could see was the solid undercast and one solitary puff of black smoke in the sky, evidently made by two 100-pound bombs as they collided in midair. All bomber formations were routed in line astern, and after the target, had to fly a traffic pattern south across the Cherbourg Peninsula, then a right turn flying about 75 miles west, and then another right turn flying due north, past the Jersey and Guernsey islands, and back to Bassingbourn.

It was a thrilling occasion; but for our crew, it was a very easy raid. There was no need for the extra boxes of ammunition we had stashed throughout the plane. We didn't see a single enemy fighter, and there was no flak over the target or along our route.

On the evening of June 5, Theron Dosch and his landing ship tank (LST) set off for Normandy. He was to operate into the Gold, Utah, and Omaha beaches.

I was just sick as could be. I could hardly do my job. Until we got into combat, I was the quartermaster steering the ship, up in the chart room. I was sick most of the time. There were ships as far as you could see, in all directions, and there were airplanes going across all the time. At one elevation, one altitude there would be eight Spitfires protecting us, and then 1,000 or 2,000 feet above them would be maybe eight more American P-51 fighters. We had just magnificent air cover. I don't remember too much opposition directly, until late in the evening when we picked up casualties. A plane came over but we had a barrage balloon with a cable attached, and I remember the bomb just missing us . . .

I had thought I was going to be killed. I got my picture taken with all my battle stars; how I would have looked "if I'd lived through D-Day."

1944

JUNE 13
The first V1 flying bombs are launched against England from the Pas-de-Calais, France

JUNE 22
President Roosevelt signs the Servicemen's Readjustment Act, better known as the "GI Bill of Rights," providing funds for postwar housing and education

Landing craft on exercise in English waters, rehearsing for the Normandy landings in France. At left, a French veteran of World War I greets Canadian troops of the South Saskatchewan Regiment as they push inland from the Normandy beaches

When I got home and told my mother about that she was very annoyed that I would think that I wasn't going to live.

Lance Corporal Norman Travett was with the Devonshire Regiment, that landed on Gold Beach.

You could see the shells going over. You could see burning assault craft. The aircraft were bombing and the battleships were firing shells over you. We had to jump into the water. It came to our waist. Whilst you were wading ashore—and I lost a couple of friends this way—the beach had been bombed and had left bomb craters in the water, which you could not see. Some people walked into these craters and were drowned because of the weight of their packs.

We had to run up the beach. There was still considerable enemy firepower. In no way could you

---

JULY 6

Americans launch an offensive in Cherbourg, France. Allies prepare for next phase in Normandy

JULY 9

After a long and bitter struggle, Caen, France, falls to the British and Canadians

1944

possibly advance until this troublesome pillbox had been destroyed. We lay there in our wet trousers, water oozing out of our boots, for what seemed ages. Eventually the pillbox was silenced. That was when I saw my first dead Germans. Gruesome. Those chaps had probably been called up for service like myself and had no wish to be where they were. They didn't stand a chance really, not there.

By the end of the day, the Americans had sustained 6,000 casualties, the British and Canadians 4,300. The figures were lower than expected. Most of the U.S. casualties had been incurred on the steep, heavily defended "Bloody Omaha." Prudence Portman did not forget the U.S. paratroopers.

Quite a number of these didn't come back. The villagers felt it. They were very sad about it. Quite a lot of them were killed.

On the other side of Europe, Royal Marine Edward Hill was in a German prisoner of war camp in Poland.

We knew within 24 hours that they'd landed on the Normandy beaches, six minutes after midnight, as precise as that, purely by word of mouth across the

During the D-Day operation, Canadian officers in Courselles-sur-Mer study a captured German model of the beaches. Above right, Nursing Sisters H. O'Donnell, T. M. Woolsey, and J. MacKenzie enjoy a cup of tea after arriving at Arromanches in France, July 1944

1944

JULY 17

Field Marshal Erwin Rommel, now commanding Germany's "Atlantic Wall" coastal defenses, is seriously wounded in France when his staff car is attacked by South African Spitfire pilot Squadron Leader Le Roux

JULY 20

Hitler is wounded in an assassination attempt when a briefcase bomb explodes at his Rastenburg headquarters

continent. It had come all the way across with prisoner of war drivers or civilians driving lorries. Look at the languages you had to compete with! Yet the detail was exact, incredible.

Six days after D-Day, Private Patrick Lewis and his armored regiment landed at Bernières-sur-Mer. They got a mixed reception.

French people were waving to us and wishing us luck. But when we got to know the farming people, we were surprised at their attitude. They were telling us that we were screwing everything up. The Germans had allowed them to farm their land and they got pretty good pay for it. We didn't have any fresh food for a couple of days. So we were going to the local people to see if we could get anything to cook up with our bully beef for a bit of flavor and they were asking for money. I thought they could give us a few potatoes.

The troops decided "we 're fighting for your people, we're hungry and we want food and we'll take it."

We started getting shot at by farmers. Three people were walking together across the field and suddenly the guy in the center got hit with pellets.

By the end of June, the Americans had captured Cherbourg and headed south across the Cotentin Peninsula. Farther east, the key town of Caen was a target for Anglo-Canadian forces. On July 7, the Allies unleashed an aerial bombardment. Patrick Lewis:

When the attack on Caen got going, we were really

AUGUST 5

1,000 Japanese POWs attempt to break out of a prison camp at Cowra, New South Wales, Australia; 234 are killed and 108 wounded

AUGUST 9

The deportation of 72,000 Jews from the Lodz ghetto in Poland to the Auschwitz extermination camp begins

1944

having a hard time. We were surprised. Considering the RAF had bombed them the night before, where did all the Germans come from? It was just shell after shell, and aircraft coming in. A real war was going on. So many troops and tanks and aircraft coming in made me realize what war is like, the real thing.

It was 28 days after D-Day that Albert Cunningham of the Second Canadian Road Construction Company hit the Normandy beaches. Soon after Caen fell, he arrived.

Caen was flattened. The only building left standing in the middle—there were piles of rubble everywhere—was a whorehouse. There was a constant stream of men up and over the rubble and down into the whorehouse. And the cathedral.

They were desperate to get supplies up, and they couldn't get through the city because of the streets being blocked. So they gave up trying to clear the streets and said, "We'll make a bypass. We'll go from A to B around the city."

That's an engineer's dream, not to have to ask, "Can I pull your house down?" You just pull it down. They just knocked everything down in their path and made a road. We had a target date to get done. It was a beautiful road. It looked like a motorway ...

Hitler fired his commander in the west, Gerd von Rundstedt. On July 17, Erwin Rommel was injured by Allied strafing. On July 20 came the famous assassination attempt on Hitler at his headquarters in Rastenburg, East Prussia. Rommel was implicated in the conspiracy and forced to committed suicide in September. Also implicated and hanged was Lieutenant General Paul von Hase, uncle of Karl Günther von Hase. The latter recalls:

AUGUST 25

Paris is liberated by the Allied troops

SEPTEMBER 2

20-year-old pilot and future president of the United States George Bush is shot down in the Pacific while flying a Grumman Avenger on a bombing mission. His two crew members are killed in the incident but Bush survives to be picked up by a submarine

Above, an American column snakes through the devastated town of Saint-Lo, in Normandy. At left, Canadian troops come ashore at Arromanches in France, July 1944

An emotional return—the Second Canadian Infantry Division marches into Dieppe, where many Canadian lives were lost in the raid two years before, on September 3, 1944

SEPTEMBER 6

In response to the progress being made by the Allies in Europe, blackout rules in Britain are relaxed and the training of Home Guard units comes to an end

SEPTEMBER 8

The first V2 rocket lands in London, killing three and injuring 10. Fired from a mobile launcher in German-occupied The Hague, the rocket's 192-mile journey takes only five minutes

1944

pigs in the road. I see two RAF guys walking. I slowed down and said, "What are you doing up here?"

He said, "We're souvenir hunting."

I couldn't believe it. I said, "Get the hell out of here, or you'll be coming under fire."

"What do you mean?"

I said, "A battle's just going on up the road here."

There was half a dozen tanks there waiting for ammunition. When they are all loaded up, they said, "There's one more tank, you wait here."

They all cleared off. I crossed the road, there's a farmhouse. I thought I'd go and see if there's any fruit in the orchard. No sooner had I got near the orchard than two Canadian soldiers come with two prisoners.

They said, "What are you doing?"

I said, "Well, I'm here, I've just delivered ammunition."

"Oh good," they said. "Then you can take these two prisoners."

I said, "I can't take any prisoners. How can I drive a tank and keep an eye on prisoners?"

So they said, "You're not taking them?"

I said, "No, I can't do that."

They walked back into the orchard. The next thing I hear "bang! bang!" I looked through and there's the two Germans lying dead—which was a shock to me. Then a bombardment started. Outside the farmhouse there was an old iron bathtub turned upside down, lying on its side. I got under the bathtub. The bombardment eased off and I went into the back porch of the house. A shell hit part of the upper structure and I was half covered in bricks and bits of wood. I was just going to try to get myself out when I see a German half-track come through, loaded with German soldiers. They had come up the road that I'd come up. They went through. I cleared myself out of the house and got in the tank. Then I got a few yards down the road, I see a guy wandering around the field. I'm shouting, "Get out of there, there'll be mines in that field!" His tank had been hit and the rest of the crew had been killed. He was in a state of shock and confusion, and I got him in the tank to take him back. Towards the end of the road, there's the two RAF guys lying dead. I assumed it was the half-track full of Germans.

I was interrogated by a General Meisel. I just said, "I'm against the plot, but I don't think that the people who made this plot did this out of dishonorable attitude. I think they did it since they felt this was a way to help Germany." I got away with that.

Wehrmacht paratrooper Herbert Holewa was skeptical.

So long as the German flag was going up, they were for it. Now it was going down, they wanted to jump the sinking ship.

On August 15, the Allies landed in southern France. Four days later, in the north, the Allies began crossing the Seine. Meanwhile, Patrick Lewis had been detailed to a recovery tank, clearing bodies from burned-out tanks, retrieving damaged armor. One morning he was ferrying ammunition, solo, up to a Canadian frontline unit.

I drove out of this field. There were a couple of dead

1944

OCTOBER 7

One crematorium at the Auschwitz extermination camp is destroyed when the prisoners stage a revolt. The uprising is ruthlessly crushed

OCTOBER 9

The Canadian government establishes departments of Reconstruction, Veterans' Affairs, and Health and Welfare

The Arc de Triomphe forms the backdrop for the Liberation Day Parade, Paris, August 26, 1944. At left, Corporal O. Hoffman of Illinois, Corporal M. Shanebrook of Illinois, Private J. Vetter of New York, Corporal W. Lucas of Oklahoma, and Corporal F. Mascard enjoy a beer at a sidewalk café in newly liberated Paris

At right, manning this antiaircraft gun in Paris are privates S. Lano of Maine and F. Baird of Vermont, along with Corporal F. McGee from Texas and Sergeant D. Robbins from California

OCTOBER 14

The Nazis announce that Field Marshal Erwin Rommel has died of his wounds. In fact, he was forced to commit suicide after having been implicated in the July 20 attempt to kill Hitler

OCTOBER 20

130,000 U.S. troops land at Leyte in the Philippines, including General MacArthur, who announces to the people of the Philippines that he has returned

1944

Soon after, Patrick Lewis was hit and invalided back to England.

U.S. General George S. Patton's Third Army swept into Brittany in early August, followed by the Eighth U.S. Corps. The Germans fell back, turning Breton ports into fortresses. Herbert Holewa had marched from Cologne to Brest, in Brittany. The Eighth Corps took Brest on September 14. Four days later, the U.S. Army caught up with Herbert Holewa.

> We were taken back in a lorry to a makeshift POW camp. We very well treated. Most of the Americans in that unit were of German descent. Then we got the K-rations. The K-rations were fantastic. On the first of November, we landed in Southampton.

At left, United States Army Air Force fighter ace Captain John Godfrey from Rhode Island, who scored 36 kills before being brought down behind enemy lines in 1944. Despite attempting to escape, he spent the last six months of the war as a POW in Germany. Below, pitched battles were fought in bitterly cold conditions in Belgium during the winter of 1944-45

NOVEMBER 8

Churchill informs the public that Germany's V2 rocket campaign is the cause of the explosions across southeast England

NOVEMBER 8

In Holland, the First Canadian Army's long, hard-fought and triumphant Schelde campaign is over

Privates H. Brookey of Oklahoma and J. Dixon of North Carolina, right, gaze at the ruins of Cologne Cathedral, Germany, destroyed by Allied bombing

On August 24, General Leclerc's 2nd Free French Division took Paris. Channel ports were falling to the Canadians—including Dieppe, on September 1. The British took Brussels on September 3, and Antwerp a day later. On September 17, Operation Market-Garden began. Conceived by Field Marshal Montgomery, it aimed to establish a bridgehead across the Rhine at Arnhem. It ended on September 25 in defeat for its British, American, and Polish combatants.

On December 16, a last, vast gamble from Hitler focused on the Ardennes, the very territory where, less than five years before, General Heinz Guderian's blitzkrieg had led to the fall of France. Hitler's goal was to capture Antwerp and cut the Allied armies in two. Bad weather had grounded Allied aircraft and the Germans launched 30 divisions against an unsuspecting five U.S. divisions.

At Bastogne, which became a symbol of U.S. defiance, nine German divisions besieged the Americans. On December 22, General Hasso-Eccard von Manteuffel proposed "honorable surrender" to the U.S. commander Brigadier General Anthony C. McAuliffe. The famous reply was "nuts."

When the weather improved, Allied air power reasserted itself, and U.S. generals Patton and Hodge demonstrated that lightning war was no longer the preserve of the Wehrmacht. By mid-January, the Battle of the Bulge was over and, with it, Nazi hopes.

In those last days, the consequences of Hitler's 1941 invasion of the Soviet Union came home to Germany. A Nazi war—of a size and genocidal horror unparalleled in world history—was met on January 12, 1945, with the war's greatest offensive. The Soviet Red Army threw 3.8 million soldiers into battle.

Karl Günther von Hase was posted to a German eastern border "fortress" where the defending troops were expected to fight to the last man.

> It was a normal town with some very slight fortifications. The strategic reasoning was to have a few places behind the front line to stop the Russian offensive. The orders were to defend it at any cost.

> There were soldiers from all parts of the army. We were quite successful, but then we decided it was no use, we were already about 100 km behind the front. We prepared a spearhead to go out of the fortress and to surprise the Russians. It was pointed to the east. We were successful in getting out of the

NOVEMBER 27

The RAF uses of the 12,000-pound Tallboy bomb for the first time on a German city in a raid on Munich, causing damage to more than 600 buildings

DECEMBER 3

The Home Guard is decomissioned after providing service to the war effort since 1940

1944

fortress. We had the bad luck then of crossing a Polish division, and a Russian division. They immediately attacked—and we were dispersed.

Lance Corporal Norris, a POW in Berlin, was force-marched east.

We could hear the Russian artillery now really laying down huge barrages. We were soaked through. We were eating raw potatoes from the fields. With a huge revving of engines, we saw the T-34s coming in. Everybody was embracing each other. And we were free, at that moment.

The Germans' long-range artillery was now centering on where we had been liberated. We saw strange three-ton lorries with ramps attached to them being driven up. There must have been about 200 to 300 of these lined up.

Suddenly we saw a Russian officer. He went along the line. He looked to his left, he looked to his right. He took out a sword. With the dropping of the sword we heard and saw something which was almost like Dante's Inferno. This was the Stalin Organ, the Russian Katyusha. And they were pouring these rockets on the retreating German forces. You could follow the trajectory. They were falling like rain.

1944

DECEMBER 16

In the Ardennes, the Battle of the Bulge, a last-ditch attempt by the Germans to divide the Allied thrust toward Germany, begins

DECEMBER 24

Manchester is hit by V1 bombs air-launched by Heinkel He-111 bombers. The city center is hit by a single bomb, while the rest fall in the outskirts

At left, the Russian and American armies meet at Torgau in April 1945. Major General Reinhard of the U.S. 69th Infantry shakes hands with Major General Rusakov of the Soviet 58th Guards

Allied soldiers on the steps of St. Peter's Basilica in Rome, 1944

DECEMBER 29

RCAF Flight Lieutenant Dick Audet sets something of a record in France by destroying five German planes in only ten minutes

DECEMBER 31

Heavy fighting at Leyte, in the Philippines, inflicts huge losses on both sides. The campaign will ultimately claim 60,000 Japanese lives and leave 15,000 Americans dead or wounded

1944

Overlord—The D-Day Landings

At daybreak on the morning of June 6, 1944, the largest invasion fleet ever assembled arrived off the French coast. Operation Overlord, the Allied invasion of Europe commanded by General Eisenhower, was underway. The armada comprised over 5,000 ships and 8,000 aircraft, coordinating after months of planning and training to deliver almost 150,000 men to five designated landing areas covering 62 miles of Normandy's beaches at the base of the Cotentin Peninsula.

The Normandy coastline between Le Havre and Cherbourg was not as intensively fortified as the Pas-de-Calais area. There the distance between England and France is just over 20 miles. This was where the Germans expected the Allied invasion to come. Nevertheless, Normandy's defenses were thorough. Thick wooden posts were driven into the ground, creating bizarre denuded forests in open fields to deter glider landings. Behind the beaches, fields were flooded to impede invaders, coastal gun emplacements covered the approaches to the shore along with networks of concrete bunkers and machine-gun nests along the shoreline. Land mines littered the beaches and wooden or steel posts topped with land mines, submerged at high tide, provided deadly obstacles for landing craft or amphibious tanks.

The Germans, however, still expected the Allied assault farther east. Various ruses were employed to encourage this misconception including, on the eve of the invasion, a handful of ships at sea combined with aircraft dropping "window" (strips of tinfoil) to create erroneous radar images of a phantom fleet heading for Pas-de-Calais.

The real invasion got underway on the night of June 5, having been postponed for 24 hours due to bad weather. The first Allied combat troops to land as part of Operation Overlord were British and American airborne forces.

The map below shows the approximate basic routes taken by different elements of the invasion force. The flight paths of the airborne divisions have been especially simplified as they took off from bases throughout southern England

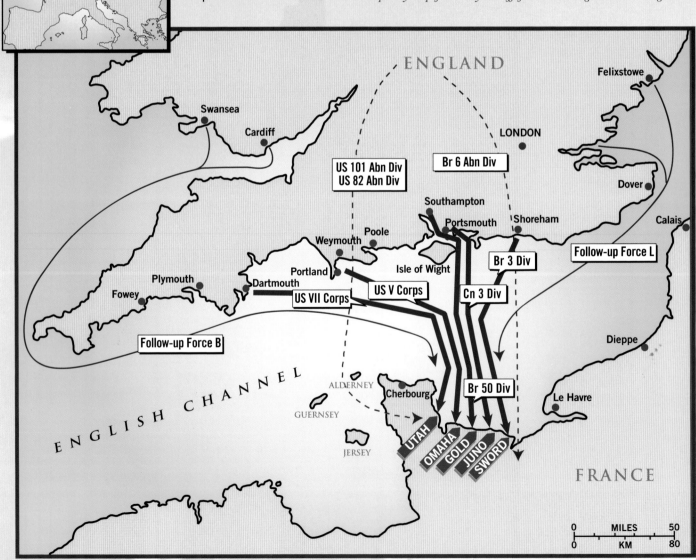

THE U.S. AIRBORNE ASSAULT

American airborne troops took off from bases in southern England at 22:15 hours. The 82nd and 101st airborne divisions, 13,000 paratroops, were charged with securing the exit routes from Utah Beach as well as capturing or destroying vital road, rail, and bridge links. Their flight path down the western flank of the invasion group kept them clear of friendly fire from Allied gunners, but on reaching their drop zones they experienced heavy flak. Almost 25 percent of the 101st Division's paratroops landed outside their battle area; the 82nd fared little better. Despite the confusion of the drop and heavy casualties (around 2,500 in total on D-Day), the paratroops achieved almost all of their objectives.

UTAH BEACH

The U.S. VII Corp's 4th Infantry Division, comprising the 8th, 12th, and 22nd infantry regiments, were charged with taking Utah Beach. With the landings timed to make the best use of the incoming tide, Utah was the first area to be attacked, elements of the 8th Infantry hitting the beach on time at 06:30 hours. Fortunately for them it was the wrong beach. Strong currents and high winds had driven their landing craft over a mile to their left where they came ashore on a far less heavily defended beach. By noon, the 4th, supported by the 70th Tank Battalion, had fought their way four miles inland and linked up with the 101st Airborne. By 18:00 hours, 21,000 troops and 1,700 vehicles had landed at Utah. They suffered losses of 20 dead and 200 wounded.

OMAHA BEACH

Separated from Utah by 10 miles of cliffs, Omaha Beach was the landing area for the U.S. V Corp's 29th Infantry Division (comprising the 115th and 116th infantry regiments) and the 1st Infantry Division (16th and 18th infantry regiments). They were supported by artillery, tanks, the Special Engineer Brigade, and two Ranger battalions. Altogether the assault force totaled 34,000 men. Strong winds and high seas sank many of the landing craft and amphibious tanks and drove the assault craft off target. Despite heavy naval bombardment of the German defenses, the assault troops came under heavy fire. By nightfall V Corps had managed to push one and a half miles inland but were still in a precarious position. They suffered 2,400 casualties.

FORCES B AND L

Follow-up forces B and L brought further manpower as well as the ingenious and vital "Mulberrys"—prefabricated floating harbors that were set in position off Omaha and Gold beaches, allowing troop and supply ships to dock before the Allies had actually captured any sizable port.

THE BRITISH AIRBORNE ASSAULT

The British 6th Airborne Division, which included the 1st Canadian Parachute Battalion, crossed the English Channel to the east of the main invasion force with orders to capture or destroy several key bridges, eliminate a gun battery, and secure the eastern flank of the invasion area. The first soldiers to land at 00:16 hours were 181 glider troops of the 2nd Oxfordshire and Buckinghamshire Light Infantry. The Ox and Bucks gliders landed within yards of their target—the Canal de Caen Bridge. The first D-Day objective to be captured, the bridge was later renamed Pegasus Bridge in honor of the paratroops' winged horse divisional insignia. In total, the 6th suffered 650 casualties.

GOLD BEACH

At 07:25 hours the tide made the timing right for the British XXX Corp's 50th Infantry Division, comprising the 8th Armored Brigade, 47 Royal Marine Commando, the 151st Brigade, the 56th Brigade, the 231st Brigade, and the 69th Brigade, to attack Gold Beach. Beach defenses and stubborn German resistance held up their advance. A naval barrage helped the assault troops fight their way off the beach. By the end of the day, XXX Corps had linked up with the Canadians to their left, advancing up to eight miles inland. Twenty-five thousand men landed on Gold Beach with about 1,000 casualties.

JUNO BEACH

At 07:55 hours Juno Beach was stormed by British I Corps's 3rd Canadian Division comprising the Canadian 2nd Armoured Brigade, the Canadian 7th, 8th, and 9th brigades, and 48 Royal Marine Commando. By now the tide was rising fast and many of the beach obstacles were covered by water. Nearly a third of all of I Corps's landing craft were destroyed or damaged on their way to the beach. Despite this, the assault wave fought its way off the beach and house to house through Bernières, capturing the coastal town by midmorning. By nightfall, the Canadians were in a strong position, and over 21,000 men had come ashore. They suffered almost 1,200 casualties.

SWORD BEACH

The 3rd Division of British I Corps comprised the British 8th, 9th, and 185th brigades, the 27th Armored Brigade, 3 Commando, 4 Commando, 6 Commando, 41 Royal Marine Commando, and 45 Royal Marine Commando. The 3rd Division was allocated the Sword landing area, and attached to 4 Commando was a detachment of 176 French troops, ensuring that native Frenchmen were among the first of the liberators to arrive on French soil. The 3rd Division's job was to take the town of Ouistreham, link up with the 6th Airborne Division, and press inland to capture Caen. Caen proved impossible, but they did land 29,000 men during the course of the day, suffering around 1,000 casualties.

Note: Casualty rates may not seem high given the large number of troops who came ashore, but most who landed did so later in the day, when the beaches had been cleared of the enemy.

You cannot exaggerate the horror of Dachau. The G.I.s were, most of them were sick at their stomach. It was, if anything, worse than the descriptions that have been heard.

AMERICAN FIGHTER PILOT
JAMES GOODSON

CHAPTER NINETEEN

HORRORS OF NAZI RULE

Genocide is not unique to World War II, but Adolf Hitler's regime made it a core faith. A mystique developed, was encouraged, and still persists around Nazism; in reality, it was a society ruled by a conspiracy of thugs, racists, psychopaths, and murderers. Amid the moral chaos created by Hitler and his associates, anyone could become a victim. First, they were Germans, then they were from all European states. Specific groups were targeted, denied their humanity, slaughtered without compunction— people with disabilities, Slavs, Gypsies, homosexuals, political opponents, and most of all, Jews.

As soon as the Nazis came to power, Jews were excluded from the civil service and the professions. Within two years, the Nuremberg race laws stripped citizenship from any German with a Jewish grandparent. Then the expansion began.

When the Nazis took over Austria on March 12, 1938, Harry Burger was a Viennese-Jewish teenager from an affluent family.

> I woke up on March 13 and saw nothing but swastikas. There was a tremendous amount of jubilation. The only realization I got out of this was that I had become a German-Jew, which was a horrible thing to be. Daddy said, "Don't worry about it, everything will be fine." He was the eternal optimist.
>
> You have to understand what went on in Austria.

> There was no such thing as a Jew. The religion was Hebraic, but nobody called you a Jew. Not until the Anschluss. That was the big changeover. All of a sudden, I belonged to a race. There was no such thing as a Jewish race. My religion, Israelitisches Yiddish, was like a Catholic or a Protestant, or whatever.

Harry Burger was expelled from his school as a "dirty Jew." Then the Nuremberg laws were enacted in Austria. Thus was Harry excluded from education. Jews couldn't go to movies, even to the park.

> My grandpa, who was 86, used to go down every day and sat on his favorite park bench talking to people. He looked at boats go by. One morning, he came down and he saw on the park bench "*Juden Verboten*"—Jews not allowed. He went back to his apartment, brought a chair down, set it next to the bench and sat himself down. An SS man pulled his gun out and said, "If you do that one more time, you dirty Jew, I will shoot you in the head." That was the end of sitting on the park bench.

In October 1938, distraught at the plight of his family at the hands of the Nazis, 17-year-old Polish-Jewish refugee Herschel Grynszpan shot the German Legation secretary in Paris, Ernst Vom Rath. Grynszpan said he had done it for love of his parents and people:

> It is not, after all, a crime to be Jewish. I am not a dog. I have a right to live. My people have a right to exist on this earth.

Vom Rath died on November 9, by which time scattered anti-Semitic riots were breaking out in Germany. The Nazi propaganda minister Joseph Goebbels incited violence. The SA- and SS-led mob set to work on what became Kristallnacht, the night of the broken glass. Jewish property and synagogues were destroyed and 91 German Jews murdered. Harry Burger:

> My mom and I stayed in the apartment. She didn't get arrested because we had a good caretaker who did not give out the names to the Nazis when they came to the door. I saw people being dragged through the streets by the hair, bloody, kicked.

In Berlin the next morning, 21-year-old teacher Berta Ollendorff was phoned by her mother. Her father's corner shop had been smashed, and the police had told the family to leave.

JANUARY 9
U.S. troops invade the Philippines at Luzon island, 107 miles from Manila

JANUARY 17
Polish troops fighting alongside Soviet units capture Warsaw

Above, President Roosevelt meets with King Saud of Saudi Arabia aboard a U.S. Navy vessel in Cairo, Egypt, in 1945. On the previous pages, G.I.s talk to former captives of the Nazis at Buchenwald camp in April 1945. In the background, gas ovens in the crematorium at the Dachau concentration camp

At the First Canadian Corps Headquarters in Wageningen, Holland, on May, 5, 1945, an agreement to the surrender of all German forces in the Netherlands was reached. At left, Jews were unaware of the terrible fate that awaited them as they were herded by the Nazis into city ghettos like this one in Kutno, Poland

JANUARY 19

German armies are in full retreat along the 500-mile eastern front

JANUARY 26

Russian troops find fewer than 3,000 survivors when they liberate Auschwitz extermination camp

1945

> The people in the main street stopped and watched me clearing up. I became so furious, and so full of hate that this had been done to my father, and to us, that I wasn't afraid anymore. I was absolutely cold inside, full of hate and fury.

Berta arrived in England in 1938.

In January 1939, in Berlin, Harry Burger's father's chauffeur arrived for work—in an SS uniform. He then arrested his employer. Burger senior was given the choice of giving his business to the Nazis or being sent to Dachau concentration camp. Harry Burger:

> He signed it over and he was for the first time in his life unemployed. He came home and concentrated on migration.

The family resolved to reunite with relatives in southern France, and made it. But Harry's father was later deported by the French Vichy police, and was destined to die in Auschwitz.

More than 50 percent of Germany's half-million Jews had emigrated by 1939, but Hitler's advance left the fate of more and more Jews in Nazi hands. With the invasion of Poland in 1939, some 2.5 million Polish Jews came

Canadian war bonds were sold aggressively at home, above, and on the front line, left, where privates M. Therrien, J. Laplante, and R. Gallahan of the Black Watch (Royal Highland Regiment) study Victory Bonds paperwork while manning their post

At right, a wounded G.I. is treated by medics as the Allies advance on Bologna, in Italy, 1945

JANUARY 29

Having bypassed some pockets of German resistance, Soviet troops cross the German-Polish border and are now in Germany, only 100 miles from Berlin

FEBRUARY 4

At the Yalta Conference, Churchill, Roosevelt, and Stalin meet once again to discuss the world's postwar future

under Nazi rule. Adolf Pilch was a 25-year-old Polish soldier. As resistance was overpowered, he attempted to head west and arrived in a little Polish town.

> There were three Jewish people pulling a water tank. The people said that one of them is the rabbi, the other is a distinguished lawyer, and the other again was some type of noble Jewish man. One or two soldiers surrounded them and they were having sticks and beating them, "schnapp, schnapp, schnapp," and so on.

A plague of betrayal seeped across the continent. In 1940, artilleryman William Harding, a Londoner, was captured and sent to a German POW camp in Poland. Among his fellow prisoners was a British Jew who, speaking a smattering of German, became a go-between with their captors—and had curbed violence toward POWs. He was also bartering for food with Polish civilians. But another London cockney POW, a suspected supporter of the British Union of Fascists, was unhappy with the deal he had made. A fight broke out. William Harding:

> The next day we were working. The Jew was talking to the German overseer, a civilian. This cockney shouts out, "Hey, Jew!" in a very loud voice.
> The German looked up. He said, "Juden?"
> The cockney shouted out, "Ja, ja, Jew. Juden."
> The German civilian gave the Jew a terrible uppercut and laid him right out on his back. He

FEBRUARY 13-14

The German city of Dresden is devastated following night and day attacks by 750 RAF and 400 USAAF bombers. Some 100,000 people are killed, with another 300,000 injured, as the city was full of refugees

MARCH 7

U.S. forces cross the Rhine into Germany by seizing intact the Ludendorff Bridge at Remagen

1945

smashed into him. The Jew jumped up and the pair were slogging it out toe to toe.

I thought, "My God, you've got to admire a man for sticking up for himself."

The guard went over and started to knock the Jew about with his rifle butt. The Jew lay on the ground with a lot of blood over him. The guard made him take his boots off, and he doubled him past us. He looked in a terrible mess, his face. I said to this cockney chap, "You've done a good job. You've given him a death sentence."

His reply was: "Serve the bastard right."

I had a deep hatred of Germans then. I don't go through life hating anybody, but I did then. I mortally hated them then, I did.

We went back from work that evening, we was all looking for the Jew. He was standing in the guards' compound, to attention, with his face close to the wire, with the guard nearby, sauntering around with his rifle on his shoulder. In the morning he was still there. He'd been there all night. I never heard or saw him anymore.

MARCH 11

Essen is bombed during a daylight raid made by more than 1,000 RAF bombers. The city and rail junction are crippled following the barrage of 4,700 tons of bombs

MARCH 18

Berlin endures heavy bombing once again as 4,000 bombs are dropped by Allied forces

At left, Canadian soldiers P. Rivet, A. McLean, and J. Pratte buy grapes from a Belgian farmer's dog-drawn cart. Below left, a WAAC takes time from training for war to reapply battle-damaged makeup

Accompanied by organist Staff Sergeant W. Wilkins, these soldiers and civilians share an Easter day service high in the Italian Apennine mountains in 1945

With the takeover of Poland, the Nazis confined Jews in ghettoes—to be used as forced labor, murdered, and starved. Then in June 1941, came the German invasion of the Soviet Union. The Wehrmacht's and SS's mass murders were accompanied by those of special death squads, the Einsatzgruppen who, assisted by local squads of collaborators, targeted Jews. By the end of the year, around one million Jews had been murdered.

That autumn the Nazis moved toward the "final solution"—the gassing of all Jews and other "undesirables." The final solution was already under way when, on January 20, 1942, Reinhard Heydrich summoned a group of German bureaucrats to a conference in the Berlin suburb of Wannsee to discuss details for the planned murder of every European Jew. In the new death camps, murder was the sole objective. In concentration camps, meanwhile, inmates were also being murdered, starved, and worked to death. In January 1941, Premysl Dobias, a 27-year-old Czech from the Sudetenland, was arrested by the Gestapo. By May he was in the concentration camp at Mauthausen, in Austria. There he was assigned to the granite quarry.

The SS were stationed on each side of the road. While we were passing, we were hit by rifles. The granite quarry was very, very steep, very deep, and 186 steps led to the bottom. Going down we had to run barefoot on awfully sharp granite stones, we just screamed with pain. Our feet were bleeding and in the dirt so many of them got infections and very soon died. As we passed, the SS were hitting us. Many prisoners fell on the steps, and knocked over some of the prisoners in front like cards or dominoes. The SS were laughing.

Even as the war intensified, the Nazis devoted more of their efforts to mass murder. While focusing on eastern Europe, they reached out to engulf the ancient communities of Greece and the Balkans. The Jews of western Europe, along with others, were consigned to the camps. Resistance to the final solution took many forms. In autumn 1943, Jørgen von Führen Kieler, a 24-year-old member of the Danish Resistance, heard of Nazi plans to abduct Danish Jews.

It would not have been possible to organize the rescue of the Jews within hours unless there had not been enormous public support. What was important

MARCH 23
British and Canadian forces cross the Rhine, supported by airborne landings

MARCH 27
The last V2 rocket launched at England lands in Orpington, Kent; 2,754 civilians have been killed by V2s, 6,523 have been seriously injured

1945

was to get in contact with the Jews and have them shipped over to Sweden. We had a fleet of 10 to 12 fishing boats. It took us two weeks to transport between 800 and 1,000 Jews across the Sound, without losing a single one.

Some 7,000 Danish Jews were saved. Earlier that year, the Warsaw Ghetto had risen against the Nazis in the first phase of an epic of resistance. The Jewish Fighting Organization, together with the Jewish Military Union, fought with homemade weapons as the Nazis sought to liquidate the ghetto. Final resistance was not crushed until July. A total of 14,000 Jews died in the uprising, 7,000 were murdered in the Treblinka death camp, and some 50 lived to fight alongside fellow Poles in the Warsaw uprising of August–October 1944. A quarter of Warsaw's one million population died. The Nazis then demolished most of the city.

For the Nazis the war with Poles, Russians—all Slavs—was a race war. Even if tactical alliances could have been made along the way, they saw the Slav peoples as subhumans to be murdered or enslaved. Captured British medical orderly Albert Jenkins was held in upper Silesia adjacent to a Soviet POW camp.

Above, Spotty was left behind in England by I Company of the U.S. 70th Infantry Division in the belief that they would not be allowed to take their mascot home. He was rescued by some nurses and is seen here traveling to New York on the Queen Mary *with Red Cross nurse Rosaline Palmer of Menlo Park, California. In New York, Spotty was handed over to an old infantry buddy*

At Eisenhower's headquarters in Reims, France, General Alfred Jodl signs the documents for Germany's unconditional surrender. At right, a shipboard romance blossomed for Edna McDonald of South Carolina, and George Zavoda of New Jersey as they sailed home from Europe to the United States

MARCH 29

The last V1 flying bomb to land in England hits Kent; 6,184 civilians have been killed by V1s, 17,981 seriously injured

APRIL 12

President Franklin Delano Roosevelt dies of a cerebral hemorrhage at the age of 63. Vice-president Harry S Truman is sworn in as 32nd president of the United States

Their conditions were absolutely appalling. The men were given shovels and picks to dig holes, to live in. Typhus broke out. While I was working in the cemetery, every day carts used to arrive from the Russian camp with a tarpaulin over them so that the ordinary civilian people wouldn't know what was inside.

They were stacked with naked Russian prisoners of war. They dug these mass graves and just bundled the bodies in. Fires were kept going all night, by felling trees, to thaw the ground out so that they could bury these chaps.

There were also freakish reversals of fortune. In 1944, Michael Etkind, a 19-year-old Polish Jew at Buchenwald, Germany, witnessed the arrival of an SS man as a prisoner.

He must have murdered somebody, not a Russian, not a Jew and not a Pole, but his wife or his child or somebody. Being a German, he got the best job, which was the kitchen. Suddenly a transport came from who knows where and these Russians recognized him, that he was the German who murdered so many Russians.

The Russians provoked an argument. I was on the top bunk looking down when one of the Russians hit him over the head, not very hard. As he lifted his head, he was surrounded by the Russians. They were smiling. He went pale, he realized suddenly he was in danger.

Then the Russians told him, "Remember such-and-such a camp? Remember you were hanging so many people? You remember how many of our friends you've killed? Now you're being tried."

He shook his head and said, "No, no, no. I must go."

They blocked his way. They found a rope and told him, "For what you have done, you are sentenced to death."

They hanged him horizontally. Then they took his body and threw it into the latrine.

Between 1940 and 1942, a cluster of concentration camps and a death camp were built at Auschwitz. In that place of cruelty, inmates were enslaved, subjected to inhumane medical experiments, and gassed. In October 1944, there was a camp revolt which led to a gas chamber being blown up. One day that month, Frank Bright, a 16-year-old Czechoslovakian Jew, arrived with his mother.

Somehow, I lost her, but she spotted me, walked towards me, shook my hand and walked away again. We were taken in front of somebody who would point right and left. There were lorries waiting, and those who were ill or crippled or old were told they could get on this lorry. We thought, "How nice to be so kind."

I'd seen my mother go first, and she walked to the left. I'm a bit slow on the uptake, so when my turn came, I walked forward, and simply followed where my mother had gone. I was called back and turned to the right. We were marched on a roadway between barbed wire. The soldiers said, would we let them have watches? We would lose them anyway.

I stood at an open door and there were women in there who presumably had just arrived and had their heads shorn; we too eventually had our hair cut. I'd never seen a naked woman before, but to see a naked woman absolutely shorn is a bit of a shock. Then we had to undress completely, and anybody who had supports for hernias had to put it to one side and even false teeth had to be removed. We had a shower, but nothing to dry ourselves with. It was quite cold.

G.I.s at left discover the corpses of over three dozen Buchenwald prisoners piled on a truck outside the crematorium.

While many headed home to the United States, others, like Private Royland Otter from Indiana, opposite, boarded ships headed for the unfinished war in the Far East

We were issued then with pants which were made of prayer shawls. Now that was an excellent thing, because prayer shawls were made from the finest wool, some sort of shirt and a dreadful black jacket.

On the first night, it was pitch-dark. I stood there and saw the licking flames out of the crematorium and said to myself, knowing by now what had happened: "Which of these flames is my mother?"

In January 1945, the Red Army liberated the camp. Three months later, *London News Chronicle* reporter Stanley Baron arrived at Nordhausen, a complex of tunnels inside Kohnstein Hill.

You went into the mouth of a great cave. And inside the cave there were some 30 or 40 miles of tunnels. It was the largest underground factory in Europe. And it was there that they were building the V1s and the V2s.

We saw every sign of sophisticated engineering, of man at his scientifically most brilliant. And then we went to the quarters of the slave labor. And we saw men dying. I remember in one particular dark corner waving my torch around, just seeing the glint of eyes and very weak voices tried to explain who they were. Virtually the whole of the work force there consisted of political prisoners. It was estimated afterwards that something like 20,000 Poles had died there. Spiritually it was almost the worst possible place. These people were not being destroyed because of their race. They were being used as material for this vast scientific apparatus that was producing weapons of war destined for London.

The contrast between that advanced technical ability of the Germans and what they were able to do to ordinary humanity was so great that this has struck me as a most extraordinary example of the dichotomy which can exist in the human mind. It was absolutely terrible.

Shot down just before the end of the war, held in a POW camp, helped to escape by Yugoslavs, and sheltered by members of the German resistance, American fighter pilot James Goodson entered Dachau with the first American forces.

You cannot exaggerate the horror of Dachau. The G.I.s were, most of them were sick at their stomach. It was, if anything, worse than the descriptions that have been heard.

1945

APRIL 21

Soviet troops fight their way into Berlin

APRIL 25

The U.S. First Army links up with Soviet forces at the River Elbe

The people who were responsible were the Himmlers and the Hitlers and so on. The G.I.s were just absolutely scandalized; they too were so overwhelmed by this horror that they could hardly react to it.

Hedy Epstein's father had been held prisoner at Dachau in the 1930s and probably died in Auschwitz. The German-Jewish girl had the good fortune to escape to England in 1939. By 1945, the 21-year-old was an employee of the U.S. War Department at the Nuremberg trials and there, during a trial recess, she encountered Hermann Goering.

I didn't say anything. I just looked at him. He was obviously uncomfortable and he didn't know who I was. We were given American uniforms, so he probably didn't even suspect that I would know German. He said to his defense counsel, in German:

"Who is this little one? What does she want?"

The defense counsel said, "I don't know who she is, but she obviously works for the prosecution. I don't know what she wants. Don't say anything. Don't do anything."

I'm thinking, "You know, here is Goering whom, not too long ago I would have feared mortally. Here I am—and he's afraid of me."

APRIL 28

Food is distributed to starving civilians in Holland after German and Canadian forces agree to a truce in order to relieve the famine

APRIL 28

As they attempt to escape from Italy into Switzerland, Mussolini, his mistress, and his closest Fascist cohorts are captured by Italian partisans and executed

The Nazi Camp System

Dachau—the name evokes chilling feelings of dread and revulsion for anyone with even a superficial knowledge of the atrocities committed by the Nazis in their "death camps" during World War II. Dachau wasn't the camp with the worst reputation, the camp where the most prisoners were incarcerated, or even the camp where the most prisoners were cruelly murdered. It was, however, the first of the major Nazi camps and the model for all subsequent camps. Dachau supervisor Theodor Eicke established a manual of disciplinary and penal codes for prison camps—a mandate for the torture and murder of millions of helpless prisoners throughout Europe over the coming years.

The former ammunition factory near the Bavarian town of Dachau first became a prison camp in 1933. Following a fire at the Reichstag building in Berlin, which the Nazis declared an act of sabotage by Communists, a ferocious witch-hunt began. Political dissidents of all persuasions were rounded up and imprisoned. The camp at Dachau was originally intended as a prison for Communist detainees and was run by the State Police. It wasn't long, though, before the SS took over and the reign of terror began. The first deaths at Dachau came the next day after the SS took over, when four respected members of the Communist Youth Association were murdered.

Inmates at Dachau were placed on a starvation diet and used as slave labor. Complaints were met with ruthless punishment. Beatings were commonplace and disobedience was regarded as mutiny, to be punished with death by shooting or hanging. The Nazis saw Dachau as a great success and, as the governments of the rest of western Europe looked on, reluctant to act upon the reports they were receiving, the cancerous growth of the camps began.

By the end of World War II, more than 100 major Nazi concentration camps of various types had been established all over occupied Europe from Bredtvet in Norway and Vivara in Estonia to Salonika in Greece. While Dachau defined the methods to be used for their running, the camps were utilized for a variety of sinister purposes.

Facilities like the Drancy camp near Paris were transit centers where prisoners were held prior to being sent on to other camps. Drancy was the largest center through which Jews were deported from France. In the two years up to August 1944, 61,000 Jews were processed through Drancy on their way to Auschwitz, where most of them were murdered.

Concentration camps such as Natzweiler–Struthof in the Alsace region of France used forced labor; in this case for the construction of vast mountain caves to house underground V2 rocket factories, where the inmates were worked until they dropped. Living conditions were appalling; the prisoners were dressed in rags and struggled to survive on a starvation diet.

Natzweiler–Struthof eventually acquired further facilities, a gas chamber and improved crematorium to be used for the extermination of Jews, Gypsies, those involved in religion or politics who spoke out against the Nazis, homosexual men, resistance workers—anyone, in fact, who the Nazis considered to be "undesirable." Many thousands of people died in concentration camps, but the death toll became almost

Victims of the Buchenwald camp. The camp was liberated by American forces in 1945

The above map shows only a few of the major Nazi camps but gives a good overall impression of their widespread distribution

unimaginable at the most horrific of the Nazi camps, the extermination camps.

The main Nazi extermination camps were located in German-occupied Poland, where the highly efficient rail links brought prisoners from all over Europe, but the sites were far enough east to keep them out of sight of most of the civilized world. The largest camp was at Auschwitz–Birkenau, just 37 miles west of Krakow. The others were at Treblinka, 50 miles northeast of Warsaw; Majdanek near Lublin in eastern Poland; Sobibor near the Russian border; Chelmno between Warsaw and Gdansk; and Belzec in the south. Although estimates vary, it is believed these camps were used to murder almost 3 million Jews as well as countless thousands of others persecuted by the Nazis.

While Dachau did have its own gas chamber, for some reason it appears never to have been used, although prisoners were sent from Dachau to Hartheim and yet another kind of Nazi killing facility, the euthanasia center. Six such centers were established between January 1940 and January 1941. They were located at Brandenburg near Berlin, Grafeneck near Stuttgart, Sonnenstein near Dresden, Bernburg near Magdeburg, Hadamar near Koblenz, and Hartheim near Linz in Austria. Just as they regarded the Jews as being "subhuman," the Nazis also looked upon the physically and mentally handicapped as being a lower form of life. The euthanasia, or "mercy killing" centers were designed to rid Germany of these "undesirables," at the same time freeing up bed space in sanatoriums for the use of wounded German soldiers.

By 1945, almost 300,000 innocent people had died in these facilities, including around 8,000 children.

. . . I saw the flash from the bomb which was exactly like the sort of bluish light that you get from an electrical welding operation. It was very blue and it came in exactly the opposite direction from the sun's rays, it completely eclipsed them.

BRITISH POW
NORMAN SHERRING
Nagasaki, Japan, 1945

CHAPTER TWENTY

Brighter Than the Sun

When Guam fell to the United States in August 1944, along with the Mariana Islands, the end of the war against the Japanese empire began. The Japanese mainland was within range of the world's first intercontinental bomber, the USAAF's B-29 Superfortress. In the last months of the war, B-29s fire-bombed Japan's cities but, as Allied armies and fleets closed in on Japan, a greater horror emerged from the desert of New Mexico.

In 1942, Douglas MacArthur had proclaimed on arrival in Australia—soon after quitting the Philippines—that he would return. Despite the U.S. Navy's desire to leapfrog the islands, the general got his wish. On October 21, 1944, in the wake of a vast naval bombardment and the U.S. landings on Leyte Island, the general waded ashore.

Alongside the landings, a cluster of naval engagements unfolded that would comprise the biggest naval battle in world history. The Battle of Leyte Gulf erupted between October 24 and 25, 1944. The Japanese high command threw almost all its surviving surface vessels into an attempt to wreck the landings and smash the U.S. Seventh Fleet. The result was the virtual elimination of the Japanese Navy. There was another threat, born of dedication—and desperation. On October 21, the Australian cruiser *Australia* was the first ship attacked by a kamikaze suicide pilot.

Sonarman first class Jack Gebhardt was serving on the USN destroyer *Pringle* at Leyte Gulf in November.

> The first kamikaze attack against the *Pringle* occurred the day after arriving at Leyte Gulf. The Jap planes seemed to be everywhere, and the noise of gunfire, explosions, and yelling was intense as we manned our battle stations. A light cruiser came under persistent attack by about a dozen planes and all were shot down without hitting the ship, but then suddenly a lone Jap plane dove out of the clouds and struck the ship. The explosion was ear shattering, and smoke and flames were soon belching from the stricken vessel.

The Japanese poured reinforcements into the land battle on Leyte. The *Pringle*, meanwhile, was escorting supply ships to the southern Philippine island of Mindanao.

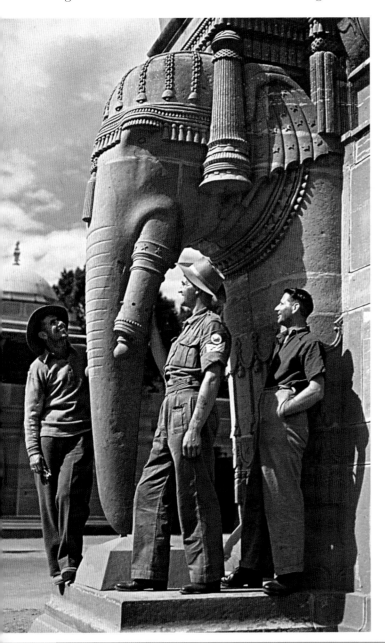

APRIL 30

Adolf Hitler commits suicide along with his wife, Eva Braun, whom he had married in his Berlin bunker the previous day

MAY 1

Leading Nazi propaganda chief and close confidant of Hitler, Dr. Joseph Goebbels orders his six children to be killed, then has an SS officer shoot both him and his wife outside the Berlin bunker

At right, Mitsubishi Zero fighters at Olita airbase in Japan, the country's last line of defense against the onslaught of U.S. bombers. On the previous pages, PFC Faris Touhy, battle weary from 48 hours of fighting on Eniwetok Atoll in the Marshall Islands, takes a coffee break (Inset). In the background, the first atomic bomb is tested at Alamogordo, in New Mexico

At right, Sailors aboard H.M.C.S. Uganda set shell fuses prior to the bombardment of Truk, in the Pacific, June 1945. Far left, British troops inspect buildings in the grounds of the residence of the Viceroy of India

A large ammunition freighter got hit and exploded in a blinding flash. When the ship blew up, the pilothouse was blown on to another ship, which exploded, and the debris rained down on the *Pringle,* almost a mile away from the blast.

Sometimes a suicide plane would pass so close overhead we could see the pilot struggling to control his aircraft before it plunged into the ocean and exploded.

On January 9, 1945, the Americans landed on Luzon, the largest Philippine island. The ensuing battles led to the virtual destruction of the capital, Manila, and the death of almost 100,000 Philippine civilians. In the meantime, Jack Gebhardt and his *Pringle* shipmates had been assigned to Admiral Chester Nimitz's invasion of Iwo Jima on February 19, 1945. The five-mile-long island, less than 700 miles from Tokyo, became a byword for heroism—and death.

For shore bombardment, the *Pringle* would anchor a few hundred yards off Iwo Jima and frequently received enemy small-arms fire from Japanese snipers. Afterward, we discovered plenty of nicks in the hull from the gunfire.

At night the sound of gunfire and explosions on the island was intense as the battle raged, and we wondered how our marines coped with the stress. We could smell the smoke, hear the sounds, and tried to comprehend the deadly conflict under way . . .

It wasn't until the end of March 1945 that Iwo Jima was secured.

In Burma, the Japanese hadn't recovered from their summer 1944 defeat by British, Indian, and Nepalese forces at Imphal, on the Indian border. In northern Burma, U.S. General Stilwell pressed on. On March 30, 1945, Mandalay fell to Commonwealth forces; a little more than a month later, Rangoon fell.

Australian entertainer Nan Kenway had also moved on. She found other work after the collapse of her 1939 English touring concert party. With her husband and partner Douglas Young, she had performed in Italy, North Africa, France, Belgium, Holland, and India. Then it was Burma's turn.

After we left the Irrawaddy at Katha, that was in Burma, the general said we were to have been sent back. And we said, "Oh please, we want to go forward

MAY 4

Field Marshal Montgomery accepts the surrender of all German forces in Holland, Denmark, and northwest Germany in a tent at Luneburg Heath, near Hamburg

MAY 7

German generals Jodl and Friedeburg sign the unconditional surrender documents at General Eisenhower's headquarters in Reims, France

1945

where there's no entertainment at all." It was only just Dougie and me. So the general very kindly said, well, if I had sufficient coverage, we could go.

We had two jeeps. I sat in the front jeep, two soldiers, rifles at the ready. Dougie sat in the back Jeep with the piano, which kept falling off. I can't tell you what the roads were like. And forward we went for nearly a hundred miles . . .

Was I a success? Oh, happy days! And they ran up a tent. There were all these lovely silk parachutes coming down with supplies. And there was the tent. And it was quite easy to find supports, loads of

bamboo and plenty of rope from the parachutes. And before you could say Jack Robinson, we had a tent.

And then they got together and thought, "Oh yes, she'll want to go somewhere."

So they went a little bit further away. And when I went along, you could have heard me laughing in Calcutta. They had dug a lovely new hole. And they'd got a sugar box. And they'd cut out just the right size. Well they knew the size, they'd been following me round the camp all day, you see. And when I went in, it was upholstered with grass and white silk parachute. I've never had a padded loo since, or before.

At right, the U.S. Army Chemical Corps maintained stocks of chemical agents and trained with tear gas to give troops the experience they would need should they ever come under chemical or gas attack. Bottom right, while chemical weapons were not used in the European theater, U.S. troops trained for the possibility of the Japanese using such tactics

With fathers in the services and mothers doing war work, nurseries like the one shown at left in Hatfield, Hertfordshire, sprang up all over England

MAY 8

VE-Day—Victory in Europe is declared and Churchill, President Truman, and King George VI make radio broadcasts as street party celebrations erupt

MAY 8

Victory celebrations in Halifax, Nova Scotia, get out of control as servicemen ransack various commercial premises, including the Keith Brewery, where they steal almost 240,000 pints of beer

In China, as the war moved to its end, most fighting against the Japanese was undertaken by communist Mao Tse-tung's forces. British nurse Evelyn White was close to Chinese nationalist forces who were fighting— but also taking in some theater.

A party came round of actors who were producing the classic Chinese play *Lady Precious Stream,* in Mandarin. The actors appeared in the most magnificent costumes, very old some of them. That was fine but the awful thing was that the men played the ladies' parts. When they started singing in the high-pitched strangulated voices and we had to listen to this for four hours, that wasn't so good.

The audience were very appreciative. All the Chinese Army seemed to spend most of the performance eating sunflower seeds, wise of them; it's full of vitamin N. That was fine, but what they would do was crack the seed between their teeth and spit out the casings. If you happened to be in the way, that was just too bad.

On April 1, 1945, units of the U.S. Tenth Army, backed by massive naval and air support, and supplemented by the newly arrived British Pacific Fleet, landed on the Japanese island of Okinawa, just 340 miles from the mainland. The battle for the island, which engaged 170,000 soldiers and marines, was viewed as another necessary step to victory. But it was also seen as a dreadful warning of what a landing on the mainland could entail.

On April 16, Jack Gebhardt's destroyer was 75 miles off Okinawa. It was dawn.

The *Pringle* was attacked by a horde of Japanese planes. Some were shot down, but one Zero got through our air defenses and crashed in a huge ball of fire. When the two 500-pound bombs on the plane exploded, it seemed like the world ended.

The ship was a burning hulk, with men stumbling dazed and bleeding from the flying debris, smoke, and flames. Just then someone yelled, "Abandon ship!" I climbed down to the gun deck where I took off my shoes and hat and laid them neatly against the

bulkhead, as if I was coming back! People can do strange things in a stressful circumstance.

Gebhardt dived into the sea and headed away from the stricken destroyer.

It all happened in less than five minutes. The Japanese plane hit and the *Pringle* disappeared. There was no explosion, only the cries of wounded men and the continuing battle.

Gebhardt gave up his life jacket to a Filipino steward who had a cramp, grabbed a piece of wreckage and floated for eight hours before he was picked up.

By the time Chicagoan Burton Stein had completed training, been transported across the Pacific, and arrived in Saipan, in the Marianas, it was the summer of 1945.

The invasion of Japan was in everyone's head; it was going to be murderous. It was going to be just the worst kind of campaigning possible.

Geoffrey Sherring had a closer view. A British Merchant Navy radio operator, his ship had been captured by a German surface raider in the South Atlantic in

MAY 13

American aircraft carrier U.S.S. *Enterprise* is hit by kamikaze strike

MAY 21

U.S. Marines take Sugar Loaf Hill, a major strategic stronghold on Okinawa

Above, a flight deck handling party sunbathes on the wing of a Royal Australian Navy Hellcat somewhere in the Pacific. Above left, Allied troops take a break during the advance along the road to Mandalay, Burma, 1945

A U.S. Marine is buried at sea from the hospital ship U.S.S. Hanford, having died from wounds sustained on Iwo Jima

MAY 23

Top Nazi Heinrich Himmler, captured by British troops while trying to escape in disguise to Switzerland, commits suicide after two days in detention

MAY 24

The second massive air raid on Japan in two days sees Tokyo hit by a force of over 500 U.S. bombers. Almost half the city is now in ruins

1945

September 1942. Soon afterward, he was handed over to the Japanese and treated savagely. By 1945 he was a prisoner in the city of Nagasaki.

> We had felt for many months that the Japanese couldn't continue the war. We used to joke about it in a mild sort of way with them. An American would come flying over; you could almost see the pilot, and we would say, "Where are the Japanese airplanes?"
>
> And they would say, "These are being saved up if there is an invasion."

In the first four decades of the 20th century, an international community of physicists—scientists from Germany, Great Britain, Italy, Denmark, France, Austria, New Zealand, Russia, Canada, Hungary, the United States, and other countries—had been exploring the vast potential energy housed in the atom. When Hitler came to power in 1933, many German-Jewish scientists moved to Great Britain and the United States.

In 1939, Albert Einstein warned Franklin Roosevelt that Germany might be developing an A-bomb. In the autumn of 1941, impressed by British atomic research, U.S. scientists urged their government to take action. It did. A team of international scientists was set up to work on the Manhattan Project, the top secret undertaking to develop an atomic bomb. The project was under the scientific direction of New Yorker J. Robert Oppenheimer. But there were concerns. There were fears that the Germans would beat the Allies to it, fears the project would fail, and there were Congressional questions about missing funds. The answer was a secret (to the Nazis, but not the Soviet Union) enterprise that stretched from New York to Berkeley and North Carolina to Washington State. On July 16, 1945, the first nuclear device was detonated at Alamogordo, New Mexico. Soon after the war, J. Robert Oppenheimer recalled:

> We waited until the blast had passed, walked out of the shelter, and then it was extremely solemn. We

At right, Hiroshima devastated by the world's first atomic bomb, on August 6, 1945

Kamikaze pilots bow serenely before setting out on the missions from which they will never return

MAY 24

U.S. marines enter Naha, capital of Okinawa

JUNE 21

Major General Roy Geiger of the U.S. Marine Corps announces that Okinawa is secure. The last great battle of the war is over

knew the world would not be the same. A few people laughed, a few people cried. Most people were silent. I remembered the line from the Hindu scripture, the Bhagavad Gita: Vishnu is trying to persuade the Prince that he should do his duty, and to impress him, he takes on his multiarmed form and says, "Now I am become Death, the destroyer of worlds." I suppose we all thought that, one way or another.

A special B-29 unit commanded by Colonel Paul W. Tibbets was trained to deliver the devices from Tinian Island in the Marianas. The first bomb, Little Boy, was flown by Douglas DC-3 to San Francisco and then loaded onto the heavy cruiser U.S.S. *Indianapolis*. Its commander was Captain Charles B. McVay.

On the fifteenth of July, I was in San Francisco and talked with Admiral Purnell and Captain Parsons, who I know were connected in an intimate way with a secret project, but I did not know what this project was. I was informed at that time that when we were ready for sea on July 16, we would proceed as fast as possible to the forward area. On Sunday, the fifteenth of July, about noon, we were at Hunters Point and they put on us what we now know was the atomic bomb. The cruiser sailed from San Francisco on July 16 for the Marianas. We arrived in Tinian the morning of July 26 and unloaded the material and the bomb.

On July 30, on its return journey, the *Indianapolis* was sunk by a Japanese submarine. Just after 8:15 a.m., Japanese time, on August 6, six miles above Hiroshima, Colonel Paul Tibbets's B-29, the *Enola Gay*, dropped Little Boy in the world's first atomic attack. Of the 320,000 people in that city that morning, some 80,000 died immediately or were badly wounded. The explosion site reached a temperature of 5,400°F.

Three days after Hiroshima, Nagasaki was A-bombed. Geoffrey Sherring and a friend had been

JUNE 28

In the Philippines, General MacArthur announces that the islands have been retaken, although pockets of determined Japanese resistance will continue to be mopped up for several months

JUNE 29

Plans for the invasion of Japan are approved by President Truman

1945

pumping water out of an air-raid shelter.

It was a beautiful day to start with, with very little cloud and a nice southerly breeze. We set alight our cigarettes and retreated back into the trench, which was roofed, to smoke in peace. The atomic bomb went off, whilst we were in there.

Bernie said to me, "I can hear a car on the road."

I said, "Don't be ridiculous, there isn't any petrol in Japan, let alone motor cars, it must be an airplane."

He said, "I'm going out to have a look."

He began crawling away from me towards the hole in the roof of the trench. As he did so, and I was looking after him, I saw the flash from the bomb, which was exactly like the sort of bluish light that you get from an electrical welding operation. It was very blue and it came in exactly the opposite direction from the sun's rays; it completely eclipsed them. It was this blue blazing light shining down a square hole in front of Bernie who hadn't fortunately reached the hole or he would have been burned, too. Then, of course, we heard the vibration and shaking which wasn't a bang by any means. It was a continuous shaking of the whole air and earth about it.

It was separated by several seconds from the flash because we were not directly underneath the bomb,

we were about 1,100 yards away. Then this thundering, rolling, shaking came along and everywhere went completely dark.

What had happened was the shock wave had rolled over us, lifting as it went all the earth and dust around us and blowing the building flat at the same time. So when we came out, in a matter of seconds, we came out into a choking brown fog.

This fog lasted for quite a while before the southwesterly breeze blew it back up the city. As it did so, we had a shower of most peculiar rain. It was in very, very large droplets about as big as grapes and it was almost entirely mud, just thick blobs of mud falling from the sky. I presume what had happened was it had fallen down through this dusty cloud and had picked up a lot of mud on the way.

We could see farther than we'd ever seen before across the city, which was all in a heap. Most of the buildings had been made of wood, and some of them nearer to the site of the bomb had already been set on fire. A number of the trees, which weren't terribly near but were nearer to the bomb, had also been set on fire.

I had run outside the camp and found a storehouse. The Japanese in charge of it must have been standing in

JULY 1

Australian troops land in force on Borneo to capture oil installations and drive back the occupying Japanese

JULY 2

Massive bombing raids continue on Japanese cities, with incendiary bombs causing horrendous damage and casualties

the doorway. His skin was completely burnt off him and he had fallen on the ground. He was a distressing sight with a lot of his insides hanging out. I was trying to make him comfortable and all the skin came off his arms in my hands just like thin wet rubber. He, of course, was in great pain.

Geoffrey Sherring and his fellow prisoners helped some numbed locals using Red Cross supplies their captors had withheld from them.

You would encounter people on the move and they would never stand still. They would never rest. They would be moving from one place to another, almost without object or aim.

By 10 p.m., the prisoners were on a hillside.

We were feeling very tired and hoping nothing more would happen, when a Japanese soldier came along. He still had his rifle and still had his bayonet fixed. He told us that the bulk of our prisoners were on the opposite side of the city, occupying a similar hillside position. He pointed out that they had no stores, food, or blankets, no nothing. He impressed this upon us. I was very much impressed by the way he went about his duties in the middle of all this terrible chaos

I got three Dutch East India men and we put buckets, of which we had a number, on thick bamboo poles and we loaded these up with tinned food of various kinds, and we folded blankets onto the poles and, carrying these burdens, we set off into the burning city.

Neither Sherring nor Burton Stein regarded the bombings as a mistake. Burton Stein:

No one that I knew regretted it at all—that this kind of a weapon had been used. All we knew was that a super weapon had been used, that it had worked and that we would not have to invade Japan. I'm not sure that we knew it was on civilians, but among anyone I knew, there was not the slightest regret, compunction about it, concern about it.

Geoffrey Sherring:

Always hovering over Nagasaki were the kites. These big brown birds were scavengers of the buzzard type. A number of them must have been hovering over there when the bomb fell. I came across two or three of them walking about in the city with no feathers on. Their feathers had been burnt off them in midair. They'd collapsed to the ground and they were wandering around on foot. Horrifying sight.

Above left, a G.I. examines the wreckage of a Japanese Zero fighter on the island of Munda, New Georgia

The Japanese delegation, led by Foreign Minister Mamoru Shigemitsu, arrives on the U.S.S. Missouri, in Tokyo Bay, to sign the documents for Japan's unconditional surrender, September 2, 1945

JULY 4
Canadian forces arrive in Berlin to share occupation duties

JULY 10
Tokyo is subjected to a raid by 1,000 bombers

1945

After work, we all got on the streetcars. I can remember one streetcar after another jammed. People had flags and were yelling and screaming. Everybody was so happy the war was over.

DOROTHY ZMUDA
On VJ-Day in Milwaukee

CHAPTER TWENTY-ONE

NEW BEGINNINGS

On May 2, 1945, Major Anna Nikulina of the Soviet Ninth Rifle Corps took a red banner onto the roof of the Reich Chancellery in a Berlin that was devastated by the final engagement between the Soviet Red Army and the Nazi Wehrmacht. It was a symbolic moment, a sign that the wars of the world were almost over. Nightmares had been coming true for more than a decade; now a dream of peace was being realized. But at what cost? The triumph for civilization had left an estimated 30 million refugees on the move in Europe alone. Along the route of the eastern front, from Moscow to Berlin, hardly a building was standing. Among the living there was the struggle for survival and, amid traumatic memories, a struggle for the future.

One day in 1943, in the Hampshire village of Medstead, in southern England, 17-year-old Iris Pilons was in The Castle, the local pub. There she met Emil, a 27-year-old private in the Canadian Army. She was with her parents.

> They liked him. I liked him. We fell in love. He was the man that a good many women hope they will meet, and very few seldom do. His mates and me called him "Happy" because he was such a happy-go-lucky fellow. He really was.

They married in February 1944.

> I walked to the church in a borrowed wedding dress from a neighbor. In those days of rationing you couldn't get a wedding dress. The wedding reception was in the public house, which closed at 10 p.m. sharp. It was snowing, I remember quite clearly. We had a very happy fortnight, two people together, keeping one another happy and enjoying one another's company.

When the honeymoon was over, Emil went to Scotland. On June 13, 1944, he landed in France. Belgium,

Although he had seen the war through almost to its conclusion, President Roosevelt died, aged 63, before hostilities ended. His funeral cortege at left makes its way along Constitution Avenue in Washington on April 14, 1945. On the previous pages, the end of the war is celebrated at a holiday camp in England, summer 1945. In the background, locals at a street party in Holland embrace freedom after six years of occupation

Top right, Corporal Iris Stead of Clapton, London, and Private Alwe Lock of Wimbledon enjoy the flower market in the Grande Place, Brussels, October 1944. Bottom right, a boy proudly wears his father's posthumous Victoria Cross, Britain's highest award for bravery. His father died in Italy.

JULY 14

Italy declares war on Japan

JULY 14

A ban on Allied troops fraternizing with local women in Germany is lifted

Holland, and Germany followed. While Emil was taking the fight to the enemy, Iris had given birth to their son. Emil came back for the christening in April 1945.

> I hadn't seen him in between when we were married, and the christening. I can see him now on the Central Station in Southampton. He kissed me before he left. It was a lovely day, one of the hottest Aprils we'd had in years. He got in the coach that was taking him to London. He waved to me out of the carriage window. He was serving with the Canadian Foresting Corps, and he was killed in a road accident, by a tram, with a fractured base of the skull, on April 16, 1945, within two days of leaving my home. I'd got within three weeks of going to Canada. I was looking forward to it. I was young. I was in love. He was such a nice chap. He really was. I didn't hear for three weeks. I was writing to a dead man and I didn't know it.

On April 30, 1945, Adolf Hitler, the man who had unleashed over a decade of barbarism, had committed suicide and the war in Europe came to an end. For one-time Viennese teenager-turned-Italian-partisan Harry Burger, the closing days of war saw him with a new uniform, provided by the U.S. Army's 101st Airborne.

> They got some water, washed me—I had scabies, they treated me with sulfur—put me into shape and put an armband on me which said "Italian Partisan." It was a good-looking khaki uniform and I loved it. The next day, we had automobiles all of a sudden. It was a Lancia convertible—one of the most fabulous automobiles ever made—taken from the Germans. We shot for Cuneo; as we got into the city, we could see no activity, no more Nazi flags. There was just a few Italian flags, a few English flags, and a few American flags. There was nothing happening. Sunrise started as we got to the big bridge on the way to Torino. Our driver suddenly stopped and we were cursing him out. He said, "You better get out of the car and have a look."
>
> The middle section of the bridge was missing; we were at the verge of falling 900 feet. We returned to Cuneo and our guys were starting to come in when the American Army finally came into Cuneo. The first group were Hawaiians, and the first thing they did, they went into a coffee house and set up a little swing combo and taught the Italians girls how to do swing.

On May 7, the German High Command surrendered—May 8 was declared Victory in Europe, VE-Day. Michael "Flip" Pallozola of the USAAF was on base, in eastern England.

Revellers celebrate VE-Day on Sparks Street in Ottawa, Ontario, May 8, 1945

> They closed the base down. Nobody could get out, nobody could get in, for three days. They had 24-hour movies. They had kegs of beer. They had a big three-day party. But we were not allowed to leave the base.

When peace came to Canada's North Shore (New Brunswick) Regiment, it was in Ostersander, Germany. Their padre, R. M. Hickey, was finishing Mass.

> A babble of voices and some cheering started outside. Then, someone rushed in and shouted, "The war is over. It's over!" The news of the German surrender on the Canadians' front had been picked up on the wireless. Everybody took it quietly. One fellow said, "Well, I guess that's it, eh, father?" Most of the lads just stood there, watched me take off the vestments, then quietly walked away. Like myself, they were thinking hard; memories rushed in fast and stilled expressions.

At William Ash's prison camp, there was a grim settling of accounts.

> One of our people was trading cigarettes to one of the guards for some eggs. And a German *feldwebel* saw them—and shot the British prisoner of war who was engaged in this. This was within a couple of days of the end of the war . . . and this poor chap was trying so desperately to stay alive.
>
> We were liberated by the British Guards Armored Brigade. One of the officers in the brigade was told about this *feldwebel*. He shot him—just like that—which was fine, really. It saved all the trouble of postwar trials.

On VE-Day, Ellen Harris was in the House of Commons headed for Whitehall, center of British government.

> I was standing right underneath the balcony when they shouted and shouted for Churchill. He came out on the balcony and he flung his arms out. And he said, "Londoners, I love you all," and said a few words. It was short and sweet, but lovely for the Londoners. And he finished up once more, "Londoners, I love you all!" The cheers! It was a wonder the clouds didn't come down.

1945

JULY 26

The defeat of the Churchill government is confirmed in Britain. Clement Attlee replaces Churchill at Potsdam, Germany

JULY 26

The Allies broadcast "The Potsdam Declaration"—their demands to Japan for an unconditional surrender

watching these streetcars of mad people going past, yelling and screaming. Everybody just quieted down, and it was just flat silence, then a couple of blocks later they started up again.

That I remember; I could never forget that.

Six years after donning Mickey Mouse gas masks, young Londoner Sylvia Townson celebrated VJ-Day in Mountain Ash, Wales—to where she had been evacuated following the 1944–45 V-weapon blitz on London.

Crowds pack Times Square in New York to celebrate VE-Day. At left, Allied POWs celebrate their release from Aomori Camp near Yokohama, Japan

But hanging over VE-Day celebrations was the specter of the continuing war with Japan. Iowa-born, 24-year-old Signe Cooper was serving with the U.S. Army Nurse Corps in Assam, India.

I don't know exactly when I heard the news about VE-Day. But I do remember about VJ-Day because when the corpsman came to say the war was over, I can remember exactly where I was standing and I said to him, "We have heard this all week, how do we know this isn't just another rumor?"

He said, "This really is not a rumor. This is really it."

On VJ-Day, advertising layout artist Dorothy Zmuda was at work in Milwaukee.

After work, we all got on the streetcars. I can remember one streetcar after another jammed. People had flags and were yelling and screaming. Everybody was so happy the war was over. And the streetcar was going down National Avenue, and it came in front of Wood Hospital. But here on the ground are sitting all these veterans, some without legs, in wheelchairs with their legs covered, with a blanket, and they're just sitting there watching us,

AUGUST 2

The war's heaviest air raid is launched against Japan, with 800 U.S. aircraft dropping 6,000 tons of incendiary bombs; 80,000 Japanese die

AUGUST 6

Colonel Paul Tibbets drops an atomic bomb on the Japanese city of Hiroshima from his B-29 Superfortress. Over 80,000 people die instantly

1945

They had an enormous street party and the children had a fancy dress party. And because I'd just come from London, I didn't have any fancy dress of my own. So this dear old mam, an 80-year-old lady, dug into her wardrobe or her attic. And, somewhere from her past, she managed to produce a Japanese kimono which was absolutely beautiful, and wound that around me. She had a fan and parasol and those Japanese shoes, pieces of wood with ribbons attached—very difficult to walk in—and some artificial chrysanthemum. And I went along—it seems extraordinary but there you are—celebrating the end of the war in Japan dressed as a Japanese lady.

And I won the fancy dress.

The war was over, but not everyone was celebrating. Iris Pilons:

Everybody else was laughing and joking and enjoying themselves and I was crying my eyes out. You could do nothing else. Your partner was gone. He'd never come back. In my circumstances, the chances of me remarrying were practically nil. I never did, because I never found another man quite like him. I wish he was here now, this very minute.

Her grief was shared by many. The estimated—and no precise figures are possible—war dead of the United States was 290,000; Canada, 45,000; the United Kingdom, 350,000—of which 50,000 were civilians.

Those tragic figures were modest compared with the global scale of death. In the little country of Holland 6,000 soldiers had died and 204,000 civilians. In Yugoslavia 300,000 soldiers and 1.4 million civilians, in Poland 123,000 soldiers and 4 million civilians, in France 250,000 soldiers and 350,000 civilians, Italy 400,000 soldiers and 100,00 civilians, Japan 2 million soldiers and 350,000 civilians, Germany 4.5 million soldiers and 2 million civilians, China 2.5 million soldiers and 7.4 million civilians.

In their policy toward the east, the Nazis had

1945

AUGUST 8
The Soviet Union declares war on Japan

AUGUST 9
A second atomic bomb is dropped on the shipbuilding center of Nagasaki; 35,000 are reported to have died, almost twice that number injured, and 5,000 people are claimed to have simply "vanished"

Above, two women accused of collaborating with the Nazis are paraded through the streets of Paris in shame, their clothes torn asunder and their heads shaved. At left, bomb damage had caused a severe housing shortage in Britain, and prefabricated buildings, manufactured in sections and assembled on site, provided a swift and supposedly temporary solution for families like the Hickmans, at left. Some of the World War II "prefabs" are still in use today

Citizens of Mönchengladbach, Germany, show white flags outside an underground shelter as the U.S. Ninth Army enters the city

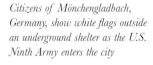

AUGUST 10

The Japanese broadcast a response to the Allies' surrender demands, accepting the general terms of the unconditional surrender, but insisting that their Emperor must remain at the head of the nation

AUGUST 10

Taking the Japanese announcement as the end of the war, crowds head for Times Square in New York to celebrate, but the party fizzles out

1945

anticipated 30 million Soviet dead. In the war that followed, an estimated 10 million Soviet soldiers and 10 million civilians died.

During the closing stages of the war, U.S. fighter pilot James Goodson, shot down over Germany, was caught in a USAAF raid on Berlin while in transit by rail as a POW.

> When it was all over, we came out and there was pure mayhem all around the station. People dying and God knows what. My captors asked me if I would parole myself—and help them rescue people.
>
> For the first time I realized the havoc that we were causing down below.
>
> From 35,000 feet you looked down and see flashes, puffs of smoke. You know there are people down there, but it doesn't really penetrate. But when you are in it, down there, the whole thing is different. I remember going into a cellar where a woman was dying. I was trying to pull her out, and she said, "No, forget me, I'm dying." But she rolled over and she puts this baby girl in my arms and she says, "Take care of my baby."
>
> I said, "I'll try."
>
> She said, "You're not German."
>
> I said "No."
>
> She said, "Who are you?"
>
> I pointed up and said, "I'm one of them."
>
> And she says, "I don't understand, but promise me to take care of my baby."

AUGUST 11

The Allies concede that the Emperor can remain, but all control will rest with the Supreme Allied Commander.

AUGUST 12

An accidental press announcement of the Japanese surrender sparks a series of surrender reports in the media and widespread premature celebrations in Ottawa

In London in those final days of war, artist Eleanor Hudson was running a mobile canteen around west London during the V-weapon attacks.

> There was this square where these very beautiful trees—in late summer I think it was—were so blasted, they were lost in a fog of dust. I saw stark-like trees in winter, every leaf—they had been in full leaf—every leaf was blown off. And it was sad to see this, this wrecked square covered, as in snow almost, with the blast, the dust, and the bare trees. I was so delighted a month later or two to realize that there was another spring, in very late summer or early autumn. The trees hadn't finished their life and they had put out new leaves. I thought it was a delightful miracle.

In the aftermath of victory—and Japanese surrender—Burton Stein was on guard duty at Arakabasan in Palau, the Philippines.

> The Japanese battalion there were starving. They nourished themselves by coming in on very, very small boats at night, and throwing grenades into the water and scooping up the fish. We were sitting there on guard duty and a grenade would scare the hell out of you. That would lead to a whole lot of shooting and nonsense. Then we discovered what they were about, so after that, we watched them very carefully, and when we saw a boat, we would hail them. And what we convinced them of was that we had no wish to deny them their bloody fish; if they wanted to use their grenades, that was fine, but just whistle or let us know. This got to be so familiar that at one point I exchanged pictures with a Japanese soldier. He gave me a picture of his family, which I carried around for years, I don't know why, and I gave him a picture of a girlfriend. And we talked in the strange way that people who don't understand each other talk—a good deal of smiling and reassuring and the guns are all away, which was charming, human, and not very military.

VJ-Day meant that Flip Pallozola was not going to the Pacific.

> It was about three weeks after that, the first part of September, that we were sent back to the States. We came back on the *Queen Elizabeth* and there were

AUGUST 12
Police clear a crowd of 100,000 from Times Square, all anxiously awaiting the announcement of the end of the war

AUGUST 14
Japan's Emperor Hirohito issues a formal notice of ceasefire to all of his forces.

1945

were 15,000 of us, sleeping in the swimming pool, everywhere, but it was an enjoyable trip. It was only about four and a half days. It took us 10 days to go over in the Liberty ship.

And when we pulled into New York Harbor, I was so emotional that I cried, and I wasn't alone.

When you come through, up the Hudson, and you see the Statue of Liberty—after what has happened in the world—it was just overwhelming to us. We were the first large group from Europe to come back after VJ-Day. There were people hanging out of all the windows of all those big buildings. All of the fire ships were shooting their water up and they had balloons, which were a protection against air raids. It was a tremendous welcome. I couldn't believe it.

One of the things that I remember is that an airplane had run into the Empire State Building, and there was this big hole. And the other thing was how loud the foghorn was. My eardrums just tingled.

With the war over, people began to assess their past and future. For Canadian Albert Cunningham, the army was the place where he had grown up.

When you are 17, you are not a man. Three and a half years among men, nothing but men, you grow up, you become self-sufficient.

In 1942, teacher Vivian Sekey of Forestville, Wisconsin, married. In 1943, she had a son, but with teacher shortages, soon returned to the classroom.

I became a better American going through this with my family, and I wanted peace, oh I wanted peace so bad. It just never seemed it was going to come. I just appreciated my country so much more. You take things for granted. I thought, America, this is the most wonderful place to live and I know I'm a better American because I now have so many memories of what we did. I am just very happy that I lived through that period. It made me a better person, a more compassionate person. I think I'm more interesting,

A truce was called prior to the German surrender in Holland to allow food to be distributed to starving civilians. At left, German soldiers guard a Canadian food truck while talking to its Dutch driver

At right, the Victory Parade in London—troops march under Admiralty Arch into the Mall heading toward Buckingham Palace. Above right, Mrs. R. Whitley, a volunteer Red Cross nurse, lights a cigarette for Ralph Haynes, who was in transit at the Patuxent Naval Air Station in Maryland

AUGUST 14

VJ-Day—Victory in Japan. Once again, the streets of the Allied home countries are packed with jubilant crowds bent on celebration. Up to two million people flood the streets around New York's Times Square

AUGUST 19

Rationing of gasoline and fuel oil ends in America

and grew up a lot. I really grew up in those years when I had to take over responsibilities and many sacrifices. I'm happy for that, but I'm sad for the ones that gave their lives.

For Burton Stein, the end of the war saw an ember of hope that had been kindled in vain during the conflict finally extinguished.

All of my friends, including kids who were a bit older, had gone into the war with great enthusiasm. Several of them had been killed before I went into the war. Boys that I'd played baseball with, and who were a couple of years older, and therefore objects of some admiration. Being in the war was the right place to be.

My sense was that Russia were our allies and a lot of the propaganda during the war was that the world would really be different after the war, precisely because the Soviet Union were our friends, our allies, and that the big enemies had been defeated and it's got to be a different world. The terrible realization after the war was that it wasn't going to be a different world, a new world, that the enemies were being lined up again and we were being led into a kind of national hysteria about some damn thing or other—Harry Truman's policy. It was terribly disillusioning.

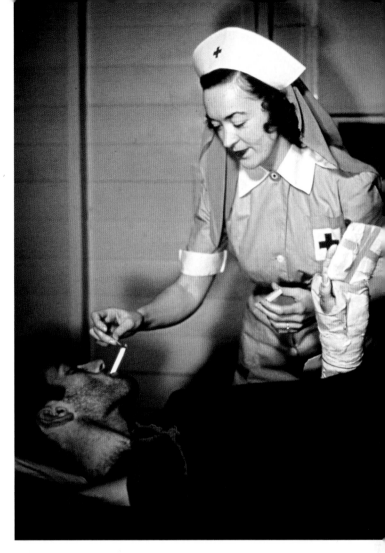

SEPTEMBER 2

As the Supreme Allied Commander in the region, General Douglas MacArthur accepts the formal surrender of the Japanese when surrender documents are signed on board the U.S.S. *Missouri* in Tokyo Bay

SEPTEMBER 17

The commandant of Belsen and 44 Belsen and Auschwitz guards go on trial at Luneberg Heath in Germany

1945

Nurse Evelyn White, back in England from China, married a vicar.

> People, whether they're Russian, Chinese, Japanese, Indian, American, we all have the same hopes and fears. We all want to live as long as God allows us to in peace, or comparative peace. We all want our children to grow up; we don't want our sons to be thrown into another war. There's something missing in our makeup or in our leadership or we've got the wrong leaders, which makes nations go to war or want to go to war. I don't know the answer. I wish I did.

Karl Günther von Hase was captured by the advancing Red Army and sent to a prison camp in Stalin's Soviet Union. The poverty in the area surrounding the camp was so great that locals were begging from the Wehrmacht prisoners.

> I was better treated than the Russian prisoners in Germany, which is a very great shame for the German Army, and for Germany. The Russians did not wilfully try to make the prisoners die. They tried to give them a chance of survival—but by Western standards this chance was low.

Released British prisoner of war Reginald Reading arrived back in his devastated hometown of Coventry on VE-Day.

> The following Christmas I had a German ex-prisoner of war—he hadn't been repatriated—in my home over Christmas. Everybody thought I was crackers. But I let him spend his Christmas with me. By that time I realized we'd got to start again somewhere, and it was only up to us. If we could keep this friendship with each other, well, there was a chance, because the world had gone crazy through war.
>
> I've met his people and my family have met them, and we've grown a great friendship between our families.

Iris Pilons visited her husband's homeland a decade after the war. And she raised her Anglo-Canadian son.

> The Canadian authorities were very sympathetic. They gave me first-class treatment. I can never thank them enough. It's their money that's paid for it. When I look back, I think, how did I cope? All I can say is, I did my best.

In his last days with the Italian partisans, Harry Burger returned to the mountains, hunting fleeing SS personnel. A month after VE-Day, he was discharged from the partisan unit, found his mother, and headed back to Nice, in southern France. He was interned there for three weeks as an "enemy alien"—along with detained SS personnel—and then released.

> The Tommy Dorsey Orchestra was in town. My mother gave me a couple of francs and I bought some used clothes. And I walked the streets and saw people, people that I thought I knew. They looked funny, they looked very skinny. The women all had their heads shaved. They looked like they were in peasant clothes, Russian clothes, and they all had a tattoo on their arm. These were all people who used to live there—Jewish people. It took a couple of weeks before they started telling us about horrors of the death camps.

He went in search of visas for the United States to join the Burgers' American relatives. Getting them was a very slow process for Harry and his mother. But, in Marseilles, they met with success.

> The consul said, "I want you to raise your right arm as allegiance to the flag," and all of that stuff.
>
> I said, "Whatever you say."

1945

SEPTEMBER 25

Soviet embassy cipher clerk Igor Gouzenko gives evidence of a Soviet spy ring operating inside Canada to the *Ottawa Journal* and, later, the Department of Justice

OCTOBER 24

When its charter is ratified by the member states, the United Nations officially comes into being

Eventually, the Burgers sailed from Rotterdam, bound for New York.

> We arrived, I looked out and I saw the Statue of Liberty. And an American I became buddy with, he put his arm around me and said, "See? What you see here, this is your freedom. This might not be the best thing in the world, but it is certainly heaven on earth as far as the world goes."

The ship docked at Hoboken, New Jersey.

> The immigration people came aboard and had our papers and passed us through. My English was little bit rough. And the fellow says, "Well you might want to clear that up but it is a good thing you speak English, anyhow." And he says, "Have a good life, go out and get yourself a Social Security card and in five years you can become a citizen and you are going to be OK."
>
> When my left foot touched the gangplank, I knew I was home. I got a job the next day and I have been working ever since.

At left, U.S. servicemen dance with Japanese partners in the newly opened Oasis of Ginza nightclub in Tokyo

Peace at last—G.I.s take photos for keepsakes as their time in Europe comes to an end

OCTOBER 29

The U.S.S.R. announces that it will build its own atomic bomb

NOVEMBER 20

Nazi war crimes trials at Nuremberg begin with, among others, Hess, Goering, and von Ribbentrop in the dock

1945

INDEX

PICTURE CREDITS

BIBLIOGRAPHY

Mark Arnold-Foster, *The World at War* (Collins 1973)
Antony Beevor, *Berlin: The Downfall, 1945* (Penguin Viking 2002)
Hugh Brogan, *The Penguin History of the United States of America* (1990)
Michael Burleigh, *The Third Reich: A New History* (Macmillan 2000)
Angus Calder, *The Myth of the Blitz* (Jonathan Cape 1991)
Angus Calder, *The People's War* (Jonathan Cape 1960)
I.C.B. Dear (General Editor), M.R.D. Foot (Consultant Editor),
   The Oxford Companion to World War II (Oxford University Press Paperback 2001)
Bernt Engelman, *In Hitler's Germany* (Methuen 1988)
Eric Hobsbawm, *Age of Extremes: The Short Twentieth Century, 1914-91* (Michael Joseph 1994)
Michael Howard, *The Invention of Peace* (Profile Books, 2000)
Philip Kaplan and Richard Collier, *The Few* (Seven Dials Cassell 1989)
Ludovic Kennedy, *Pursuit: The Sinking of the Bismarck* (William Collins 1974)
Ronald Lewin, *Ultra Goes to War* (Hutchinson 1978)
Charles Messenger, *The Second World War in the West* (Cassell 1999)
Jean Michel, *Dora* (J.C. Lattès, Livre de poche, 1975; Weidenfeld & Nicholson 1979)
Martin Middlebrook, *The Nuremberg Raid* (Allen Lane Penguin Books 1973 revised 1980)
Richard Overy, *The Battle of Britain* (Penguin 2000)
Purnell's History of the Second World War (1966)
Reader's Digest The Canadians at War, 1939/45 (Reader's Digest 1969)
David Reynolds, *From Munich to Pearl Harbor: Roosevelt's America and the Origins of the
   Second World War* (Ivan R. Dee 2001)
David Reynolds, *Rich Relations: The American Occupation of Britain* (Harper Collins 1995)
Richard Rhodes, *The Making of the Atomic Bomb* (Simon & Schuster 1986)
Graham Rhys-Jones, *The Loss of the Bismarck* (Cassell 1999)
Sheila Rowbotham, *A Century of Women* (Viking, 1997)
William L. Shirer, *The Rise and Fall of the Third Reich* (Simon & Schuster 1960)
Michael E. Stevens (Editor), Ellen D. Goldlust (Assistant Editor),
   Voices of the Wisconsin Past: Women Remember the War, 1941-45
   (Center for Documentary History State Historical Society of Wisconsin 1993)
A.J.P. Taylor, *English History, 1914-1945* (Oxford University Press 1965)
Studs Terkel, *The Good War* (Pantheon Books 1984)
Philip Warner, *The Battle of France 1940* (Cassell 2001)
H. P. Willmott with Tohmatsu Haruo and W. Spencer Johnson, *Pearl Harbor* (Cassell 2001)
Derek Wood and Derek Dempster, *The Narrow Margin* (Hutchinson 1961)
Chronicle of the 20th Century (Longman Chronicle 1988)
The Great Battles of World War II (Hamlyn 1972)
Chronicle of America (Chronicle Publications 1989)

CD CREDITS

Count Basie—"One O'Clock Jump"
Count Basie—"Jumpin' at the Woodside"
Artie Shaw—"Begin the Beguine"
The Andrews Sisters—"Bei Mir Bist Du Schöen"
The Andrews Sisters—"I'll Be With You in Apple Blossom Time"
Frank Sinatra—"Saturday Night"
Bing Crosby—"Too Marvelous for Words"
Bing Crosby—"The Folks Who Live on the Hill"
Bing Crosby—"The Bombardier Song"
Billie Holiday—"Fine and Mellow"

All musical excerpts © 2003 River Productions Ltd. MCPS. All rights of the owner of the work produced reserved. Unauthorized copying, hiring, public performance and broadcasting of this record prohibited.

ACKNOWLEDGMENTS

It was Toby Buchan and Gabrielle Mander at Michael O'Mara Books in London whose dedication led to this project, and the wonderful editorship, research, and humor of Rod Green that saw it through. The perception, diligence, and vitality of Magdalena De Souza made her an invaluable research assistant. Karen Dolan and Rhian Mackay were vital to the CD production, as was the creativity of Mike Thornton of One Stop Digital and producer Bob Dickinson. At the IWM's Sound Archive I received unfailingly helpful, informed assistance from Margaret Brooks, Richard McDonough and John Stopford-Pickering, whose tactical skills saw me through many a crisis. Author Eric Hill donated his interviews on the 1941-42 battle for the Philippines. I would also like to thank the archivists and researchers at the Center for Documentary History at the State Historical Society of Wisconsin, and the U.S. Naval Institute Oral History Collection. Lastly, I would like to thank the interviewees, without whom there would have been no Allied victory—and no book.

ABOUT THE AUTHOR

Nigel Fountain has a degree in History and Politics from the University of York. He is a writer, broadcaster for the BBC, and journalist working for a number of newspapers in England, including *The Times*, *The Guardian*, and *The Daily Telegraph*. Nigel specializes in military and historical subjects, particularly those based upon archival material. His other books include two titles with documentary CDs, *The Battle of Britain and the Blitz* and *Women at War*. He lives in London.

CONTRIBUTORS

William Allister
Edward Ardizzone
Ruby Armbust
J. Arthur
William Ash
Dr. Paul Ashton
Brian Atkins
David Balme
Stanley Baron
Tony Bartley
Nancy Bazin
Roland Beamont
Percy Beaton
Edward Bedford
Rubie Bond
John Bowie
Frank Bright
Harry Burger
Bert Carlton
Francesco Cavalera
Malcolm Champlin
Francis Codd
Signe Cooper
Yvonne Cormeau
Virginia Cowles
Spencer Coxe
William Crawford
Albert Cunningham
Edward Davies Scourfield
John Day
Premysl Dobias
Theron Dosch
Anne Duncan
Hugh Dundas
Charles Dunphie
Bernt Engelman
Hedy Epstein
Ruth Erickson
Michael Etkind
Douglas Fairbanks Jr.
Mitsuo Fuchida
William Garthwaite
George Gay
Jack Gebhardt
Herbert Gollop
Charles Goodson

James Goodson
Benny Gordon
Harold Gower
John Graham
George Green
William Gregory
Herschel Grynszpan
William Harding
Elizabeth Harris
Ellen Harris
Martin Hastings
George Henderson
Edward Hill
Eric Hill
Dr. K. E. Hinrichsen
Vera Holdstock
Herbert Holewa
Dorothy Hont
Rosemary Horstmann
John W. Howland
Eleanor Hudson
Howard Instance
Hugh Janvrin
Albert Jenkins
Charlie Johnson
Rose Kaminski
Dorothy Keating
Nan Kenway
Tom King
James Kirk
Louise Kroeger
Richard Leacock
Patrick Lewis
Reginald Lewis
Joseph L. Lockard
Robert Maloubier
Derek Mayne
Colin McMullen
Charles B. McVay
Dollard Ménard
Jean Mills
Michael Moran
Ross Munro
Ernest Munson
Sylvia Munson
L. W. Murray

Catherine Niblock
Norman Norris
Sir Richard O'Connor
Berta Ollendorff
J. Robert Oppenheimer
Louis Ortega
Michael "Flip" Pallozola
Kenneth Pattisson
Josephine Pearce
Jon Pensyl
Marika Phillips
Adolf Pilch
Iris Pilons
Diana Pitt Parsons
Joseph P. Pollard
Prudence Portman
Elizabeth Quayle
Reginald Reading
Harry Ree
Colin Ryder-Richardson
Peter Salmon
Roger Sandstedt
Orville Schlef
Vivian Sekey
Norman Sherring
Myrtle Solomon
Lee Soucy
Burton Stein
John Thach
Sylvia Townson
Norman Travett
Madeline Ullom
Jørgen von Führen Kieler
Erwin von Hase
Karl Günther von Hase
Lilias Walker
Gilman Warne
Stephen Weiss
Evelyn White
Jesse White
Frederick Winterbotham
Petrea Winterbotham
Nan Winton
Beatrice Wright
Allan Younger
Dorothy Zmuda